Contents

For a free download of suggested answers to the Apply it questions visit www.illuminatepublishing.com/btec_psych_rg_answers

Introduction

Exam advice

Please note: The advice, answers and comments given here are not from the exam board but are our interpretation of 'the rules of the game'.

Knowing is not enough; we must apply.

Leonardo da Vinci

Apply it

The 'Apply it' boxes throughout this book contain questions to help you practise all your skills, especially application.

These are exam-type questions, very much like the real thing. They include scenarios because the majority of exam questions are scenario-based.

The Unit 1 exam

Unit 1 (Psychological Approaches and Applications) is externally assessed by one exam. You will be awarded a mark for the whole paper, which will contribute to your grade of Distinction (D), Merit (M), Pass (P), Near Pass (N) or Unclassified (U).

The exam is 1 hour 30 minutes long and the total number of marks available is 72.

The paper is divided into three sections (Section A, B and C), each worth 24 marks. Each section contains material from both content areas A and B.

The Unit 3 exam

Unit 3 (Health Psychology) is externally assessed by one exam. Again, you will be awarded a mark for the whole paper, which will contribute to your grade of Distinction (D), Merit (M), Pass (P), Near Pass (NP) or Unclassified (U).

The exam is two hours long and the total number of marks available is 70.

The paper is divided into three sections (Section A, B and C), with 20 marks for Section A, 20 marks for Section B and 30 marks for Section C. Each section may contain material from all content areas A, B and C.

Types of exam questions

AO1 Description (with or without scenario) e.g. *State, Give, Name, Describe, Identify* Unit 1 + Unit 3	*State what is meant by the term 'vicarious learning'. (1 mark)*
	Give **one** *assumption of the biological approach. (1 mark)*
	Identify **one** *type of conformity. (1 mark)*
	Name **one** *route to persuasion of the elaboration-likelihood model. (1 mark)*
	Describe any **one** *stage of the transtheoretical model. (3 marks)*
AO2 Application (to scenario) e.g. *Describe, Explain, Justify* Unit 1 + Unit 3	Jak became a vegan at university when she lived with students who were vegans. She is still a vegan many years later as are most of her friends. Molly went out with Jak for a while and became a vegan during this time. But when the relationship ended Molly went back to eating meat. *Explain* **one** *possible reason from the social approach why Molly became a vegan. (2 marks)*
	Taz gave up gambling online. But they told a friend they had relapsed, saying, 'I missed the excitement of going online. I saw the flashing lights, the sounds and colours, and I remembered how much I enjoyed gambling.' *Describe how the learning approach could help us understand why Taz has relapsed. (3 marks)*
	Adi drinks alcohol every day. He admits this is bad for his health but he enjoys it. Adi's best friend says he should cut down. Adi knows his friend will help him but he has tried to cut down before and it didn't work. *Explain how the theory of planned behaviour could predict the likelihood of Adi cutting down his drinking. (2 marks)*
AO3 Evaluation (with or without scenario) e.g. *Explain, Compare* Unit 1 + Unit 3	*Compare normative social influence and informational social influence as explanations of conformity. (3 marks)*
	Arwa sells chilli sauces and most of her sales come from the bandwagon effect because people don't want to 'miss out'. Arwa is considering running a two-for-one offer. *Explain* **one** *alternative way to understand how the offer could lead to higher sales of Arwa's chilli sauces. (3 marks)*
Extended writing (with or without scenario) e.g. *Analyse, Discuss, Assess, Evaluate* Unit 1 + Unit 3	*Discuss how the cognitive approach can help us to understand aggression. (9 marks)*
	Mia identifies as a girl. She won a school prize for creative writing. Mia's dad praises her for helping her brother with homework. But he wasn't so keen on Mia playing rugby. Mia follows several beauty influencers online. *Assess how the behaviourist and/or social learning approaches can be used to understand Mia's gender. (9 marks)*
	Will is a single father and has a demanding job. He can't always get child care and never feels on top of his work. He has no time to relax or to see friends. Will feels so stressed he cannot cope and has been to see his doctor. *Evaluate* **one** *talking therapy that could help Will reduce his stress levels. (6 marks)*

Pearson BTEC National

Applied Psychology

Revision Guide

Cara Flanagan • Rob Liddle

Illuminate
Publishing

Published in 2023 by Illuminate Publishing Limited, an imprint of Hodder Education, an Hachette UK Company, Carmelite House, 50 Victoria Embankment, London EC4Y 0DZ

Orders: please contact Hachette UK Distribution, Hely Hutchinson Centre, Milton Road, Didcot, Oxfordshire, OX11 7HH.
Telephone: +44 (0)1235 827827. Email: education@hachette.co.uk.
 Lines are open from 9 a.m. to 5 p.m., Monday to Friday. You can also order through our website: www.hoddereducation.co.uk

© Cara Flanagan and Rob Liddle 2023

The moral rights of the authors have been asserted.

All rights reserved. No part of this book may be reprinted, reproduced or utilised in any form or by any electronic, mechanical, or other means, now known or hereafter invented, including photocopying and recording, or in any information storage and retrieval system, without permission in writing from the publishers.

British Library Cataloguing-in-Publication Data

A catalogue record for this book is available from the British Library

ISBN 978-1-913963-23-1

Printed by Ashford Colour Press Ltd

Impression 3
Year 2024

Hachette UK's policy is to use papers that are natural, renewable and recyclable products and made from wood grown in well-managed forests and other controlled sources. The logging and manufacturing processes are expected to conform to the environment regulations of the country of origin.

Every effort has been made to contact copyright holders of material reproduced in this book. If notified, the publishers will be pleased to rectify any errors or omissions at the earliest opportunity.

Editor: Nic Watson
Layout: Stephanie White, Kamae Design
Cover design: Helen Townson
Cover photo: PremiumVector / Shutterstock

Acknowledgements

Adobe Stock © p4 Yury Zap; p5(b) Sashkin; p7(t) techiya, (b) ViDi Studio; p10 Nikolai Sorokin; p11 Jacob Lund; p12(l) janvier, (r) ольга шабашова/EyeEm; p14 khosrork; p15 pixarno; p16 karichs; p17 Ljupco Smokovski; p18 Ben; p19 LIGHTFIELD STUDIOS; p20 LIGHTFIELD STUDIOS; p21 Anatoliy Karlyuk; p22 jstaley4011; p23 pelooyen; p26 Markus Bormann; p27 Viacheslav Yakobchuk; p28 DisobeyArt; p30 LIGHTFIELD STUDIOS; p31 JackF; p32 rocketclips; p33 Antonioguillem; p34 Wayhome Studio; p35 luengo_ua; p36 fizkes; p37 PheelingsMedia; p38 lithiumphoto; p40 Ljupco Smokovski; p41 Mauricio G; p42 airdone; p43 Seventyfour; p44 nenetus; p46 nerthuz; p48 Kateryna_Kon; p50 DANIELMANUEL; p51 Jacob Lund; p52 asiandelight; p53 Rawpixel.com; p54 cherylvb; p55 LIGHTFIELD STUDIOS; p56 pathdoc; p57 Elnur; p58 Paolese; p60 yuromanovich; p61 Urupong; p62 brgfx; p63 Kenishirotie; p64 artnazu; p66 Wayhome Studio; p67 motortion; p68 Ranta Images; p69 Pixel-Shot; p71 Cultura Creative; p72 A.KaZaK; p74 peopleimages.com; p75 Patryk Kosmider; p76 Waseem Ali Khan; p78 ikostudio; p79 cunaplus; p80 Diane; p81 Mangostar; p82 Jihan; p83 kei907; p84 fizkes; p85 Rido; p86 hbrh; p87 pixs4u; p89 Yuliia; p90 sofiko14; p91 natanaelginting; p92 Studio Romantic; p93 Studio Romantic; p94 Photographee.eu; p95 pikselstock; p97 VERSUSstudio; p98 Rawpixel.com; p99 esdras700; p100 Antonioguillem; p101 Wayhome Studio; p102 Alexey Stiop; p103 R. Gino Santa Maria; p106 NopponPAT; p108 rh2010; p110 aijiro; p111 Maksym Yemelyanov; p112 Monkey Business; p113 ThamKC; p114 Nejron Photo; p115 auremar; p116 auremar; p117 Travel Faery; p118 william87; p119 Tupungato; p120 puhhha; p121 amenic181; p122 NDABCREATIVITY; p123 Prostock-studio; p124 peopleimages.com; p125 Miroslav Alterov; p126 olly; p128 lukszczepanski; p129 peopleimages.com; p130 Olena; p131 220 Selfmade studio; p132 LIGHTFIELD STUDIOS; p133 Comeback Images; p134 Vadim Pastuh; p135 insta_photos; p136 Prostock-studio; p137 pathdoc; p138 WavebreakMediaMicro; p139 Fotos 593; p140 AmanWoody; p141 Monika Wisniewska; p142 Wayhome Studiop 143 zinkevych; p144 Andrey Popov; p145 Peakstock; p146 gstockstudio; p147 Electric Egg Ltd.; p148 SeanPavonePhoto; p149 Rido; p150 Mediteraneo; p151 Daisy Daisy; p152 shintartanya; p153 Alessandro Biascioli

Shutterstock © p5(t) iQoncept; p6 fizkes; p13 Alessia Pierdomenico; p39 valeriya_sh; p45 Alex Mit; p47 SciePro; p49 Alex Mit; p65(phone) 12bit, (people) Ground Picture, (emoji) Jan Engel; p70 AJP; p73 fotofeel; p77 frantic00

Creative Commons

p34 Photograph of Ivan Petrovitch Pavlov. Photogravure after Lafayette Ltd. Wellcome Collection, London. Public Domain Mark. CC BY 4.0 (https://creativecommons.org/licenses/by/4.0)

Other illustrations © Illuminate Publishing

About the authors

Cara has written some of the best-selling textbooks for A-level students for more than 30 years, having also been a teacher and senior examiner. She also organises and speaks at student conferences and is senior editor of the student magazine *Psychology Review*. She is looking forward to slowing down and spending more time walking and travelling.

Rob was an A-level Psychology teacher, head of department and an examiner for more than 20 years (greetings to students of KGV Southport and Winstanley College!). He is now the co-author of almost 20 BTEC, A-level and GCSE Psychology books. In his spare moments, Rob likes nothing better than to pluck away skill-lessly at his guitar. He spends the rest of the time contemplating the benefits of CDs and wondering when *Frozen 3* is coming out.

Exam advice

… it's how you use it.

What to do for a distinction

If you could go into the exam with all of your textbooks, you might not get top marks. 'How can that be?', we hear you ask. It's because exams are not just about knowing a set of facts – you also have to explain these facts and organise them in a meaningful way. It's not just what you know, but how you use your knowledge.

Effective description (AO1)	If a description question starts with the word *Identify*, *State* or *Give* and is worth 1 mark, then all you have to do is provide a brief answer. Accurate knowledge is all you need for a good answer – you get 1 mark for accuracy, or zero marks if inaccurate.
	Questions that start with *Describe* or *Explain* require more (and are worth more marks). They need development, they require you to demonstrate you understand, possibly by giving an example.
	For example (see what we did there?):
	Question: *State what is meant by the term 'schema'. (1 mark)*
	Answer: A schema is a mental packet of beliefs and expectations.
	Question: *Explain what is meant by the term 'schema'. (2 marks)*
	Answer: A schema is a mental packet of beliefs and expectations. For example, you have a schema for trains which includes what they look like, what they are for and what happens when you want to get on or off.
Effective application (AO2)	Questions with a scenario test your understanding because you have to use the information you have learned to explain something new. You can only do that if you understand the concepts.
	Almost every sentence of your answer should be related to both the scenario and the theory/concept you are using.
Effective evaluation (AO3)	For effective evaluation you should do at least two of the following three things (the PET rule): • Point – state the point you wish to make (strength or weakness). • Explain/Elaborate/provide Evidence – give some substance to support the point you are making. • This suggests that… / Therefore… / This means… – end with a mini-conclusion. What does the point tell us? We have made every evaluation point in this book PET-friendly.
Effective structure	Examiners are human so you need to help them award you marks. You can do this by organising your answer clearly. For example, make sure sentences follow logically from each other, use paragraphs, finish one point before going on to the next.
Less is more	Try to cover fewer points but, with each one, provide detail, explanation, examples, etc. Don't write everything you know and hope the sheer volume of facts will impress the examiner. They need to know that you understand it.

REVISION BOOSTERS

We've included some top tips to boost your revision, based on the advice on these Introduction spreads. There's a booster on almost every spread, so there's always something new for you to try.

Preparing for the exam

You will sit external exams on the topics in Units 1 and 3. Exams mean revising, but the secret is that revising should happen now. Start revising as you go along.

We have divided this book into spreads. Each spread represents one 'chunk' of the specification, shown at the top left of the spread.

Context is king

When you make a point of evaluation, make sure it applies to the concept, theory or scenario in the question. If your point could apply to *any* concept, theory or scenario, then it is a weak point.

Exam advice

Nailed it.

Timing

Timing is always important in exams because it is a fixed amount.

You must spend enough time on each answer in relation to the marks – not too much otherwise you won't give full enough answers to other questions.

How long should you spend on each question? For both Units 1 and 3, a very rough (but useful) rule of thumb is 'one minute per mark', bearing in mind you have to read and think as well as write.

How much should you write? Of course, there is no firm answer to this question. But here is a (very) rough guide.

A 9-mark extended open-response answer should be between 320 and 360 words and take about 13–15 minutes. A 6-mark answer should be between 200 and 220 words and take about 8–10 minutes.

Some lower-mark questions can be answered quickly. You don't have to, but you could 'bank' time to spend on the higher-mark questions.

But remember the thing that really matters – the quality of your answer is always more important than how many words you write.

Have confidence!

Self-efficacy is covered in Unit 3 (see page 94). The research shows that when you believe in your abilities, you expect to do well and often this will boost your performance (just don't get overconfident!).

Have things around you which remind you of your successes. Before the exam, remind yourself how much studying you have done and again think of your successes. Raise your self-efficacy.

Question 'rules' to consider

One / Two	Give **one** assumption of the cognitive approach. *(1 mark)*
	Explain **two** reasons for Theo's aggression. *(4 marks)*
	You must write about the exact number of 'things' in the question, otherwise you'll lose marks or waste time.
Evaluate / Assess	These are special terms because they require you to come to a conclusion (e.g. make a judgement about something). *Analyse, Discuss* and *Compare* do not require a conclusion.
Compare	*Psychologists believe there are different types of conformity. Compare **two** types of conformity.* *(3 marks)*
	When comparing two things, your answer must include both a similarity and a difference. You also need to bring the 'things' together (e.g. types of conformity) and not treat them separately (see the next spread for an example).
Examples / Types / Factors / Ways / Reasons / Effects	Any of these could appear in a question, so it's important you know what they are. Note that a question can tell you to include an example. But even if it doesn't, it's still often a good idea to do so.
Consider	*Evaluate the extent to which the biological approach can explain Theo's aggression. In your answer you should consider the roles of genetics and evolution.* *(9 marks)*
	The question may help you by giving a prompt about what to include. But that means you must include it.

Command terms

This is a selected list of the words that tell you how to answer questions.

Name	Recall a feature or characteristic using correct terms.
Describe	Give an account in which sentences are developed from each other (linked). Justification (reasons why) is not required (unlike *Explain* below).
Explain	Sentences should be linked to provide an element of reasoning. Reasoning involves justifying a point or example (e.g. saying why).
Justify	Give reasons/evidence to support a statement.
Discuss	Identify and explore all aspects of the issue/situation, with reasoning/argument (conclusion not needed).
Evaluate	Consider various aspects of a subject's qualities in relation to its context, such as strengths or weaknesses. Come to a judgement (conclusion), supported by evidence.

Revision advice

Five steps to effective revision

Step 1: Construct revision cards	For every spread you study, create a card for revision (if you wish, you can create more than one card, e.g. where there are two obvious topics on the spread). On the card draw a table with two columns: • Column 1 = cue word(s). • Column 2 = a small amount of text to remind you of important information. The great thing about using these cards is: • You reduce what you have to memorise (just the cues). The rest is engraved in your memory through practice. • If you keep making these cards throughout your course, you will have them all ready for revision.

Description

Topic *Life events*

Cue	Description
Big events	*e.g. marriage.* *Not everyday events.* *Require psychological adjustment.*
Holmes and Rahe	*1960s developed the SRRS.*
SRRS	*43 events.* *Add up LCUs.* *Divorce = 73 LCUs.*
Illness	*More likely the more LCUs.*

Evaluation

Practical uses – self-report	*People are experts on events and hassles so ask them, valid measure.*
Retrospective recall	*Recall events/ hassles from past, could be inaccurate, underestimate health impacts.*

Step 2: Check your cues work	Cover the right-hand column on your revision card and, for each cue, write down what you can recall from the right-hand side. Then check how much you remembered. Maybe you need to add a word or two to your cue to help you?
Step 3: Test your recall again	Repeat step 2 and see if you remember more this time.
Step 4: Test memory of cues	See if you can just recall the list of cues. In the exam all you need to remember is the cues and then the rest should be available to you. Psychological research shows that cues are the best way to enhance recall, and also that testing enhances memory.
Step 5: Practise writing timed answers	There is no substitute for practising what you will have to do in the exams – writing answers in timed conditions without your cue cards. Practice is especially important because answering questions isn't just about recalling knowledge. You need to practise applying your knowledge and understanding to scenarios. This revision guide contains a wide variety of exam-type questions you can use.

Right on cue

There are snooker cues and there are other cues – a cue is a thing that serves as a reminder of something else. Actors know they must come in on cue – a reminder or signal.

Psychologists have investigated the value of cues in remembering. They act as a reminder of what else you know.

In the revision card on the far left the key words in the first column can serve as a cue to remember the contents in the second column, which in turn can trigger more information you have stored in memory.

Active revision

Our memories evolved to store important information and not waste time on unimportant information. Therefore, you have to do something to make the information more meaningful. Compose a song using the key words and sing it. Have a debate on the topic with friends. Make up a quiz for your friend. Anything more active than just making notes.

Assessment advice

Example questions and answers	Marker's comments

Unit 1: Tahlia wants to buy some wireless earphones but she doesn't know which ones are best. She saw an advert for Airbuds which showed lots of happy people enjoying the product. But Tahlia has noticed that the music students in the college seem to prefer Earpods.

Explain how social proof might influence Tahlia's decision on the earphones she will buy. (2 marks)

Answer: Tahlia is unsure so she looks to others for guidance about which earphones to buy. Music students have more knowledge about music than the average, so Tahlia will trust their opinions and buy Earpods.	**Comments:** The first sentence shows correct understanding of social proof, related to the scenario. The second sentence is a linked explanation of how this affects Tahlia's decision. 2 marks.

Unit 1: *There are several different approaches in psychology. They differ in terms of how they explain behaviour.*
Compare the biological approach with **one** *alternative approach in psychology.* (3 marks)

Answer: One alternative is the cognitive approach. A similarity is both approaches look at how activity in the mind/brain affects behaviour. Both approaches also use brain scanning methods to investigate what is going on in the mind or brain.	**Comments:** The student gets 1 mark just for identifying an alternative approach. The 'rule' for a *Compare* question is that the answer should include both a similarity and a difference. But the student has given two similarities. Both of them are appropriate but only one can gain the second mark. Because the answer does not include a difference, it cannot get the third mark. This is a non-scenario question, so no application is needed. The marks are for evaluation/AO3. 2 marks.

Unit 3: Rajul knows she is addicted to smoking. Her friends have pointed out that she might get lung cancer or heart disease. Rajul knows she is at risk and would like to stop.

Her friends have bought her nicotine patches but she doesn't use them and hasn't done anything else to give up. Rajul seems to believe she is powerless to change her own behaviour. Her attitude is one of, 'Whatever will be will be, there's nothing I can do about it.'

Explain how Rajul having an external locus of control affects the likelihood of her giving up smoking. (2 marks)

Answer: Rajul believes she is powerless and that her smoking is determined by external factors outside her control. Therefore, she does not believe she can do anything to give up smoking, which is why she didn't use the nicotine patches.	**Comments:** The student gets 1 mark for identifying a feature of external LoC in Rajul. The second mark is for applying this to Rajul's chances of giving up smoking. This is done well and even uses a specific example from the scenario. The key words in the answer are 'she does not believe' because this shows the link between external LoC and behaviour. It is not enough to say 'Therefore, she will not give up smoking.' 2 marks.

Unit 3: Noah has an early memory of his parents having a party where lots of people were smoking. As a teenager his group of friends all smoked. He watched carefully how they did it. Everyone cheered when Noah smoked his first cigarette. That was when he really became part of the group and he's still friends with most of them. Now he is trying to give up and hasn't smoked for two days. He is keeping his lighter in his pocket 'for good luck'.

Explain **one** *way in which learning may play a role in the initiation of Noah's smoking addiction.* (2 marks)

Answer: A smoking addiction like in Noah can be started by social learning such as vicarious reinforcement. A child might see someone else smoking so this person is a role model (could be a parent). The child feels the model's pleasure from smoking so they imitate it and believe they will get the same experience and rewards from doing it.	**Comments:** The student has given a generic answer with no application to Noah at all. So although the answer is 'correct' (and quite detailed for 2 marks), it is not appropriate because it completely ignores all the useful information in the scenario. This is a pity because the answer only has to have some context somewhere (although more than just Noah's name). 0 marks.

Assessment advice

Example questions and answers	Marker's comments

Unit 3: The UK government devises a campaign to encourage people to exercise more, called 'Let's Get Britain Moving'. As part of this, a TV advert is filmed which is fronted by a major sports celebrity who has also been a fashion model. The advert points out the dangers of being inactive and the benefits of exercise.

Ellis watches the advert and realises that they could improve their health by exercising more. But they worry that they don't have the time or motivation.

Assess the effectiveness of the Hovland-Yale theory in predicting whether Ellis will be persuaded to exercise more.

(9 marks)

Answer: The Hovland-Yale theory predicts whether Ellis will exercise more depending on three aspects of the campaign.

First, the source of the campaign's message. A person will be persuaded to change their behaviour if the source has credibility and attractiveness. The source in the advert is a sports celebrity, who is credible because they are an 'expert' on physical activity. They have personal experience of being fit. They were also a fashion model so they probably are physically attractive. Because of the halo effect, Ellis might believe the celebrity is also knowledgeable about exercise.

Second, the message itself. The message will be persuasive if it has emotional appeal for Ellis. It has a fear threat because it shows the dangers of being inactive. But this is not enough on its own to persuade Ellis. However, the campaign also highlights there is a way to avoid negative outcomes – it can show Ellis how they get positive benefits from exercising. One part of the message may make Ellis afraid, but the other part may relieve their fear, so they are more likely to exercise.

Finally, there is the audience, i.e. Ellis themselves. If Ellis is an intelligent person, they may feel they are being manipulated by the campaign and resist changing their behaviour. On the other hand, as Ellis is aware they are lacking fitness, perhaps they have low self-esteem. People with low self-esteem are easier to persuade so Ellis may be more likely to exercise.

However, some research shows that people with high self-esteem are easier to persuade but just less willing to admit to being persuaded. This means the theory makes the wrong prediction about Ellis's behaviour. Also, the theory may well predict that Ellis will become more positive about the idea of exercise. But changing Ellis's attitude may not be enough to change their actual behaviour. Therefore, the theory cannot predict that Ellis will exercise because it is only describing the factors that contribute to their attitude.

In conclusion, the model could be effective in predicting that Ellis will exercise because two of the three aspects of the campaign are favourable. But this may just mean Ellis has a more positive attitude towards exercise, without actually doing any.   368 words

Comments: A very important rule of 9-mark extended open-response questions is that there are 3 marks for AO1, 3 for AO2 and 3 for AO3. So, the answer has to include a balance of description, application and evaluation, even though the command term is AO3.

The student's knowledge and understanding of the theory are accurate and thorough. Description is fairly detailed and has some depth. The answer covers all three factors in the theory rather than leaving one out.

At almost every point in the answer, the theory is applied to Ellis. The focus is on predicting Ellis's behaviour and whether the theory is able to do this. But there are vague elements too, e.g. 'A person will be persuaded to change their behaviour…' instead of 'Ellis will be persuaded to exercise…'.

The student has given two weaknesses of the theory which are both appropriate but neither is developed in much detail.

The command term is *Assess* so the student has drawn a conclusion. It is slightly repetitive of the previous point but otherwise a balanced judgement and applied to Ellis.

Overall, this is a very good answer. The reason it does not get full marks is because each skill could have been just a little bit more developed, especially the evaluative element (e.g. '…the theory makes the wrong prediction' is a bit vague).

Looking at the table below, the AO1 in this answer is bottom of level 3, the AO2 is middle of level 3 and the AO3 is top of level 2. So overall, bottom of level 3 = 7 marks.

Level	Mark	Knowledge and understanding	Gaps or omissions	Points are relevant to the context of the question	Links made to context	Discussion/ analysis/ assessment/ evaluation	Considers different aspects and how they interrelate
1	1–3	Isolated elements.	Major.	Few.	Minimal.	Limited.	Generic assertions.
2	4–6	Some accurate.	Minor.	Some.	Not clear.	Partially-developed.	Some, but not always in a sustained way.
3	7–9	Mostly accurate and detailed.	None.	Most.	Clear.	Well-developed.	A range, in a sustained way.

This is called a levels-based mark scheme because an examiner decides on your mark by determining the level that best describes your answer. The criteria in this table are adapted from the exam board's marking guidance.

Content area A

Assumptions of the four approaches

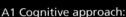

SPEC SPOTLIGHT

A1 Cognitive approach:

- Behaviour is a product of information processing.
- The brain can be compared to a computer (computer analogy) – input, processing and output.

A2 Social approach:

- Behaviour occurs in a social context (influenced by people around us).
- Wider culture and society influence people's behaviour.

Comparing the brain to a computer is a key assumption of the cognitive approach.

Apply it

In a meeting of a company's management team, the chief executive explains her plan to save the company from closing down. The other managers show signs of agreement, nodding their heads, saying 'yes, that's right' and making approving noises. But Shana doesn't think the plan is a good idea, so she keeps very quiet.

*Referring to an example from the scenario, explain **one** key assumption from the social approach.* **(2 marks)**

REVISION BOOSTER

Get organised!

This is a great topic for making sure your revision notes are organised. You've got four approaches and two assumptions for each approach. A revision table is a perfect way to arrange your notes.

Assumptions of the cognitive approach	
Behaviour is a product of information processing	'Cognitive' means related to thinking/mental processes. We are **information processors** – internal mental processes (e.g. reasoning, remembering) work together so we make sense of the world.
	A model (theory) explains how information from the environment is processed at each stage. Processes work together.
	E.g. you see a dog: you notice it (perception), focus on it (attention), recognise it (memory), name it (language).
The brain can be compared to a computer	Computers process information so the mind is compared to a computer. In both cases there are three stages:
	• Information goes in (input). • It is changed and/or stored (processing). • It is used to respond to the environment (output).
	The brain is the central processing unit ('hardware') which codes information, changing it from one format to another ('software').
	This approach contributes to the development of artificial intelligence (AI).

Assumptions of the social approach	
Behaviour occurs in a social context	'Social' means other members of your species, who influence our behaviour because humans are 'social animals'.
	E.g. conformity: you 'go along' with friends even if you disagree with them so you are not the odd one out. So, social context (your friends) affects behaviour.
	Social pressure is so powerful we just have to think about how others behave, they do not have to be present.
	Social interaction may influence behaviour more than an individual's disposition (their **personality**).
Wider culture and society influence people's behaviour	Behaviour can be understood/explained in terms of two broad types of **culture**:
	• Individualist cultures (e.g. UK and USA) – focus is on an individual's needs, where each person should achieve their potential and pursue their own goals (e.g. in a relationship, partners' happiness and 'being in love' matter).
	• Collectivist cultures (e.g. China and India) – priority is the needs of the family and community before the individual (e.g. in a relationship what matters is family approval, being 'in love' is less important).

Unit 1 Psychological approaches and applications

Assumptions of the four approaches

Assumptions of the behaviourist and social learning approaches

Behaviour is a learned response to environmental stimuli	Things in the environment bring about learning. If you touch a hot pan, you are hurt and learn not to do it again. If you smile when you ask a favour, you get what you want and learn to do it again.
	There are two main forms of learning:
	Classical conditioning Learning by association (Pavlov) – dogs salivated when they heard a door open because they associated noise of the door with food.
	Operant conditioning Learning by consequences (Skinner) – if a behaviour produces a pleasurable consequence (reward) it will be repeated. The environment **reinforces** (strengthens) the behaviour.
Behaviour can be learned from observation and imitation	Learning can occur through **observation/ imitation** of other people's behaviour (Bandura).
	E.g. child observes parents'/carers' behaviour (**role models**) and imitates it if they see behaviour rewarded (with praise, money, etc.). This is **vicarious reinforcement** (i.e. the model's behaviour is rewarded, not the child's).

Assumptions of the biological approach

Behaviour is influenced by central nervous system (CNS), genes and neurochemistry	Everything psychological is firstly biological, so behaviours, thoughts, feelings have a physical basis.
	Central nervous system (CNS) Consists of the brain and spinal cord, the body's control centre. Different areas of the brain perform different functions (e.g. language, **aggression**). Damage to the brain/CNS seriously affects these functions.
	Genes 'Units' of DNA (inherited from parents) interact with environment. Many behaviours are passed down generations.
	Neurochemistry Brain **neurotransmitters** (**serotonin**, **dopamine**, etc.) affect behaviour (e.g. dopamine is disrupted in schizophrenia).
Behaviour is a product of evolution	Genetically-determined behaviours that are successful continue into future generations (= natural selection, Darwin).
	Behaviours and characteristics enhancing an individual's chances of survival and reproduction are selected.
	E.g. someone with good hunting skills is more likely to thrive and survive (they have food to eat). So they are more likely to reproduce successfully. Their skills (e.g. fast reactions) are passed onto offspring.

SPEC SPOTLIGHT

A3 Behaviourist and social learning approaches:

- Behaviour is a learned response to environmental stimuli.
- Behaviour can be learned from observation and imitation.

A4 Biological approach:

- Behaviour is influenced by central nervous system (CNS), genes and neurochemistry.
- Behaviour is a product of evolution.

Imitation of other people's behaviour is one way children learn.

Apply it

Larry organised a cake sale for Children in Need. He distributed flyers, with images of cakes and other sweet goodies. When people turned up, he gave them a free cake and cup of tea. He put on a demonstration of cake-making for people who had never baked. Larry sold lots of cakes and raised lots of money.

*Referring to an example from the scenario, explain **one** key assumption from the behaviourist/social learning approaches.* *(2 marks)*

Key concept 1: Characteristics of three memory stores

Content area A

Unit 1 Psychological approaches and applications

SPEC SPOTLIGHT

Characteristics of sensory, short-term, and long-term memory (encoding, capacity, duration).

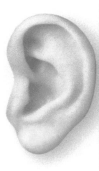

Ear is echoic memory. Eye is iconic memory.

Apply it

Nikita was daydreaming again. Her friend said to her, 'Did you hear what I just said?' Nikita immediately replied, 'Yes, you said something about going out tonight.'

1. Name the memory store that allowed Nikita to give this reply.
   (1 mark)

Later that day, Nikita heard a song on the radio that she liked. The presenter said the title of the song and the name of the band. Nikita thought, 'I must make a note of that on my phone.' But by the time she found her phone, she could only remember the name of the band.

2. Using your knowledge of short-term memory, explain **one** reason why Nikita could not remember all of the information.   *(2 marks)*

The name of the band was 'The Cars'. But when Nikita recalled the name the next day, she thought it was 'The Motors'.

3. Using your knowledge of encoding in long-term memory, explain why Nikita made this error.   *(2 marks)*

4. Discuss **one** characteristic of Nikita's memory.   *(3 marks)*

Duration

Sensory memory (SM)	All stimuli pass into SM, which is made up of five stores, one for each sense, e.g.: • Iconic memory – visual stimuli last less than 0.5s. • Echoic memory – auditory (sound) stimuli last 2–4s.
Short-term memory (STM)	Temporary memory store lasts up to 30s (Peterson and Peterson). Maintenance rehearsal increases duration and information may then pass into LTM.
Long-term memory (LTM)	Potentially permanent store for rehearsed material (lifetime). E.g. recognising names/faces after 50 years (Bahrick *et al.*).

Capacity

Sensory memory	Very high capacity, e.g. over one hundred million cells in each retina (eye) with each cell storing visual data.
Short-term memory	Limited-capacity store, between five and nine items ('magic number 7 ± 2', Miller).
Long-term memory	Practically unlimited, LTM stores everything we learn so forgetting is due to lack of appropriate retrieval **cues**.

Encoding

Sensory memory	All stores convert information into a form that can be stored. SM has different forms of encoding depending on the sensory store, e.g.: • Visual encoding in iconic store. • Acoustic (sound) encoding in echoic store.
Short-term memory	Uses mainly acoustic encoding (sounds of words). **Baddeley's study** Participants learned lists of words and recalled them immediately (STM). Errors were based on mixing up sounds (e.g. recalling 'cat' instead of 'cap'), therefore acoustic.
Long-term memory	Uses mainly semantic encoding (meaning of words). **Baddeley's study** Participants learned lists of words and recalled them after 20 minutes (LTM). Errors were based on mixing up meanings (e.g. recalling 'big' instead of 'large'), therefore semantic.

Key concept 1: Characteristics of three memory stores

One strength is that knowledge of memory stores has practical applications.

For example, researchers have found that a technique called 'chunking' increases the capacity of STM.

15 letters is more than double the average STM capacity, e.g. C A R D O G L I T P E N B U Y. But these letters can be reorganised into: CAR DOG LIT PEN BUY, which is five bigger items ('chunks'), well within most people's STM capacity.

This shows how understanding the characteristics of memory stores can help to improve memory.

What do Nelson Mandela and a sensory memory store have in common? That's right, they're both iconic.

Another strength is evidence of memory stores with different characteristics.

For instance, one characteristic of memory stores is their duration.

Information in the iconic store (vision) lasts for about 50 milliseconds (Sperling), in STM up to about 30 seconds (Peterson and Peterson) and in LTM up to a lifetime (Bahrick *et al.*).

Therefore SM, STM and LTM must be separate memory stores because they differ so much in duration (and also encoding and capacity).

REVISION BOOSTER

This topic is a goldmine of practical ways to improve your memory. The key for a student revising for exams is to improve long-term memory. The real skill, however, is not so much getting information into memory, but getting it *out*. We'll have a lot more to say about this in later boosters.

For now, bear in mind that long-term memory can be improved by organising the material you want to learn. For instance, use plenty of headings and bullet points at different levels. Organising material forces you to think about it more deeply, which is much better than simply reading or copying.

One weakness is that a lot of research is not typical of everyday memory.

Participants in studies often have to remember letters, digits and consonant syllables which have no meaning, e.g. 'YCG' in Peterson and Peterson's study.

But memories in everyday life are about useful things (faces, facts, places, etc.), much more meaningful than materials used in many studies.

This means that the different characteristics of the memory stores may not be so clear when we use our memories in everyday life.

Apply it

Lena is a junior doctor in a hospital A&E department. Recently a patient was admitted by ambulance and a paramedic handed him over with these words:

'This is Sam, 25-year-old male, respiratory rate is 18, heart rate is 130, blood pressure 115 over 65, temperature 36.9, oxygen sats 96%, Coma Scale score is 13, administered 10 mg morphine 15 minutes ago.'

Lena repeated this information over and over to herself until she started treating Sam. Lena forgot Sam's blood pressure but a nurse was able to remind her. Lena thought the morphine was administered 50 minutes ago.

1. Identify the memory store that Lena was using to remember the handover information. *(1 mark)*

2. Explain **one** reason why Lena forgot some of the information. *(2 marks)*

3. Explain **one** reason why Lena thought the paramedic said '50 minutes' rather than '15 minutes'. *(2 marks)*

4. Describe **one** way in which the scenario illustrates the duration of Lena's short-term memory. *(2 marks)*

Key concept 2: Remembering

SPEC SPOTLIGHT

Remembering (recognition, recall and the importance of cues).

It's usually much easier to recognise someone than to recall their name.

Recall	
Free recall	Retrieval from a memory store without 'assistance'.
	E.g. in a research study you read a list of words, put it to one side and write down all the words you remember.
Cued recall	Retrieval from memory with assistance from a **cue** ('trigger').
	E.g. in a research study you read a list of words, put it to one side and are told the first letter of each word.
	We have more in memory than we think and can recall 'forgotten' information when triggered by the right cue.

Recognition	
Recognition memory	When we remember something because we have encountered it before.
	E.g. you know someone's name when you hear it.
	E.g. in a multiple-choice question with answers, you know the correct one when you see it.
	This shows we store more in LTM than we can access through free recall.

Cues	
Meaningful cues	The cue is directly relevant to the material we want to remember.
	E.g. the cue is 'STM' – 'S' cues retrieval of 'short', the word 'short' cues retrieval of other meaningful material (duration, capacity, etc.).
Cues without meaning	The cue is not directly relevant to the material but occurs at the same time we learn it.
	E.g. a random event such as a thunderstorm happens at the same time you learn something about STM. When a storm happens again, it might cue recall of information about STM.

Apply it

Vash is listening to Popmaster on the radio. He often can't think of the answers, but when he hears them he thinks, 'Of course, I remember that song now.'

1. *Identify the type of remembering that Vash is experiencing.* *(1 mark)*

Vash is doing a multiple-choice test at college. He says to his friends, 'Multiple-choice questions are a lot easier than normal exam questions where you have to come up with the answers.'

2. *With reference to Vash's comment, explain **one** difference between recognition and recall.* *(2 marks)*

Vash has a new technique to help him revise. He writes notes in a table on a card. Each row of the table starts with a couple of key words, followed by more information. He then tries to remember the key words. Vash's exam results have improved since he started revising like this.

3. *Explain how Vash's revision technique has improved his exam results.* *(2 marks)*

4. *Discuss the importance of cues in Vash's experience of remembering his college work.* *(3 marks)*

Key concept 2: Remembering

One strength is practical applications of retrieval cues.

Mnemonics are memory aids based on psychological knowledge that use cues to trigger retrieval of information from long-term memory.

E.g. BIDMAS (where each letter stands for one maths operator) reminds you of the order of operations, 'Richard Of York Gave Battle In Vain' helps retrieve the colours of the rainbow.

This shows how understanding the role of cues can help us to improve memory.

A mnemonic for guitar strings:
Every Adult Dog Growls Barks Eats.
Well, they do when I'm playing.

Another strength is support for cues from many research studies.

Participants learned and remembered lists of words from categories (animals, clothing, etc.). Some participants were given headings as cues, others not (Tulving and Pearlstone).

When they had to recall the lists, participants who were given cues remembered significantly more words than participants without cues.

This finding shows that cues are important in retrieving memories that would otherwise be 'forgotten', and also that cued recall is superior to free recall.

One weakness is some cues are not important in everyday remembering.

The environment in which you learn (e.g. classroom) provides some context-related cues to retrieve information later (e.g. physical layout, background noises, smells).

But context-related cues are not as powerful in everyday life as meaningful cues (e.g. BIDMAS), because environments at learning and retrieval are usually different (e.g. classroom and exam room).

Therefore, not all cues are equally important and some are relatively useless in everyday situations.

REVISION BOOSTER

Vash (see Apply it on facing page) is definitely onto something. Cues are your gateway to memory improvement. Use cue words to trigger your memory of other words. There are lots of ways to do this. Here's one suggestion (more later):

- Actively read a page of notes – that is, highlight or circle the key terms, concepts, theories, etc. as you go.

- Write each of these (just one or two words) on the back of a post-it note (or card).

- On the front of the post-it/card, write a question to which the answer is the word or two on the back.

- Stick the post-it notes up, choose one and have a go at answering the question.

Apply it

A psychologist is training Lena and other junior doctors in how to improve their memories to better retain handover information (see previous spread).

The doctors role-play a handover in pairs. Lena is given some information and 2 minutes later she correctly remembers the patient's blood pressure. She cannot remember the patient's heart rate, but when her partner tells her, Lena says, 'Oh yes, I remember that now.'

The psychologist says that memory can be improved by using cues.

1. Identify **one** example of recognition and **one** example of recall from the scenario. (2 marks)

2. Explain **one** reason why Lena was able to recognise some information but not recall it. (2 marks)

3. Describe **two** ways Lena could use cues to improve her memory. (4 marks)

4. Discuss the importance of cues in Lena's remembering of handover information. (3 marks)

A1: Cognitive approach

Key concept 3: Reconstructive memory

Content area A

Unit 1 Psychological approaches and applications

SPEC SPOTLIGHT

Reconstructive memory, including the role of schema (shortening, rationalisation and confabulation).

A video recorder. Ancient technology. Not how memory works.

Apply it

Finn is a teacher. He watches a recording of the interview for his job from the previous month. Finn thinks to himself, 'I thought they asked me about coursework marking but there's nothing in this recording about that.'

1. Using **one** concept from reconstructive memory, explain why Finn remembered being asked about coursework marking. **(3 marks)**

Amber was on her way home from school when she saw a robbery. She told the police it was a betting shop that was robbed but other witnesses said it was a jewellers.

2. Explain **one** way that reconstructive memory can help us understand what Amber remembers about the robbery. **(3 marks)**

3. One feature of reconstructive memory is shortening. Explain how Amber's recall of the robbery might demonstrate shortening. **(2 marks)**

4. Referring to Amber's experience, discuss the view that memory is reconstructive. **(3 marks)**

What is reconstructive memory?

Memories are not reproductions (Bartlett)	Memories are reconstructions and we retrieve memories by rebuilding them again. • Memory does not record events like a video recorder. • We store fragments of information and to recall them we build (reconstruct) them into a meaningful whole. • So, memory is not always a totally accurate record of events.

Role of schema in memory

Schema is a mental structure or 'package'	**Schema** contain stored knowledge about the world. E.g. we have a schema for 'mother', 'teacher', 'party', and many many other concepts. Schema develop through personal and shared cultural experience, e.g. what you expect a 'birthday party' to include. Schema affect what we store in memory and later retrieve.
War of the Ghosts (Bartlett)	Participants heard an Inuit folk tale, with concepts that were unfamiliar to them, e.g. 'canoes', 'arrows'. They recalled the story in ways that made it more familiar – to fit existing schema, making it more meaningful and easier to recall.
Schema reconstruct memory in three ways	**1. Shortening** We leave out parts of an event that don't fit our schema (e.g. unfamiliar details), so the stored and retrieved memory is shorter. Bartlett's participants did not recall supernatural elements because they were unfamiliar. **2. Rationalisation** We recall events in a distorted way so they fit our existing schema (elements of the event did not match schema but now they do and make more sense). Bartlett's participants replaced unfamiliar words with familiar ones (e.g. 'guns' and 'boat' instead of 'arrows' and 'canoe'). **3. Confabulation** We invent parts of an event to fill in any 'gaps', to match schema and make retrieval meaningful (this is not random and not the same as 'lying'). Bartlett's participants incorrectly recalled details to make the story more coherent.

Key concept 3: Reconstructive memory

One strength is that reconstructive memory explains problems with EWT.

One of these problems is that eyewitness testimony (EWT) in criminal court trials is based solely on what the eyewitness can recall of what they saw or heard.

But the person's recall may be affected by their schema, e.g. seeing someone with a gun and expecting them to be a man. So, people do not always recall events accurately as recall can be affected by expectations of what 'should' happen.

This means evidence in court is never based on EWT alone as it can be inaccurate, a very important application of this research.

Does this fit your schema for 'older man', 'knitting' or even 'punk rocker'? What effect would this have on your recall?

Another strength is evidence from Bartlett's research.

Bartlett's participants did not recall many details of an unfamiliar story (*The War of the Ghosts*). Instead, they tried to make sense of what they heard before storing it in memory.

Recall of the story changed significantly, with evidence of shortening, rationalisation and confabulation, as predicted by reconstructive memory theory.

This shows that we reconstruct memories from elements that are influenced by our schema, often making recall inaccurate.

One weakness is that recall of some memories can be very accurate.

For example, we can often remember the details of situations when they are personally important or unusual.

For example, in Bartlett's research, participants often recalled the phrase, 'Something black came out of his mouth' because it was quite unusual (distinctive).

This shows that people may not always reconstruct memories, and some memories can be relatively unaffected by schema.

REVISION BOOSTER

Use mnemonic rhymes. A mnemonic is simply anything that improves memory. An example is putting the concepts you want to remember into unusual sentences. Then you try to make the sentences rhyme. For example, here's a rhyming mnemonic to link the main concepts on this spread:

You reconstruct your memory by schema.
I'm not being a dreamer.
Schema make memories shorter,
By maybe a quarter.
Rationalisation makes the memory twisted,
It's schema-assisted.
And confabulation fills in the gaps.
This isn't lying or random, and that's a wrap!

Apply it

Graeme is chatting to his boss Velma about his first day working in the café two years ago.

Graeme says, 'I remember having trouble with the tablet we used to take orders. I didn't know where anything was, so I had to keep asking Gaby to help me.'

Velma says, 'But we didn't use tablets then, we used pen and paper. We've never had a Gaby working here.'

1. Give **one** example of rationalisation from the scenario.
   (1 mark)

2. Give **one** example of confabulation from the scenario.
   (1 mark)

3. Explain why Graeme's description of his first day in the café may not have been accurate. Use **two** concepts from reconstructive memory in your answer. *(6 marks)*

4. Discuss reconstructive memory as a way of understanding why Graeme's recall may not have been accurate. *(3 marks)*

AO1
Description

Key concept 4: Cognitive priming

SPEC SPOTLIGHT

Cognitive priming, including the role of cognitive scripts and different types of priming (repetition, semantic and associative).

These two go together like…

Apply it

Phoenix saw a vlog on fishing. At the supermarket later, going past the freezers, they suddenly thought, 'I fancy chips for tea.'

1. *State which type of cognitive priming is demonstrated in this scenario.* **(1 mark)**

2. *Explain how this type of cognitive priming can be used to understand Phoenix's behaviour in the supermarket.* **(3 marks)**

Rafi overheard some colleagues talking about their holiday plans. Later on, scrolling through Insta, Rafi immediately noticed someone had posted a video of their holiday in Lanzarote.

3. *Explain, using your knowledge of cognitive priming, why Rafi noticed the video so quickly.* **(3 marks)**

Coco ordered a coffee at a local café. When she got home, her partner was singing a song. 'I recognise that. It's 'Coffee Shop' by Red Hot Chilli Peppers.' Coco's partner replied, 'You never normally remember song titles.'

4. *Identify the type of priming experienced by Coco and explain how it accounts for her being able to recall the song title.* **(4 marks)**

What is cognitive priming?

Priming means 'preparing'	Seeing or hearing one stimulus (the 'prime') affects your response to a later related stimulus (you process it faster).
	The prime triggers related concepts in memory, so activation is quicker when the second stimulus occurs (examples below).
	You do not know your response is influenced because priming occurs below your level of awareness.

Types of cognitive priming

Repetition priming	You see/hear the prime. When you see/hear it again later you process it more quickly than you would have done.
	E.g. you overhear 'avocado' (the prime). You are now 'primed' to notice (process) it more quickly if you hear/see the word again later (or see an actual avocado).
Semantic priming	You see/hear the prime. When you later see/hear a stimulus similar in meaning you process the later stimulus faster.
	E.g. you see/hear 'computer' (the prime). You are now primed to notice (recognise or recall) semantically similar words (e.g. you process 'laptop' faster because it has a similar meaning).
Associative priming	You see/hear the prime. When you later see/hear a stimulus that is often associated with the prime, you process the later stimulus faster.
	E.g. you hear the word 'fish'. You are now primed to notice (recognise or recall) anything usually paired with this in memory. In our **culture** this is likely to be 'chips'.
An example of how cognitive priming works	Cognitive priming is 'mentally setting you up in advance to behave in a certain way', which could explain the influence of adverts.
	E.g. you watch a TV advert that shows snacking as fun, which primes you (in advance) to associate snacks with something positive. You then eat a lot of snacks.
	This was the experimental group in a study by Harris *et al.* They compared a group of students primed by 'snacking' adverts with a group of students who did not see adverts or who saw non-food-related adverts. Students primed by adverts ate more snacks than students not primed by adverts.

Key concept 4: Cognitive priming

One strength is that priming can help us prevent cognitive causes of obesity.

For example, advertising can affect how many snacks people eat because of cognitive priming (Harris *et al.*, facing page).

Understanding the effects of priming means we might prevent this from influencing obesity (or direct the influence towards healthy eating instead).

This means that education and legislation (although politically difficult) could help to prevent obesity.

Priming might help explain the effects of TV advertising on eating unhealthy snacks.

Another strength is a possible link between video gaming and aggression.

Priming might explain the link, e.g. in one study students read a scenario in which someone is accidentally pushed so they spill their drink (Möller and Krahé).

Frequent players of violent video games were more likely to interpret the push as deliberate and more likely to choose physical **aggression** in response.

This shows that playing violent video games may prime some people to think and behave aggressively, supporting the concept of associative priming.

REVISION BOOSTER

Examples are really useful in two ways. They boost your revision because they help you to understand a concept. They're also useful in exam answers for developing a point and showing the examiner your knowledge. You might even be asked to identify an example of a concept in a scenario.

There are four examples of priming on this spread, including the one about the influence of TV advertising. Think carefully about how the example illustrates the concept. Once you feel you've really understood a concept, you can come up with your own examples to reinforce your understanding.

One weakness of cognitive priming is that it is very difficult to study.

This is because priming studies are hard to replicate. Replication means a study is repeated using the same procedure, an important feature of science.

If the replication produces the same outcome, then we know that this is not a fluke. But replications of priming studies often produce different outcomes.

This suggests that the concept of priming is not scientific which means we cannot be confident that the theories are correct.

Apply it

Wes filled in a magazine questionnaire. One of the questions was, 'What is your favourite colour?'. His response was 'yellow'. Later on, a friend asked Wes if he would like some fruit. 'I'll have a banana please,' he replied.

1. *Explain why semantic priming is the most appropriate type of cognitive priming to understand Wes's reply.* **(3 marks)**

On her way out to work, Tam's flatmate says, 'Don't forget to get some cat food on your way home.' Later on, Tam notices a small hole in the skirting board. 'I bet a mouse did that,' he thinks.

2. *Describe **one** type of priming that could be used to understand Tam's comment.* **(3 marks)**

Ricky is at the cinema enjoying the adverts before the main feature. One advert is for popcorn. Halfway through the film, Ricky feels hungry so they go into the foyer and the first thing they notice is the popcorn machine.

3. *Explain how repetition priming might affect Ricky's behaviour in the foyer.* **(3 marks)**

4. *Select **one** of these scenarios. Discuss the extent to which cognitive priming can explain the behaviour in that scenario.* **(3 marks)**

A1: Cognitive approach

Key concept 5: The role of cognitive scripts

SPEC SPOTLIGHT

The role of cognitive scripts (memory scripts, person perception).

The language of cognitive scripts comes from the theatre, with roles, scripts, scenes, props and so on.

Memory scripts

What is a memory script?

A memory script contains our knowledge of what happens in social situations, how we should behave and what the consequences could be.

E.g. the restaurant script includes our knowledge and expectations of the setting (the restaurant), props (menus, tables, etc.) and actors (waiting staff, customers, chefs, etc.).

Features of memory scripts

Using the restaurant script example, memory scripts:

- Are broken down into scenes ordered by time, e.g. enter restaurant, sit at a table, order, eat, pay the bill.
- Concern multiple goals, e.g. satisfy hunger, enjoy the occasion, impress a partner, etc.
- Are dynamic and become more refined and detailed with experience (including from TV and other media).
- Are influenced by **culture**, e.g. in most restaurants in China, customers expect to find a table themselves.
- Influence memory – we remember events that are consistent with a script (because they match what we expect), but we may also remember events that are inconsistent (they stand out).

Person perception

What is person perception?

When we meet someone new, we quickly categorise them, mentally placing them into a group or 'type' (often on the basis of what they look or sound like).

How person perception works

Making assumptions Once we have categorised a 'new' person, we fill in the gaps in our knowledge of them with information from memory about that category.

E.g. I categorise someone as 'outgoing', so assume they are also impulsive and loud because these all 'go together' in my memory.

Stereotyping and bias My knowledge of which characteristics go together can be wrong because it is partly based on stereotypes (see page 28). I assume the other person is representative of a group – they are 'this *type* of person'.

Person perception is affected by our own **cognitive biases** (see next spread) which can distort memory. What we recall about the person is not objectively accurate but matches the category we put them in.

Apply it

Rowan is sitting an Applied Psychology exam. They arrive at the exam hall 15 minutes before the start, locate their seat on the chart, take everything they need out of their bag and put the bag in the designated area. When the exam starts Rowan reads the front of the paper carefully and then reads the questions twice. They put their hand up when they need more paper.

1. Give **two** examples from the scenario that could be part of Rowan's memory script for taking an exam. (2 marks)

2. Explain **one** way that memory scripts could be used to understand Rowan's behaviour in the exam hall. (3 marks)

3. Discuss the extent to which memory scripts can help us understand Rowan's behaviour in the exam hall. (3 marks)

Key concept 5: The role of cognitive scripts

One strength is we can make person perception more accurate and objective.

We often inaccurately judge someone's **personality** when we first meet them. These may be based on stereotypes (what they 'should' be like), which is undesirable because stereotypes are usually negative.

Instead, we could make sure we take the time to properly get to know someone without making instant 'snap' judgements about their personality.

Therefore, by knowing how person perception works, we can resist the tendency to negatively stereotype others.

Person perception is about how we try to 'work out' what someone is like.

Another strength is evidence to support the role of memory scripts.

If you are presented with a routine event where the steps are in the wrong order, you usually recall them in the correct order because the correct order matches the script stored in memory (Bower *et al.*).

For instance, a 'getting ready for college' script might be presented as 'get dressed, get out of bed, wake up', but you recall it as 'wake up, get out of bed, get dressed'.

This finding supports the argument that cognitive scripts strongly influence how we remember everyday events.

REVISION BOOSTER

It's never too early to remind you to make your evaluation points PET-friendly. If you do get asked to discuss a concept, explanation, behaviour, etc., the question will be worth 3 marks. So, stick to one point and develop it like this:

- 'P' is the evaluative **point** (e.g. a strength or weakness) – start by saying what it is.

- 'E' is your **explanation** of the point (also called elaboration), which could include an example.

- 'T' refers to a concluding sentence that begins with something like, **'This shows that…'** or 'This means that…' – here you explain what the evaluative point tells us about the theory, explanation, etc.

One weakness is we may assume a script is guiding behaviour when it isn't.

When someone behaves in a way consistent with a script, they might be doing so because they are **imitating** other people and therefore following external **cues** rather than a script (e.g. when eating in a restaurant).

Also in person perception, my judgement of a stranger might be guided more by how others respond (external cues) than by information stored in memory.

Therefore, scripts and internal processes are not always important influences on behaviour.

Apply it

Euan works as a barista in a busy coffee shop. He is introduced to a new colleague called Ettie. As they shake hands, Euan thinks Ettie seems 'standoffish' and not very interesting. However, after a while Euan thinks Ettie is more friendly.

Later on, Euan describes Ettie to a friend: 'Ettie was OK but she's a typical boring person. I don't think she's going to do very well in this job.'

1. Identify **two** examples from the scenario that demonstrate person perception. *(2 marks)*

2. Explain how the concept of person perception can help us understand Euan's comments. *(3 marks)*

3. Discuss the extent to which person perception is a useful way to understand Euan's comments. *(3 marks)*

Key concept 6: Cognitive biases

Content area A

Unit 1 Psychological approaches and applications

SPEC SPOTLIGHT

Cognitive biases, including fundamental attribution error, confirmation bias and hostile attribution bias.

It could happen. But we're more likely to think the homework is missing because the student is lazy.

Apply it

Sylvia was passing a colleague in the corridor at work and said 'hello' but the colleague did not reply. 'What a rude and impolite person,' thought Sylvia.

1. Name **one** cognitive bias demonstrated in this scenario.
   (1 mark)

2. Justify your answer to question 1.
   (2 marks)

Later that day, the colleague quietly explained to Sylvia why they had ignored her earlier. Sylvia replied, 'I don't like your tone, you need to calm down.'

3. Identify the type of cognitive bias shown by Sylvia and explain why it may be a reason for her comment. *(3 marks)*

4. Discuss the extent to which the concept of cognitive bias can explain Sylvia's comment.
   (3 marks)

What are cognitive biases?

Bias is a 'prejudgement'

Cognitive bias = how our thinking can 'prejudge' or 'lean' in one direction.

Negative effects Cognitive biases are automatic (no thinking) so how we process information (what we notice and remember) becomes flawed. Biases undermine our ability to make rational decisions.

Positive effects Cognitive biases simplify how we view the world. They are 'shortcuts' that help us make decisions quickly.

Fundamental attribution error (FAE)

Explaining other people's behaviour

We can understand the FAE from individual words in the term.

Attribution We try to explain the reasons for other people's behaviour.

E.g. if your friend is late you might attribute lateness to their personal characteristics (they don't think it's important to be on time) or to situations (the bus broke down).

Fundamental error Most people are biased towards one attribution, to overemphasise personal characteristics and downplay situations. It is the most basic (fundamental) error.

E.g. believing a student is handing in an essay late because they are lazy (a personal characteristic).

Confirmation bias

Confirming existing beliefs

We are biased towards favouring information that confirms what we already believe.

E.g. you are more sensitive to information confirming your existing view of the football team you support.

We notice, store and easily recall confirmatory information. But we ignore or reject information that challenges our beliefs and we don't look for contradictory information.

Hostile attribution bias (HAB)

An aggressive bias

Someone with a HAB:

- Wrongly believes another person's behaviour is threatening (hostile) when it is actually neutral, e.g. an accidental bump in a crowded pub.
- Believes the other person is hostile because that is what they are like (personal characteristic), but this ignores the situation (crowded pub).

Key concept 6: Cognitive biases

One strength of cognitive biases is application to real-world behaviour.

For example, we can overcome confirmation bias by deliberately seeking out information that contradicts our existing views.

We can do this by reading a variety of news sources and applying critical thinking skills to political parties, football teams, etc.

This is useful because, by understanding cognitive biases, we can improve our decision-making and reduce negative effects on behaviour.

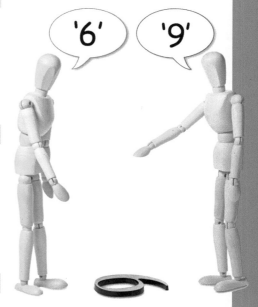

Another strength is the link between hostile attribution bias and aggression.

People with a strong HAB often behave aggressively. While behaving like this, they may experience a temporary increase in their hostile attributions.

This is a vicious circle because the temporary increase in attributions makes further **aggression** even more likely (Tuente *et al.*).

This shows the central role of a HAB in aggressive behaviour, and also a potential way of tackling it (by turning hostile attributions into neutral ones).

One weakness is that the FAE only exists in some cultures.

In individualist **cultures** (e.g. USA), people generally value individual needs above the needs of the wider community. So, behaviour tends to be attributed to individual characteristics.

However, in collectivist cultures (e.g. China) the group or community is prioritised over individual needs. So, people tend to attribute behaviour to situational factors rather than to **personality**.

This suggests the FAE may not be a 'fundamental' feature of human **information processing** after all.

Is it a '6' or a '9'? We can reduce confirmation bias by exposing ourselves to a variety of different views.

Apply it

Sasha supports a lower-league football club. All of her friends are also supporters and she is part of a supporters' Facebook group. When her team wins, she likes to read posts about the matches. But she prefers not to bother when they lose.

A group of supporters were drinking in a pub before a match. The brother of one of her friends asked Sasha how the team were doing. Sasha said 'very well indeed' even though the club had lost in a cup final the previous season.

1. Give **one** example of confirmation bias from the scenario. *(1 mark)*

2. Explain why confirmation bias is the most appropriate cognitive bias to understand Sasha's behaviour. *(3 marks)*

When her friend's brother pointed out the team had lost the final, Sasha said this was an aggressive comment and that he should leave the pub.

3. Identify the type of cognitive bias shown by Sasha and explain why it may be a reason for her comment. *(3 marks)*

4. Discuss the usefulness of cognitive biases in understanding Sasha's comment and/or behaviour. *(3 marks)*

REVISION BOOSTER

There's a type of bias that could cause you problems in the exam if you're not careful. It happens when you see one word in a question that you 'grab onto' without giving enough thought to the rest of the question.

You think, 'I recognise that word from my revision,' and then you launch into your answer immediately, relieved that you've found something you know about.

So firstly, make sure you cover all the concepts, theories, etc. for each topic. Basically, if it's on a spread in this guide, you need to know it.

Secondly, in the exam, take time to read the question carefully before even thinking about answering it. And read the accompanying scenarios carefully too.

A2: Social approach

Key concept 1: Conformity

SPEC SPOTLIGHT

Conformity (normative social influence and informational social influence).

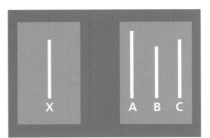

The line X on the left-hand card is the standard line. The lines A, B and C are the three comparison lines. The participants had to say which of the comparison lines was the same length as the standard line (the answer was always obvious – here it is C).

Apply it

Students in a psychology class are working in groups to answer some questions. Calvin gives an answer and gradually the other students agree with him. Shann is not sure about Calvin's answer but agrees with the rest of the group anyway.

1. Give **one** example of conformity from the scenario. *(1 mark)*

2. Explain **two** ways that the concept of conformity could be used to understand why Shann agreed with the other students. *(4 marks)*

3. Discuss the effectiveness of conformity in explaining why Shann agreed with the other students. *(3 marks)*

Later in the lesson, the students discuss a question before writing their answers down. Most of the group agreed on an answer but Shann was unsure. In the end, Shann wrote down a different answer from the other students.

4. Explain **one** reason why Shann wrote down a different answer from everyone else. *(2 marks)*

Conformity

What is conformity?	Choosing to 'go along' with other people by agreeing with their opinions or behaving as they do. The result of 'invisible' pressure from others, they do not tell us how to behave or what opinions to have.
	Two main processes explain conformity (Deutsch and Gerard).
1. Normative social influence (NSI)	**Group norms** Behaviours and beliefs considered to be 'normal' in a group. Norms guide behaviour and 'glue' the group together. We conform to these norms to be liked by the other group members and avoid being rejected.
	Emotional process NSI is about how you *feel*, so it is stronger in stressful situations where people have a greater need for social support.
2. Informational social influence (ISI)	**Information** Often we are unsure about what behaviours or beliefs are right or wrong.
	E.g. if most students in a class agree on one answer, you may accept it because you think they are probably right (they have the better information). We conform because we want to be right.
	Cognitive process ISI is about what you *think*, so is most likely in new situations where you don't know what is right or in situations where it isn't clear what is right. Also, when one person is regarded as an expert.

Studying conformity

Asch's conformity study	Students in groups of six or seven in turn stated which line out of three was the same length as another line (see diagram top left).
	One student was a genuine participant ('naïve') who did not know what the task was really about. The other students ('confederates') were told to sometimes give the same wrong answer.
	The naïve participants agreed with the wrong answers (conformed) 36.8% of the time. 75% of the participants conformed at least once.
	The students knew their answers were wrong (so not ISI). The students conformed to avoid rejection by the group (NSI).

Key concept 1: Conformity

One strength is conformity has practical applications in workplaces.

For example, 'whistle-blowers' are anti-conformists who risk their jobs to highlight malpractice in workplaces, refusing to go along with the group.

They 'rock the boat' risking rejection by colleagues (resisting NSI), and/or they do not assume other people know better than them (resisting ISI).

Therefore, having an understanding of NSI and ISI means we can take steps to counteract and resist mindless conformity.

In Asch's study, the naïve (genuine) participant was always seated either last or (as shown above) second-to-last in the group. Participants gave their answers out loud, one at a time, beginning with the first person and going round the table in order.

Another strength is Asch's evidence for NSI in his study on conformity.

Asch's participants agreed with other people in giving clearly wrong answers because they were afraid of disapproval by disagreeing publicly.

This was supported by a later study where participants wrote their answers down privately and the conformity rate fell to just 12.5%.

This suggests that we sometimes conform to avoid rejection by the majority. Conformity is less likely when this pressure is removed because you don't have to disagree publicly.

One weakness is that NSI and ISI overlap considerably.

For example, if there is a 'dissenter' present who disagrees with the group, people are less likely to conform. But why?

Perhaps the dissenter provides social support (reducing NSI) or perhaps they are an alternative source of information (reducing ISI).

This shows that we can't always be sure whether NSI or ISI is responsible for conformity. It is likely that both operate, especially in real life.

Apply it

Veronica, Amani and Cai are working a night shift at a large care home. One of the residents is showing signs of distress. Veronica says that the three of them should wait to see if the resident feels better and Cai agrees.

Amani thinks to herself, 'We should immediately call for an ambulance.' But she agrees with the other two, so they wait.

1. Identify **one** example of conformity from the scenario.   (1 mark)

2. Explain why Amani agreed with her colleagues. Use **one** concept from the social approach in your answer.   (2 marks)

3. Discuss the extent to which conformity can explain why Amani agreed with her colleagues.   (3 marks)

After an hour, Amani says to the others, 'We must call an ambulance now.' Cai agrees immediately. Veronica is unsure but agrees soon after.

4. Explain Veronica's behaviour using a different social approach concept from the one you chose in question 2.   (2 marks)

REVISION BOOSTER

The problem with learning stuff is that you often forget it. You can overcome this by using spaced repetition.

At the start of a new revision session, take a couple of minutes to briefly review the material you revised in the previous one.

After a week, review the material again. This helps to refresh the material in memory. It doesn't have to be a big deal.

For this spread you would be quickly reviewing seven things – definitions of conformity, NSI, ISI, Asch's research and the three evaluation points.

This is one reason why cue/flash cards are so useful. You can put them into different piles depending on when you last reviewed them. Make spaced repetition part of your revision routine.

Key concept 2: Types of conformity

SPEC SPOTLIGHT

Types of conformity, including internalisation, identification, compliance.

There are times when you might go along with the group for a quiet life, but you'd much rather be doing your own thing.

Apply it

When Kiana was at university, her friends invited her to go on a protest march with them. They were concerned about climate change. Kiana thought, 'I don't really know anything about this issue and I'm not that interested.' But she agreed to go with her friends anyway.

1. Identify the type of conformity shown by Kiana. **(1 mark)**

2. Explain, using the type of conformity you identified in question 1, why Kiana agreed to go on the protest march. **(3 marks)**

Ten years after the protest march, Kiana has been arrested several times and recently glued herself to a motorway in protest against climate change.

3. Explain why internalisation could be an appropriate way of explaining Kiana's behaviour. **(3 marks)**

4. Discuss the extent to which conformity can help us to explain Kiana's behaviour. **(3 marks)**

Internalisation

Definition	We genuinely agree with the group so we publicly change our view and behave like the others. The group's opinion becomes part of how we think (internalised). This is a deep and permanent type of conformity. We conform even when other group members are not present. Internalisation is most likely because of informational social influence (ISI) – we think the group view is right.
Example	Jess lived with other students who were vegans. Jess internalised their values and became a vegan herself ('the right thing to do'). Jess sees it as a complete lifestyle, not just a diet. She is still a vegan years after leaving university. **Asch's research** No evidence of internalisation because there were no meaningful values for the participants to internalise.

Compliance

Definition	We 'go along' with the group, but privately we do not change our opinion/behaviour. This is a shallow and temporary type of conformity. It ends when the group is no longer present. Compliance is most likely because of normative social influence (NSI) – we want the group to accept us.
Example	Agreeing with your friends' choice of holiday, film or nightclub so you don't 'rock the boat' or be excluded. But you don't really like any of those things. **Asch's research** This was compliance because the naïve participants knew the answers were wrong but chose to go along with them anyway – publicly agreed, privately disagreed.

Identification

Definition	We conform because we **identify** with group members (look up to them, want to be like them, etc.). This is stronger than compliance because we privately change some of our views. It is weaker than internalisation because we conform only as long as we are part of the group.
Example	Rowan is a professional psychologist who follows a code of conduct which guides how psychologists should behave. Rowan identifies with his role as a psychologist so he conforms to the code. If he changed career he would identify with a new role and conform to different behaviours. **Asch's research** Some participants may have identified with the group because they (wrongly) thought they were 'in the same boat'. But unlikely because there was nothing attractive or admirable about the group.

Key concept 2: Types of conformity

One strength is that we can apply conformity types to the workplace.

Conformity can be destructive if it leads to wrong decisions being made in the workplace, e.g. when everyone agrees with each other for a 'quiet life' (this is compliance).

Another destructive type is identification, when group members identify with each other so strongly that any outside viewpoints are not considered.

Therefore, by understanding the different types of conformity, we can target destructive conformity to improve decision-making in the workplace.

Some airplane accidents have happened because the first officer conforms with the captain's decisions even when they know they are wrong.

Another strength is research evidence for different types of conformity.

Asch's study showed compliance because participants agreed with the majority to avoid disapproval.

Participants in another study showed internalisation as they conformed because they believed others had more expertise than they did (Sherif).

These supporting studies show that people conform for different reasons, so there is more than one type of conformity.

REVISION BOOSTER

Using examples is an excellent way to demonstrate your knowledge and understanding of key concepts. For example (you see, I told you), there are three types of conformity on this spread. We have given examples of each but you could try and come up with some of your own.

Your everyday life is a good source of examples for quite a few topics in the course. Have you ever 'gone along' with others just to shut them up? Do you strongly identify with any of the groups you are part of? Making the effort to think of your own examples makes them more memorable than just reading them off the page.

One weakness is real-world conformity is less well understood.

This may be because studies are not like real-world situations, e.g. Asch's task of identifying line lengths was artificial and the 'group' was not really a meaningful group.

Also, identification is hard to separate from compliance and internalisation because it often combines features of both in real-world situations.

Therefore, conformity is oversimplified in research and may be more complex in the real world because the different types overlap.

Apply it

It's the weekend and a group of Sunny's friends invite him out to a nightclub. Sunny really hates nightclubs but he goes out anyway because he knows his friends will be unhappy if he refuses.

1. *Identify the type of conformity shown by Sunny.* (1 mark)

2. *Justify your answer to question 1.*   (2 marks)

3. *Identify **one** other type of conformity and explain how it might account for Sunny's decision to go out with his friends.*   (3 marks)

As Sunny and his friends are leaving the first nightclub, they see a man lying on the ground. Everyone is ignoring the man and walking past him. Sunny's friends are all impatient and want to get to the next club. But Sunny is a medical doctor, so he stops to help the man.

4. *Explain how identification could account for Sunny's behaviour.*   (2 marks)

5. *Discuss **one** reason why conformity is a useful way of understanding Sunny's behaviour.*   (3 marks)

A2: Social approach

Key concept 3: In-groups and out-groups

SPEC SPOTLIGHT

In and out groups – social categorisation (formation and effect of stereotypes, prejudice and discrimination).

Believing yourself to be part of a group of like-minded people brings a sense of belonging and is good for mental health.

Apply it

In 2022, only 23% of A-level Physics exam entrants were girls. There are many reasons for this gender imbalance, according to a report by the World Economic Forum. A key one is that some teachers believe that boys are 'naturally' better at physics than girls. Throughout the school years, girls more than boys feel their teachers do not expect them to do well in sciences. (Source: tinyurl.com/s42fda2w)

1. Give **one** example of social categorisation from this scenario.
   (1 mark)

2. Explain how social categorisation may lead to stereotyping in the scenario. *(3 marks)*

3. Describe **one** effect such stereotyping might have on girls.
   (3 marks)

4. Explain how prejudice and/or discrimination might arise in the scenario. *(3 marks)*

Social categorisation

What is social categorisation?	Dividing people into social groups (categories) based on their shared characteristics, e.g. **gender**, ethnicity, age.
	We view people in a category as similar to each other and different from people in another category.
In-groups and out-groups	We want to belong so we think of ourselves as a member of a category, the in-group ('us'). Being part of one group means you are not part of another group, the out-group ('them').
	Identifying with the in-group gives us a sense of belonging, **self-esteem** and status. We exaggerate differences and minimise similarities with the out-group. This means we stereotype the out-group.

Stereotypes

What is a stereotype?	A fixed view we have of a person based on our placing them in a social category, e.g. 'old people are slow'. We assume the person represents the category, usually wrongly.
Formation of stereotypes	**Social categorisation** Stereotypes are formed by increasing the psychological distance between in-group and out-group.
	Social learning theory (see page 38) We learn stereotypes by **observing** and **imitating** sources of social information (parents/carers, peers, media).
	E.g. a child hears a parent telling a racist joke and enjoys the reaction this gets (**vicarious reinforcement**), so the child is more likely to repeat the stereotype.
Effect of stereotypes	**Positive effects** Stereotypes simplify our interactions with others. By assuming they share stereotyped characteristics of a social category we save time and cognitive effort.
	Negative effects We may behave towards others in line with our stereotypes of them. We remember positive information about in-groups and negative information about out-groups (Iacozza *et al.*). Stereotypes distort and bias our social judgements.

Prejudice and discrimination

Prejudice	Stereotyping the out-group makes it easier to form negative attitudes about its members, which makes us feel good about our in-group and ourselves. Prejudice increases in-group members' self-esteem.
Discrimination	Sometimes (not always) the outcome of prejudice towards an out-group. Exclusion of people (e.g. from employment, housing, etc.) because they share a characteristic, e.g. skin colour, gender, etc. Also less obvious 'everyday' discrimination (e.g. 'microaggressions', disrespectful comments).

Key concept 3: In-groups and out-groups

One strength is that we can take steps to reduce prejudice.

For example, we can help people to see themselves as part of a bigger social category (e.g. 'human beings') instead of a smaller one (e.g. religion, gender, social class, etc.).

This emphasises similarities between in-group and out-group and lessens distance psychologically, which reduces the influence of stereotypes. You can also help in-group and out-group members to mix and cooperate towards shared goals.

Therefore, there are several ways we can counteract the negative effects of social categorisation and stereotyping to reduce prejudice.

In this drawing (based on Allport and Postman's study), a white man is holding a razor and is confronting a black man. This reverses a then-commonly-held racist stereotype (still held by some people today) that a black man is more likely to be the attacker.

Another strength is research showing how stereotypes affect memory.

For example, a participant saw a drawing (see right) that reversed a racist stereotype, then they described the drawing to another participant, who described it to another and so on (Allport and Postman).

In 50% of these sequences, participants wrongly recalled the razor was held by the black man.

This shows that a racist stereotype (the black man was the attacker) can bias memory in a way that supports the stereotype (at least in a substantial proportion of people).

REVISION BOOSTER

You will know that every subject has its own set of technical terms. Part of answering exam questions is being able to use these terms correctly, so you have to try to remember them. A technical term is a kind of shorthand, so you can use a single word like 'prejudice' instead of lots of words explaining what it means (unless the question asks you to do this of course).

It's easy to get terms mixed up, so be careful. For example, on this spread we have stereotypes, prejudice and discrimination. They are related but different. Are you confident you know which is which?

One weakness is that alternative explanations may be more effective.

For instance, some research shows that some people are prejudiced mainly because of their **personality** rather than social factors (Adorno *et al.*).

People with an 'authoritarian personality' from a harsh upbringing blame out-groups for their own failings and are more likely to stereotype and be prejudiced.

This means that prejudice cannot always be explained by social factors alone and may not be reduced without also considering personality factors.

Apply it

A recent study shows that women over 70 with breast cancer are less likely than younger women to be offered surgery as a treatment. Two GPs are discussing the study.

One says, 'I wouldn't recommend surgery for older women because they are less able than younger women to understand everything involved. None of them are fit enough for surgery anyway.'

1. Identify **one** example of stereotyping from the scenario. (1 mark)

2. Describe how social categorisation may have led to the formation of this stereotype. (3 marks)

3. Explain how the scenario also illustrates prejudice. (2 marks)

4. Explain how the prejudice in the scenario might lead to discrimination. (2 marks)

Content area A

Unit 1 Psychological approaches and applications

Key concept 4: Intra-group dynamics

SPEC SPOTLIGHT

Intra group dynamics including group cohesion, roles, common goals, groupthink and social facilitation.

Does the presence of other people improve task performance? It depends on the complexity of the task.

Apply it

A group of enthusiastic BTEC Applied Psychology students meets every week to discuss ways to help reduce stress in their college.

Justin always takes care to praise others for their contributions. Evie is a bit strict but she makes sure the work gets done. Frida says they should get some non-psychology students to join the group. The others disagree because they feel they are all doing a top job already. After some discussion, Frida agrees.

1. Apart from groupthink, name **two** intra-group dynamics and give an example of each from the scenario above. **(4 marks)**

2. Describe how the group's behaviour illustrates the concept of groupthink. **(3 marks)**

3. Give **one** other intra-group dynamic and explain how it might affect the group's behaviour. **(3 marks)**

4. Discuss the intra-group dynamics of the student group. **(3 marks)**

Intra-group dynamics	
Group cohesion	Members of cohesive groups stick together to pursue common goals. They enjoy being in the group, look forward to meeting, communicate willingly and work together efficiently.
	Group cohesion is greater when members perceive themselves as similar, externally (e.g. age) and internally (e.g. attitudes). This creates a virtuous circle – similarity breeds trust leading to more cohesion, which produces greater trust.
Roles	Three types of **roles** increase cohesion (Benne and Sheats):
	• Task roles – get work done. 'Task leaders' coordinate the work, 'Energisers' challenge the group to move forward.
	• Social roles – create harmony in group relationships. 'Encouragers' support and praise others, 'Compromisers' back down for the good of the group.
	• Procedural roles – keep the group 'on task'. 'Gatekeepers' ensure all have a say, 'Recorders' keep track of activity.
	One category of roles weakens group cohesion:
	• Individualist roles – undermine the group. 'Blockers' resist ideas but offer nothing, 'Jokesters' make light and distract.
Common goals	Well-functioning groups share goals, which increases cohesion because members feel they are 'working together'.
	Goals **motivate** members to increase effort, provide direction and give meaning. They provide a standard against which to measure progress, evaluate performance and resolve conflicts.
Groupthink	In cohesive groups members are like-minded so have a strong need to agree with each other, even when decisions are wrong. Members stop analysing decisions, do not look for weaknesses and believe the reasons for decisions are sound. They do not listen to alternatives and discourage opposing views (Janis).
	Groupthink is more likely in stressful situations and/or when the decision is very important.
Social facilitation	On simple tasks, presence of a group enhances ('facilitates') each member's performance (reduces it on complex tasks).
	We become physiologically and psychologically aroused if we believe other people are **observing** our task performance (increased heart rate, more alert). Arousal is greater when we believe we are being evaluated by others in the group (Zajonc).

Key concept 4: Intra-group dynamics

One strength is that each concept has produced practical applications.

For instance, ways to avoid groupthink include encouraging criticism, involving people from outside and breaking the group into smaller subgroups (Janis).

Also, there is evidence that greater cohesion in therapy groups reduces symptoms of **depression** (Crowe and Grenyer).

These findings show that improving intra-group dynamics can have benefits for individuals, groups and organisations.

How cohesive are the groups you are part of in your school or college? Do you share common goals or have clearly defined roles?

Another strength is evidence supporting some intra-group dynamics.

For example, groups perform better when members believe their role is recognised because the focus is on the group's goals rather than personal goals (Thürmer *et al.*).

Also, groupthink can be avoided by having a 'Devil's Advocate', a group member who challenges agreement by asking questions and offering alternative views (MacDougall and Baum).

Therefore, there is strong evidence that intra-group dynamics have a real impact on the functioning of many groups.

REVISION BOOSTER

We focus throughout this guide on questions that require you to apply your knowledge to scenarios. That's because these are by far the main type of exam question. However, although they are relatively rare, non-scenario questions do sometimes come up. They are usually worth 1 or 2 marks only.

One weakness is evidence challenging intra-group dynamics.

For example, group roles are often vague and overlap, which means members may not understand their roles, so performance suffers.

Also, group performance improved by 12% when members worked towards group goals, but it improved by 31% when members worked towards both group and personal goals (Gowen).

These findings show that the links between intra-group dynamics and performance are complex and not yet fully understood.

You can answer them without referring to the scenario. They are mostly definition-type questions such as, 'State what is meant by social facilitation'.

For revision purposes, keep track of terms for each topic. Make a list and learn the definitions so you can reproduce them in the exam.

Apply it

Job satisfaction in a major retail organisation is very poor. In order to address this, a group is formed of 20 employees, one from each part of the organisation. Their job is to come up with strategies to improve satisfaction throughout the company.

However, the group is failing to come up with any useful ideas. There is a lot of squabbling between group members and no one seems to know what they are meant to be doing.

1. *Explain how common goals could improve the intra-group dynamics of the group.* *(3 marks)*

Mia, one of the group members, says that one reason the group is doing badly is because the task is too complex.

2. *Using the concept of social facilitation, explain how the group's performance could be improved.* *(3 marks)*

3. *Explain, using **one** other concept from intra-group dynamics, how the group might improve its performance.* *(3 marks)*

4. *Discuss the extent to which intra-group dynamics can help us understand the performance of this group.* *(3 marks)*

A2: Social approach

Key concept 5: Influences of others on the self

Unit 1 Psychological approaches and applications   Content area A

SPEC SPOTLIGHT

Influences of others on self-concept (self-esteem, self-image); self-efficacy.

Most of us generally interact positively with people in certain admired roles, which contributes to their self-esteem.

Apply it

Shay is a nurse in a major city hospital. Their appraisals show they are very good at their job, especially in their relationships with patients. They make excellent contributions to team meetings and are very helpful with junior staff. Shay thinks their most positive quality is their compassion for patients. However, they know they are not so good with paperwork and accept that they need to improve in this area.

1. *Identify evidence in the scenario that shows Shay may have high self-esteem.* (1 mark)

2. *Explain **one** way in which the influence of others may have contributed to Shay's self-esteem.* (2 marks)

3. *Give **one** example of Shay's self-image from the scenario.* (1 mark)

4. *Explain how the influence of others may have affected Shay's self-image.* (2 marks)

5. *Discuss the influence of others on Shay's self-concept.* (3 marks)

Self-concept

What is self-concept?	How you see yourself (e.g. 'I am a friendly person') is part of your self-concept. This is influenced by others, by how they evaluate you and provide their feedback. Other people are 'mirrors' in which we perceive their judgements of us (Cooley's 'looking-glass self'). There are two key components to our self-concept: **self-esteem** and self-image.
Influences of others on self-esteem	Self-esteem is the extent to which we accept and like ourselves. People with high self-esteem have a positive self-image, accept themselves and have confidence in their abilities. High self-esteem is linked to psychological well-being. Interacting with others is a key source of self-esteem (Argyle): • Others react to us in ways that make us feel good, e.g. they agree with us, make positive comments, etc. • We compare ourselves to people whose qualities we believe are less desirable than our own, e.g. less successful, attractive or clever than ourselves. • We play social **roles** that are widely admired (e.g. nurse, parent/carer). Other roles carry social stigma (e.g. ex-prisoner, drug user) and are linked with low self-esteem.
Influences of others on self-image	Self-image is your awareness of your mental and physical characteristics, based on your beliefs about yourself from experience. E.g. someone with a positive self-image may be satisfied with their body shape/size. Self-image is also based on feedback from others, especially people such as parents/carers, teachers and peers. Usually a positive self-image develops from positive feedback but people do not always interpret feedback accurately.

Self-efficacy

What is self-efficacy?	How confident we are that we can achieve a successful outcome, e.g. in performing a task. Someone with high **self-efficacy** is confident they are able to get a high grade in an exam, so they feel good about themselves (self-esteem) and have a positive view of themselves (self-image).
Influences of others on self-efficacy	Two main ways other people influence self-efficacy (Bandura): **Social modelling** Observing **role models** achieving success increases your belief that you are capable of doing the same, especially if you perceive them as similar to yourself. **Social persuasion** Using positive feedback (encouragement) can increase someone's self-efficacy, overcoming their self-doubt, persuading them they are capable of achieving success (discouragement lowers self-efficacy).

Key concept 5: Influences of others on the self

One strength is that the self-concept can have positive practical uses.

In one study, underperforming schoolchildren improved academic achievement and had fewer behavioural issues after attending workshops to increase self-esteem (Lawrence).

Other groups of children received only counselling or class teaching (comparison groups) and improvements were not as great in these groups.

This suggests that self-esteem is an important factor in well-being and academic achievement.

Revision, practice and past success all contribute to a student's self-efficacy.

Another strength is evidence that other people influence our self-esteem.

A review of 52 studies concluded that fulfilling and supportive relationships with others increase our self-esteem (Harris and Orth).

Also, there is a positive feedback loop because having high self-esteem in turn improves the quality of our relationships (poor relationships lower self-esteem, creating a negative feedback loop).

This shows that there is a reciprocal (two-way) link in which self-esteem and other people influence each other.

One weakness is that the different aspects of self are poorly defined.

Some definitions of self-concept include 'beliefs' about the self, but others include 'feelings'. Many concepts overlap, e.g. self-image and self-esteem may be almost the same thing.

This demonstrates the 'jangle fallacy', the assumption that two identical things are different just because we give them different names.

This vagueness limits our understanding of ideas such as self-concept and the practical benefits we can derive from them.

REVISION BOOSTER

Most students are full of enthusiasm at the start of their revision. But it doesn't take long for this to wear off so revision becomes a bit of a slog. Here are some suggestions to help you stay motivated:

- Inject some variation into your revision. You'll have a timetable and some things will be routine, but shake things up a bit. Use different techniques, practise memory improvement as well as revising.

- Cue/flash cards are great revision tools. But don't wait for a revision period, make them as you go through the topics on the course. Carry your cue/flash cards round with you and use them to test yourself in quiet times.

- Sleep well (more on this later) and don't spend all your time revising.

Apply it

Talia was about to start work on a BTEC Applied Psychology assignment. She produced a plan for each stage of the work and the days and times she would do it. She watched a video on YouTube of someone using Gantt charts to plan projects and then produced a plan for each stage of her work.

Talia felt less stressed knowing she was well-organised and that she did well on previous assignments. She knew planning was her main weakness, so tried hard to improve it. She got very good feedback for the project and her friends asked her to show them how to plan better.

1. Identify **two** examples of Talia's self-concept in the scenario. *(2 marks)*

2. Explain **two** ways in which the influence of others may have contributed to Talia's self-concept. *(4 marks)*

3. Give **one** example of Talia's self-efficacy from the scenario. *(1 mark)*

4. Explain how Talia's self-efficacy may have been influenced by others. *(3 marks)*

5. Discuss the influence of others on Talia's self-concept and/or self-esteem. *(3 marks)*

Key concept 1: Classical conditioning

SPEC SPOTLIGHT

Classical conditioning – learning by association, to include the role of the unconditioned stimulus, unconditioned response, neutral stimulus, conditioned stimulus and conditioned response.

There are plenty of stimuli in the environment that trigger instinctive or unlearned responses.

As Rudi looked at the menu at his favourite restaurant, he soon started feeling hungry. But halfway through his meal he felt sick and experienced hot sweats and cold chills. Now, every time he thinks about the restaurant, Rudi feels sick.

1. Identify in this scenario the UCS, the NS and the CR. **(3 marks)**

2. Using **one** concept from the behaviourist approach, explain why Rudi feels sick every time he thinks about the restaurant. **(3 marks)**

3. Discuss how effective this concept is in explaining why Rudi feels sick every time he thinks about the restaurant. **(3 marks)**

Rudi runs a business selling candles. Sales are down, so Rudi plans to reduce the price of some candles.

4. Describe, using classical conditioning, how Rudi's plan could increase the sales of candles. **(3 marks)**

Classical conditioning	
What is classical conditioning?	Learning through association takes place when we associate two stimuli with each other (Pavlov).
	The two stimuli are an unconditioned (unlearned) stimulus (UCS) and a neutral stimulus (NS). **Classical conditioning** of a behaviour occurs through three stages (see diagram below).
Before conditioning	The smell of food is a UCS because it triggers an unlearned automatic response (salivation). Salivation is an unconditioned response (UCR).
	Any other stimulus that does not produce the target response is a neutral stimulus, e.g. the sound of a bell or a tap on the wrist will not produce salivation.
During conditioning	The UCS and NS are repeatedly presented to the individual close together in time ('pairing'). Pairing has the strongest effect when the NS occurs just before the UCS.
After conditioning	After several pairings, the NS is no longer 'neutral' and on its own produces the same response as the UCS.
	The NS is now a conditioned stimulus (CS) and the response it produces is a conditioned response (CR).

Before conditioning
The dog naturally salivates to the smell and appearance of food (but not to the sound of a bell).

Food (UCS)  Salivation (UCR)

During conditioning
The sound of a bell is repeatedly presented at the same time as food, so the dog salivates.

Food (UCS) Bell (NS) Salivation (UCR)

After conditioning
The dog now salivates to the sound of the bell without food. A new stimulus–response association has formed (classically conditioned).

Bell (CS) Salivation (CR)

The Russian Nobel Prize-winning physiologist Ivan Pavlov kept dogs in his laboratory for experiments. He noticed that the dogs started salivating when they saw the research assistant coming to feed them. Pavlov investigated whether his dogs could learn an association between food and a new stimulus, in this case the sound of a bell.

Key concept 1: Classical conditioning

One strength is that classical conditioning is the basis of a therapy.

This is aversion therapy, in which a person addicted to gambling is given a painful electric shock (UCS) while reading gambling-related phrases (NS).

The shock produces a UCR of discomfort and/or **anxiety**. After several pairings, the NS becomes a CS and produces the same discomfort/anxiety (now a CR).

This shows that classical conditioning has useful applications that can reduce psychological suffering and improve quality of life.

You need more than classical conditioning to explain fear of flying.

Another strength is human learning can occur by classical conditioning.

For example, a nine-month-old baby known as 'Little Albert' initially showed no fear when he played with a white rat (Watson and Rayner).

But after the rat was paired several times with a loud noise, Albert became afraid of the rat, crying and crawling away from the rat even when there was no loud noise.

This shows that classically conditioning a fear response to a neutral stimulus is quite straightforward, at least in very young children.

REVISION BOOSTER

Hopefully the diagram on the facing page will help you understand the concept of classical conditioning. But it has another use.

It's possible that an exam question might present you with a similar diagram with terms missing. Your job would be to fill in the missing terms, for example write the UCS or CR in the correct place, or whatever.

Therefore, a good revision exercise is to choose another conditioned behaviour and create your own diagram, with a section for 'before', 'during' and 'after' conditioning.

One weakness is that the range of behaviours learned is limited.

Classical conditioning can explain how simple 'reflex' behaviours are learned, but more complex behaviours involve other types of learning (see the next two spreads).

For example, classical conditioning can explain how a phobia of dogs is acquired but cannot explain how the phobia then continues over time (e.g. how we learn to avoid dogs).

This means classical conditioning is just a partial explanation of learning, with limited applications.

Apply it

Tay started playing online fruit machines a few months ago and can now think of little else. When Tay isn't playing, they are thinking about when they can next go online. Tay knows they are addicted.

Tay gets a lot of pleasure from the noises and colours of the gambling websites they visit. Tay particularly enjoys the anticipation of waiting for the fruits to line up on the wheels.

Now, whenever Tay sees a bowl of fruit or goes into the fruit and veg section in the supermarket, they feel a little bit of excitement.

1. State what is meant by 'learning by association'.
   (1 mark)

2. Identify the conditioned stimulus and the conditioned response in this scenario.
   (2 marks)

3. Explain, using your knowledge of classical conditioning, why Tay feels excitement when they see a bowl of fruit or when they see fruit at a supermarket.
   (3 marks)

4. Discuss the effectiveness of classical conditioning in explaining Tay's behaviour.
   (3 marks)

Key concept 2: Operant conditioning

SPEC SPOTLIGHT

Operant conditioning – learning by consequences, to include the role of positive reinforcement, negative reinforcement and punishment, motivation (extrinsic and intrinsic rewards).

If your motivation is mainly extrinsic, what happens when the rewards stop coming?

Enya is a sixth-form student. Every time a student gets a question right in a BTEC Applied Psychology class, the teacher praises the student. When this happened to Enya, she tried even harder to answer more questions.

1. *Describe, using operant conditioning, why Enya tried harder to answer questions.*
   (3 marks)

Enya's brother Denny is 10 years old and his room is a total mess. His mum is always telling him to tidy up but he never does. So one day, Denny's mum took his Xbox off him and told him he couldn't play on it until he tidied up. It took two days, but Denny tidied his room in the end.

2. *Explain the role of punishment in Denny's behaviour.* *(2 marks)*

3. *Explain how Denny's mum could use (a) positive reinforcement and (b) negative reinforcement to encourage Denny to tidy his room.* *(4 marks)*

4. *Discuss the extent to which operant conditioning can help us understand Denny's behaviour.* *(3 marks)*

Operant conditioning

What is operant conditioning?	Learning by consequences of a behaviour, i.e. forming a link between a behaviour (the operant) and its consequence (the result that follows it).
	The probability of the behaviour being repeated increases or decreases depending on the consequences.
Consequence 1: Reinforcement	**Reinforcement** *increases* the probability of a behaviour being repeated. There are two main types:
	• **Positive reinforcement** Occurs when a behaviour is followed by a pleasurable consequence, which could be something tangible (food, money) or intangible (a smile, praise). The consequence reinforces the behaviour, so it is more likely to happen again.
	• **Negative reinforcement** Occurs when a behaviour is followed by the removal of an unpleasant stimulus. E.g. the removal of **anxiety** negatively reinforces avoidance of a spider, making avoidance more likely to be repeated.
Consequence 2: Punishment	Punishment *reduces* the probability of a behaviour being repeated. There are two main types:
	• **Positive punishment** Occurs when a behaviour is followed by an unpleasant consequence (a slap, harsh words).
	• **Negative punishment** Occurs when a behaviour is followed by the removal of something pleasant (being fined or grounded, i.e. removal of money or freedom).
Motivation	Behaviour is **motivated** by a desire to achieve goals or satisfy needs. Motivation is driven by extrinsic (external) and intrinsic (internal) rewards through operant conditioning.
	Extrinsic rewards Come from other people, e.g. parents/carers, teachers, friends. Gaining a reward motivates us to behave in a certain way.
	E.g. writing an essay to gain a high grade.
	Intrinsic rewards Come from within yourself, e.g. your own enjoyment, interest. The behaviour is rewarding in itself, you do it for its own sake and not for an external reward.
	E.g. doing a hobby for a challenge, volunteering for a charity, doing a certain degree because you find it interesting.
	Intrinsic motivation is desirable because achieving goals without external rewards is fulfilling and raises **self-esteem**.

Key concept 2: Operant conditioning

One strength is that there are practical applications in education.

For example, good work and behaviour are reinforced by extrinsic rewards (e.g. praise, gold stars). Students' self-esteem is raised through intrinsic rewards (e.g. setting their own targets).

Furthermore, punishment is often used in schools and by parents/carers to reduce undesirable behaviour (e.g. isolation, detention, 'naughty step', 'grounding').

This shows that operant conditioning has wide uses in the real world as well as theoretical importance.

Avoiding revision makes it harder to revise next time. Thanks a lot, negative reinforcement.

Another strength is support from both human and animal studies.

Many lab studies of operant conditioning in animal species (e.g. rats and pigeons) reliably show that animal behaviour is influenced by reinforcement and punishment.

Human studies have also discovered brain areas and structures linked with reinforcement of behaviour through rewarding pleasure (e.g. Chase et al.).

Therefore, research supports the view that operant conditioning is a key form of learning in many animal and human behaviours.

REVISION BOOSTER

Use operant (and classical) conditioning to your advantage. Give yourself rewards for revising!

A break is itself rewarding and helps you refocus your attention. But think of some other rewards too. For instance, when I've done a certain amount of work, I make myself a nice mug of tea (yes, I know, I'm easily pleased).

Do something that will only take a short time, not something that's a time-killer such as watching telly or playing games. Also, don't let negative reinforcement get a look in. Don't reward yourself by avoiding revision.

One weakness is that operant conditioning is not a full explanation.

Operant conditioning can explain some complex behaviours that **classical conditioning** cannot, e.g. how a phobia is maintained over time by **negative reinforcement** of avoidance.

However, this may explain how the existing behaviour is strengthened or weakened but does not explain how the phobia first appears.

This means operant conditioning is an incomplete theory that does not account for all behaviours.

Apply it

Herbie thinks back to his childhood and remembers how he used to tell his mum jokes all the time when he was a little boy.

1. Using the concept of positive reinforcement, explain why Herbie kept telling his mum jokes. *(2 marks)*

Herbie has a phobia of spiders. He avoids going into any room where he thinks there might be a spider.

2. *Explain how operant conditioning can be used to understand why Herbie avoids going into some rooms where he thinks there might be a spider.* *(3 marks)*

3. *Discuss the effectiveness of operant conditioning in explaining Herbie's joke-telling and/or room avoidance.* *(3 marks)*

Herbie works as a hairdresser. He likes being paid more than the minimum wage and gets even more for any overtime he does. He also finds the work interesting and has decided to start a course to gain a higher qualification in hair and beauty.

4. *Explain how this scenario shows that Herbie may be motivated by (a) extrinsic rewards and (b) intrinsic rewards.* *(4 marks)*

Key concept 3: Social learning theory

SPEC SPOTLIGHT

Social learning theory – learning through observation, imitation, modelling and vicarious learning.

In social learning, the model doesn't always have to be the adult.

Apply it

Safiya is a junior wheelchair basketball player. She is attending a camp where members of the England team provide coaching. In one session on shooting, Safiya carefully watched the coach as she showed each of the steps involved in this skill. When it was Safiya's turn, she followed the steps involved and scored a perfect shot.

1. Identify from the scenario **one** example for each of:
   (a) observation and
   (b) modelling. **(2 marks)**

2. Explain Safiya's behaviour using social learning theory. **(3 marks)**

3. Explain how the coaches could use vicarious learning to improve Safiya's basketball skills. **(2 marks)**

4. Discuss social learning theory as a way of understanding the effect of coaching on Safiya's basketball skills. **(3 marks)**

Social learning theory (SLT)	
What is social learning theory?	Behaviours can be learned indirectly by **observing** and **imitating** another individual whose behaviour is **reinforced** (Bandura). Bandura and his colleagues demonstrated **social learning** in a series of famous studies known as the 'Bobo doll studies'.
Modelling	**Modelling** has two meanings: • A person (model) demonstrates a behaviour to another person (observer). The model is modelling the behaviour. • The observer imitates the model's behaviour. The observer is also modelling the behaviour. **Bandura et al.'s research** An adult model was aggressive towards an inflatable Bobo doll (e.g. punching, kicking, etc.).
Learning through observation	The observer pays attention to the model's behaviour → watches how the behaviour is performed → retains the model's actions in memory → imitates the behaviour. **Bandura et al.'s research** Children observed the adult model being aggressive.
Imitation	The observer is likely to copy the model's behaviour if they identify with the model. **Identification** happens because of: **Similarity** The observer perceives the model as similar to themselves (e.g. same age, **gender**, etc.). **Value** The observer values and/or admires the model (e.g. they have status, wealth, intelligence, etc.). **Bandura et al.'s research** Children behaved aggressively towards the Bobo doll, sometimes exactly imitating aggressive behaviours of the adult model. Imitation was sometimes more likely when the model and child were the same gender.
Vicarious learning	The observer is more likely to imitate a model's behaviour if the observer sees the model's behaviour reinforced (rewarded). E.g. a young girl might imitate a very thin celebrity's 'look' if she sees the celebrity rewarded with fame, status and attention. **Bandura et al.'s research** Children were more likely to imitate the model's aggressive behaviour when the model was rewarded for being aggressive.

Key concept 3: Social learning theory

One strength is SLT can help reduce children's aggressive behaviour.

This is based on the SLT explanation that children learn to imitate aggressive models in the family and media, especially when they see them rewarded.

So, there are several targets for interventions, e.g. reduce rewards for **aggression**, limit access to violent media, provide non-aggressive **role models** for children to imitate.

Therefore, SLT is beneficial because it offers practical ways of both reducing undesirable behaviours and increasing desirable ones.

Another strength is support from research into a variety of behaviours.

For example, children will imitate an aggressive adult model, especially when the model's behaviour is reinforced/rewarded (Bandura *et al.*).

Also, children may develop some phobias because they observe anxious behaviour by adults around them (Askew and Field).

This supports the SLT view that behaviours are learned through observation and imitation, and **vicarious reinforcement** plays a key role in imitation.

One weakness is social learning has little influence on some behaviours.

For instance, the occurrence of phobia is greater in identical twins than in non-identical twins, so some behaviours may be better explained by other theories (Kendler *et al.*).

As identical twins are more closely genetically related than non-identical twins, **genes** may play a greater role than social learning in some behaviours, e.g. phobias (and also **depression**).

This suggests that SLT is not a complete explanation of learning, and a full account can only be produced by considering other factors.

A bobo doll, 'bobo' being Spanish for 'clown'.

Apply it

Emil has recently started a new job as a care worker in a care home for people with learning disabilities. Although he is fully trained in his caring role and has some years' experience, he has no idea yet what the correct procedures and routines are in the care home.

1. *Explain how social learning theory could help Emil in his new role.*
(3 marks)

2. *Discuss how effective social learning theory could be in helping Emil in his new role.*
(3 marks)

One of the residents wanted to learn how to make scrambled eggs. So Emil showed the resident the steps involved. As he was cooking, Emil said to the resident, 'Isn't this fun? I'm really enjoying myself and I love the taste of scrambled eggs.'

3. *Explain the roles of modelling and vicarious learning in this scenario.*
(4 marks)

REVISION BOOSTER

A very useful memory improvement technique is to create acronyms. An acronym is made up of the initial letters of words you want to remember. But the crucial thing is that the acronym itself can be pronounced as a word, which makes it particularly memorable.

For example, on this spread we have four concepts of social learning – modelling, observation, imitation and vicarious learning. The initial letters are M, O, I and V. But as the order doesn't really matter we can rearrange these letters into MOVI (other arrangements are available).

All you then need to do is recall the acronym and the letters will trigger recall of the concepts.

Key concept 1: Influence of biology on behaviour and traits

SPEC SPOTLIGHT

The influence of biology on behaviour and traits, including introversion and extraversion.

It's not unusual for exam question scenarios to include identical twins.

Apply it

Scott is in their thirties and has experienced periods of depression throughout much of their life. Scott's dad and sister have both been diagnosed with depression.

1. Identify **two** biological influences on behaviour and explain how they could account for Scott's depression. **(4 marks)**

When Scott feels well, they are considered the 'life and soul of the party'. They like to spend time with their friends and visit new places. They have twice done a parachute jump for charity.

2. State what is meant by 'extraversion'. **(1 mark)**

3. Identify **two** behaviours in the scenario that suggest Scott is an extravert. **(2 marks)**

4. Explain how biology may have influenced Scott's extraversion. **(3 marks)**

5. Discuss the extent to which biology may be an influence on Scott's behaviour and/or traits. **(3 marks)**

Influence of biology on behaviour	
Genes	Strands of DNA inherited from parents, providing chemical instructions to build proteins in the body, which influence our physical and psychological characteristics, e.g. height and **personality**.
Neuroanatomy	Structure of the nervous system, including the brain and its different parts which have different functions, e.g. one area controls what we see (visual area), another controls movement (motor area).
Neurochemistry	Related to messages sent around the brain and body via neurons (nerve cells) and **neurotransmitters** (chemical messengers), e.g. some neurotransmitters affect mood.
Evolution	How organisms and their behaviour change over millions of years through natural selection as ancestors adapted to the environment to survive.

Influence of biology on traits	
What are traits?	Characteristics that make up a personality, e.g. someone is cheerful, friendly, intelligent, kind – these are traits. Traits do not change much between situations (stable), or within a situation (consistent) or as we get older (enduring).
Extraversion and introversion	Major personality types, i.e. collections of traits (Eysenck): **Extraverts** – outgoing, sociable, loud, friendly, seek new experiences and sensations. **Introverts** – withdrawn, shy, quiet, dislike new sensations. Extraversion–introversion (E–I) is a dimension of personality, i.e. a 'line' on which each of us lies somewhere between extreme extraversion and extreme introversion.
Biological influences on extraversion and introversion	**Genes** inherited from parents determine degree of E–I by influencing neurochemistry, i.e. activity of the nervous system. **Extraverts** – inherit an underactive nervous system, so they have to experience constant excitement to arouse it, e.g. go to parties. **Introverts** – inherit an overactive nervous system, so they have to withdraw to avoid the discomfort of arousing it further, e.g. stay at home.

Key concept 1: Influence of biology on behaviour and traits

One strength is improved approaches to reducing criminal behaviour.

For example, criminals are often extraverts who crave the excitement of new experiences and like taking risks, such as committing crimes.

Extraverts also do not usually learn through punishment and reward, so imprisonment and other punishments do not stop them from behaving antisocially and committing crimes.

Therefore, perhaps some criminal behaviour may be better dealt with using biological methods, e.g. drugs to increase the activity of the nervous system.

Extraverts love this stuff, introverts not so much.

Another strength is research into the genetics of personality traits.

Researchers compare identical and non-identical twins to calculate a 'heritability estimate', indicating the degree to which a physical or psychological trait is genetically inherited.

The heritability estimate for extraversion–introversion may be as high as 57% (Sanchez-Roige *et al.*).

This evidence supports the view that being an extravert or introvert is fairly strongly influenced by genes (i.e. mostly inherited).

REVISION BOOSTER

If the theory of extraversion and introversion on this spread is right, there could be implications for revision. As introverts prefer to avoid arousing their nervous systems, they may be better at resisting distractions and paying close attention to their revision.

Extraverts, on the other hand, like arousing their nervous systems. Perhaps, if you're an extravert, you could find a way of incorporating more 'arousing' methods into your revision. For example, doing a podcast instead of just reading (although this would probably benefit everyone). So, just for fun, it might be good to know how much of an introvert or extravert you are. You can fill in a questionnaire here to find out: tinyurl.com/mv3cz6up

One weakness is that non-biological factors can be more influential.

For instance, although genes make it more likely someone will become an extravert or introvert, this is not inevitable.

Non-biological factors (e.g. learning experiences) may be more important and provide more useful explanations of behaviour, e.g. influences from the social environment in which someone is raised.

Therefore, there is a risk of exaggerating biological influences and gaining an oversimplified view of the causes of behaviour.

Apply it

Rita has a disorder which means she cannot move her right leg very well and also has some difficulty using her right hand.

Rita has just a few close friends. But mostly Rita likes her own company and would much rather stay at home with a good book than go out. She and her partner own a business selling flowers. Rita looks after the finances and is happy to leave her partner to deal with customers.

1. Identify **one** biological influence on behaviour and explain how it may have affected Rita.   *(3 marks)*

2. State what is meant by 'introvert'.   *(1 mark)*

3. Identify **two** of Rita's traits that suggest she is an introvert.   *(2 marks)*

4. State **one** other trait that is typical of an introvert.   *(1 mark)*

5. Explain how biology may have influenced Rita's traits.   *(3 marks)*

6. Discuss the view that biology is an influence on Rita's behaviour and/or traits.   *(3 marks)*

Key concept 2: Genetics and inheritance

Content area A

Unit 1 Psychological approaches and applications

SPEC SPOTLIGHT

Genetics and inheritance, including genes, genotype, phenotype and the SRY gene.

Identical twins. Same genotype but different environmental influences, so different phenotypes.

Paloma and Ivo are siblings. Paloma is outgoing and sociable, but has had panic attacks since she was a teenager. Ivo is shy and quiet, and he has also had panic attacks for many years.

1. Identify evidence from this scenario that Paloma and Ivo:

   a) Share the same phenotype.
   (1 mark)

   b) Have different genotypes.
   (1 mark)

2. Using the concepts of genotype and phenotype, explain the similarities and differences between Paloma and Ivo.
   (3 marks)

Paloma is pregnant and would normally have an ultrasound scan of the embryo at 12 weeks. But she would like to have it after five weeks so she knows the baby's biological sex straight away. Paloma's doctor says there's no point because the baby's biological sex is not clear at that early stage.

3. Using your knowledge of the SRY gene, explain how the biological approach accounts for the biological sex of Paloma's baby.
   (3 marks)

What are genes?

Genes	Strands of DNA located on 23 pairs of **chromosomes** (in humans).
	They influence physical and psychological characteristics, e.g. hair colour, whether you have a calm temperament.
	Each individual typically inherits two copies (alleles) of each **gene**, one from each parent.

Genotype and phenotype

Genotype	An individual's actual genetic make-up, the entire collection of genes inherited from parents.
	Genotype does not determine characteristics directly because genes are expressed by interacting with the 'environment'.
	Environment has an influence even within the body, e.g. the food you eat (environment) affects its functioning.
Phenotype	How an individual's genes are expressed in their observable characteristics (e.g. brown hair, calm temperament).
	Phenotype is the result of the interaction between genotype and environmental influences.
Example: Identical twins	Identical twins inherit the same genes (same genotype) but they have different observable characteristics (phenotypes) because they experience different environmental influences.
	If one twin exercises, they look physically different from their twin because they have bigger muscles. The other twin might develop bigger muscles too, but only if their environment changes (they also go to exercise).
	The genotype–phenotype distinction shows that most human behaviours are due to an interaction of inherited (nature) and environmental (nurture) factors.
The *SRY* gene	Biological sex is determined by one pair of chromosomes, XX for female, XY for male.
	The *SRY* (sex-determining region Y) gene is on the Y chromosome.
	In typical development, it switches on other genes causing an XY embryo to develop testes.
	In the womb the testes produce the male sex **hormone** testosterone, causing the embryo to become biologically male.
	With no *SRY* gene other genes stay switched off so the embryo develops into a biological female.

Key concept 2: Genetics and inheritance

One strength is in distinguishing between genotype and phenotype.

For instance, someone at risk of **depression** (phenotype) may have the relevant genotype (genes) but they do not become depressed because they do not experience an environmental 'trigger'.

There are practical ways of reducing the likelihood of experiencing a trigger, e.g. by reducing **stress** so it does not interact with the genotype.

Therefore, although genes cannot be changed, environmental factors can be, which reduces the risk of a negative outcome.

Even an apparently simple behaviour is the result of many genes interacting with many environmental influences.

Another strength is evidence of the role of the *SRY* gene in development.

The evidence comes from very rare cases in which the 'copying' of the *SRY* gene goes wrong, resulting in a variant (mutation) of the gene.

The *SRY* gene cannot 'switch on' testicular development in XY embryos, so the individual is genetically male but develops female-typical reproductive organs (e.g. uterus).

This evidence shows that the usual role of the *SRY* gene is to initiate male biological sex development in genetically male embryos.

REVISION BOOSTER

In the pressure of an exam, students can give wrong answers to seemingly easy questions. A classic example is mixing up genotype and phenotype. You need to know which is which and there is an easy way to do this.

The word 'genotype' looks quite a lot like 'gene' and that is what you need to know. Phenotype must therefore be the behaviour or characteristic. So, for any scenario, identify the 'gene' information first. If the scenario is about identical twins, the genotype is the same. If the individuals are not identical twins, the genotypes are different.

One weakness is that the influence of genes is often oversimplified.

For instance, the phrase 'a gene *for* depression' is an inaccurate view of how genes work. Genes increase the risk of developing depression, but they do not cause it.

Human behaviours and traits are usually not caused by single genes, but by many genes, each one making small contributions in complex interactions with each other.

Therefore, oversimplified explanations of how genes work exaggerate the role of inheritance (nature) and present a misleading view of the causes of behaviour.

Apply it

Franky and Kenny are identical twins. They were raised by their mum, who tried to treat them in similar ways. As adults, Franky has been diagnosed with depression, but Kenny does not experience depression.

1. *Identify evidence from this scenario that Franky and Kenny:*
   a) *Share the same genotype.*   *(1 mark)*
   b) *Have different phenotypes.*   *(1 mark)*

2. *Explain how the biological approach helps us to understand the similarities and differences between Franky and Kenny.*
                                             (3 marks)

3. *Discuss whether genetics and inheritance can explain the similarities and differences between Franky and Kenny.*   *(3 marks)*

Galactosemia is a rare genetic disorder that makes babies unable to digest the sugars in dairy milk. It can cause life-threatening vomiting, diarrhoea and seizures. However, these symptoms can usually be avoided by replacing dairy milk with soy-based milk.

4. *Explain how this scenario illustrates the difference between genotype and phenotype.*   *(3 marks)*

A4: Biological approach

Key concept 3: Neuroanatomy

Content area A

Unit 1 Psychological approaches and applications

SPEC SPOTLIGHT

Neuroanatomy, including basic localisation of function, lateralisation and plasticity of the brain.

A gardener prunes a plant to redirect its energies into new growth, which happens in our brains too.

Apply it

Silas had a stroke which meant there was some bleeding in part of his brain. As a result, he experienced disturbing numbness and tingling sensations but only in his left arm and leg.

1. *Identify evidence of localisation of brain function in this scenario.*
   (1 mark)

2. *Explain how the evidence you identified demonstrates localisation of brain function.*
   (2 marks)

3. *Explain how Silas's experience demonstrates lateralisation of brain function.* *(2 marks)*

A psychologist tested Silas and concluded that his sensation would very likely improve over time.

4. *Using your knowledge of the biological approach, identify* **one** *reason for the psychologist's conclusion.* *(1 mark)*

5. *Explain why the psychologist believed Silas would improve.*
   (2 marks)

Localisation of brain function

Localisation of brain function: What is it?	Neuroanatomy is the structure of the nervous system including the brain, which is divided into two connected halves called the left hemisphere (LH) and the right hemisphere (RH).
	Different brain areas perform certain specific functions (localisation). If a brain area is damaged, the associated function is affected.
Localisation of brain function: Examples	The cortex is the brain's thin highly-folded outer layer that covers the inner structures (like an orange peel). It includes these major areas, which are found in both hemispheres:
	Motor area Controls voluntary movements of the opposite side of the body (contralateral control). Damage causes loss of control over fine movements.
	Somatosensory area Represents touch information from the skin on the opposite side of the body in proportion to the sensitivity of the body part. Over half of the area is devoted to the face and hands (highly sensitive). Damage causes sensory problems, e.g. numbness, tingling.
	Visual area Each eye sends information from the right 'half' of the visual field to the left visual area, and from the left 'half' of the visual field to the right visual area. Damage to one visual area can cause partial blindness in both eyes.

Lateralisation of brain function

Lateralisation of brain function	Some brain functions are lateralised ('one-sided'), found in just one hemisphere. So, the LH and RH are functionally different, one or the other is specialised ('dominant') for some functions.
	Language In most people, the main language areas are in the LH only. Damage to the RH does not usually cause language problems, but damage to specific LH areas does, e.g. difficulty speaking.

Plasticity of the brain

Plasticity of the brain: Synaptic pruning	The brain is plastic (flexible) and changes throughout life. An example of plasticity is synaptic pruning.
	At age 3 years, the brain has twice as many connections (synapses) per neuron as in the adult brain. Synapses are 'pruned' (cut back) to let new connections form in response to new demands on the brain.
Plasticity of the brain: Functional recovery	Healthy brain areas can often adapt and 'take over' functions of damaged areas. New connections are formed close to the damaged area or a matching area in the other hemisphere takes over. Recovery can be supported by rehabilitation therapy (e.g. speech and language therapy).

Key concept 3: Neuroanatomy

One strength of neuroanatomy is real-world applications to help patients.

For example, one programme uses 200 hours of device-based game-type activities targeting attention, memory, coordination, etc. to protect older people against age-related cognitive decline (Merzenich et al.).

This programme is based on brain plasticity. The activities help to support **neurotransmitter**-producing neurons that would otherwise decline with age.

This shows that understanding neuroanatomy can lead to interventions that benefit a range of conditions where brain injury or degeneration are involved.

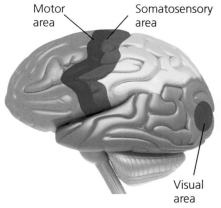

Motor area

Somatosensory area

Visual area

Three of the main areas of the left hemisphere, also found in the right hemisphere.

Another strength is research evidence to support brain lateralisation.

For example, some studies show that the right hemisphere controls our ability to make emotional facial expressions, to recognise emotions in other people's facial expressions and identify emotions in music.

Furthermore, there is also evidence that damage to parts of the right hemisphere disrupts these abilities (Lindell).

This shows there are some significant functions that are lateralised in the human brain, with one hemisphere or the other specialised for each function.

REVISION BOOSTER

This spread is a good chance for you to make your revision a bit visual. Draw an outline of the brain based on the diagram above. Practise labelling it with the main areas mentioned on this spread. Test yourself by identifying each area and explaining what they do and what happens if they are damaged. Find out where the main language areas are and add them to your diagram.

Make sure you know the difference between two similar concepts – localisation and lateralisation. Think of 'local' as a small area. Think of 'lateral' as 'one side'.

One weakness is that functions may be less localised and lateralised.

For example, thanks to advances in brain scanning, it appears that language is more widely distributed in the brain than was once thought and not completely localised.

Also, some language processing may even take place in the right hemisphere as well as in the left.

This suggests that localisation and lateralisation theories do not fully explain the organisation of language in the brain, and the same may be true of other functions.

Apply it

After Milli was involved in a car crash she was unable to speak clearly or move her right leg and arm. Milli had an injury to an area on the left side of her brain, but the rest of her brain was fine.

1. Identify evidence of localisation of brain function in this scenario. *(1 mark)*

2. Explain how the evidence you identified demonstrates localisation of brain function. *(2 marks)*

3 Explain how Milli's experience demonstrates lateralisation of brain function. *(2 marks)*

After many months of recovery, including support from physiotherapists and speech and language therapists, Milli was able to speak more clearly and could use her limbs more easily.

4. Using your knowledge of neuroanatomy, explain why Milli's speech and movement improved. *(2 marks)*

5. Discuss the extent to which neuroanatomy can explain Milli's behaviour. *(3 marks)*

Key concept 4: Organisation of the nervous system

Content area A

Unit 1 Psychological approaches and applications

SPEC SPOTLIGHT

Organisation of the nervous system, including the central nervous system and autonomic nervous system (parasympathetic and sympathetic divisions).

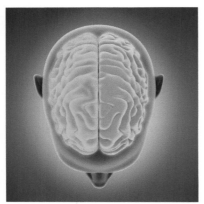

You can really see the two hemispheres of the brain in this image from above. The dividing groove is called the great longitudinal fissure.

Apply it

Scarlett is at a zebra crossing looking left and right. She decides the road is clear and starts to cross. Suddenly a car comes speeding towards her, racing over the zebra crossing and only just missing Scarlett. Scarlett feels scared, her heart races and she breathes very fast.

1. *Explain the roles of the central nervous system and the autonomic nervous system in Scarlett's response.* **(4 marks)**

After a few minutes, Scarlett's heart rate returns to normal and she feels much calmer.

2. *Name the part of the nervous system that controls Scarlett's response and explain its role in Scarlett's response.* **(3 marks)**

3. *Discuss the extent to which the organisation of the nervous system can explain Scarlett's response.* **(3 marks)**

Nervous system

Nervous system: What is it?	A complex network of cells, our main internal communication system uses electrical and chemical signals. Its two main functions are to: • Collect, process and respond to information in the environment. • Coordinate the working of organs and cells in the body.

Central nervous system (CNS)

The brain	The centre of conscious awareness where decision-making takes place. Divided into two hemispheres, connected by several structures including the corpus callosum. The right hemisphere controls the left side of the body and the left hemisphere controls the right side (contralateral). The brain's 3 mm outer layer is the cortex, where 'higher' mental processes take place, e.g. thinking, problem-solving. The brain stem connects the brain with the spinal cord and controls basic functions, e.g. sleep and breathing.
The spinal cord	A tube-like extension of the brain running down the middle of the spine, controlling reflex actions, e.g. pulling your hand away from a hot plate. Also passes signals between the brain and the rest of the body via the **autonomic nervous system**.

Autonomic nervous system (ANS)

Autonomic nervous system (ANS): What is it?	A collection of nerves passing signals between the spinal cord and body organs. 'Autonomic' means it operates involuntarily (automatically), controlling survival functions that do not need conscious attention, e.g. breathing, heart rate. It plays a key role in the body's response to **stress**. The ANS has two parts working in opposition to keep the body in balance – the sympathetic and parasympathetic divisions.
Sympathetic division	Activates physiological (body) arousal, e.g. increases heart rate, prepares the body for **fight or flight** to cope with stress.
Parasympathetic division	Activates the 'rest and digest' response to bring the body back to its normal resting state after stress has passed, e.g. reduces heart and breathing rates.

Key concept 4: Organisation of the nervous system

One strength is useful real-world applications.

For example, some actors and musicians find they experience **anxiety** and arousal that interfere with their performances, e.g. a violinist's hand shaking.

We know that this is caused by activation of the sympathetic division of the ANS and this can be prevented by drugs which reduce that activity.

This shows that understanding the organisation of the nervous system has led to effective treatments to help reduce anxiety and stress.

Another strength is support from research evidence.

For example, some research shows that damage to the spinal cord can cause body paralysis, and damage to the ANS can cause problems in responding to stress.

Researchers have also removed and destroyed parts of animals' nervous systems to see what effect this has on their behaviour.

Therefore, over time researchers have built up a 'map' of the nervous system, how it is organised and the functions of the various components.

One weakness is that the nervous system does not operate on its own.

The nervous system works together with the endocrine system (glands, **hormones**) in many behaviours (see next spread).

For example in the fight or flight response, the brain (nervous system) detects danger and sends a signal to the endocrine system to produce hormones such as **adrenaline**.

This means that our understanding of the role of the nervous system is incomplete without considering the endocrine system.

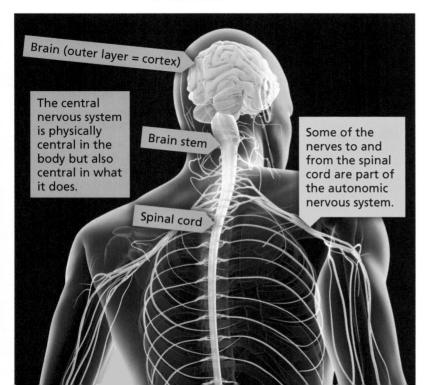

Brain (outer layer = cortex)

The central nervous system is physically central in the body but also central in what it does.

Brain stem

Some of the nerves to and from the spinal cord are part of the autonomic nervous system.

Spinal cord

REVISION BOOSTER

Some topics are harder than others. But students will disagree over which ones they are. It depends on the individual student.

But the lesson for everyone is don't avoid the tough topics in revision. In fact, you should make an extra effort to revise them so you can recall the material and apply it to scenarios.

Perhaps you know a fellow student who finds a topic difficult that you find easy, and vice versa. You can help each other!

Apply it

Wilf is a talented violinist and is playing a solo in a concert. Through the stage lights he can see hundreds of people in the audience including his friends and family.

As he gets up to play, he starts to sweat, his bowing hand shakes and he gets really worried that it will ruin his sound.

1. *Explain the roles of the central nervous system and the autonomic nervous system in Wilf's response.* (4 marks)

After a shaky start, Wilf gets into the piece and feels a lot calmer. He stops sweating and his hand is much steadier.

2. *Name the part of the nervous system that controls Wilf's response and explain its role in Wilf's response.* (3 marks)

3. *Discuss whether the organisation of the nervous system can help us understand Wilf's response.* (3 marks)

A4: Biological approach

Key concept 5: Neurochemistry

SPEC SPOTLIGHT

Neurochemistry, including the role of hormones in the stress response (adrenaline and cortisol), neurotransmitters.

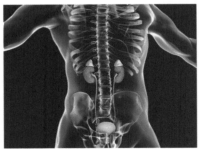

The adrenal glands (on top of the kidneys) play an important role in the stress response because they produce hormones that help the body cope.

Marlo doesn't like dogs. A big dog ran towards him the other day, barking loudly and baring its teeth. Marlo felt very scared and started shaking, his heart was racing and he was breathing fast.

1. Marlo was showing signs of the fight or flight response. Name **one** hormone that plays a role in Marlo's response.   (1 mark)

2. Describe the role of the hormone in Marlo's response that you identified in your answer to question 1.   (2 marks)

Marlo has been diagnosed with depression. He feels down most of the time and cannot motivate himself to do anything. He is sleeping poorly as well.

3. State what is meant by 'neurotransmitter'.   (1 mark)

4. Explain how neurotransmitters may be affecting Marlo's behaviour.   (2 marks)

5. Discuss the extent to which neurochemistry can explain any of Marlo's behaviours.   (3 marks)

Neurochemistry	
What is neurochemistry?	Activity of chemical substances in the nervous system, which affect brain functioning and in turn influence thinking, emotions and behaviour.

Hormones and the stress response	
Hormones	**Hormone** = 'chemical messenger' produced within glands as part of the endocrine system.
	E.g. the adrenal glands secrete the hormone **adrenaline** into the bloodstream, travelling around the body affecting any cells that have adrenaline receptors.
Stress hormones	Stress hormones regulate and control the body's response to **stress**. This **stress response** has two phases involving different hormones – immediate (acute) and longer term (chronic).
	Acute response – adrenaline When a stressor occurs, the immediate response is **fight or flight**. The sympathetic division of the ANS activates and stimulates release of adrenaline from the adrenal glands.
	Adrenaline in the bloodstream triggers arousal in the body, e.g. increased heart and breathing rates, muscular tension, pupil dilation, inhibited digestion, feeling of **anxiety**.
	Chronic response – cortisol If the stressor continues, a longer-term stress response is activated involving **cortisol**, also produced by the adrenal glands.
	Cortisol helps the body cope with stressors, e.g. it mobilises and restores energy supplies to keep the response going. Cortisol also has damaging effects on the body, e.g. it suppresses the immune system causing some people to become ill during chronic stress.

Neurotransmitters	
What is a neurotransmitter?	Chemicals that allow communication between nerve cells (neurons) in the brain and nervous system.
	Neurons are not physically connected but are separated by gaps called synapses. At the synapses, the neuron's electrical signal is converted into a chemical substance (**neurotransmitter**) that passes the signal across the synapse.
Serotonin	A main neurotransmitter in the nervous system, linked to behaviours including sleep and disorders including **depression**.
	Some psychologists have suggested that depressive symptoms may be associated with abnormally low levels of **serotonin** (but see facing page). It is currently unclear, but some antidepressant drugs may work by increasing serotonin in the synapses between neurons.

Key concept 5: Neurochemistry

One strength is that understanding stress hormones has practical value.

For example, people with Addison's disease cannot produce cortisol, so experiencing a stressor can trigger a life-threatening 'Addisonian crisis' (mental confusion, abnormal heart rhythm, drop in blood pressure).

However, there is an effective treatment of self-administered daily cortisol replacement therapy, plus awareness of stressful situations when an 'extra' injection might be needed.

This shows that a better understanding of the stress response has improved the lives of many people.

This gap is about 30 nanometres whereas a sheet of paper is about 100,000 nanometres thick.

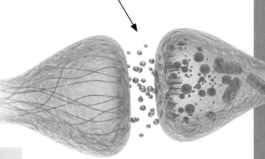

A weakness is research into serotonin and depression.

For example, a study reviewed 17 existing studies into the link between serotonin and depression, covering thousands of people with depression (Moncrieff *et al.*).

The researchers found no direct or consistent evidence that depression is caused by abnormally low levels of serotonin.

Therefore, this research suggests that neurochemistry may not play a central role in depression.

This gap is a synapse between two neurons. Molecules of a neurotransmitter (purple) drift across the synapse and attach to special receptors, which continues the electrical signal from one neuron to the next.

Another weakness is failure to take psychological factors into account.

For instance, two people can experience the same stressor (e.g. sitting an exam) but one remains calm while the other has an acute stress response, i.e. experiencing fight or flight.

These two people think about the stressor differently, with one viewing the exam as a chance to shine and the other as a 'disaster waiting to happen'.

This shows that neurochemistry is not a complete explanation of the stress response because it neglects cognitive factors.

REVISION BOOSTER

An exam question could involve you evaluating a concept, theory or model for 3 marks. This is where one of the AO3 points on the spread comes in. Notice we said 'one'...

Evaluation is much better when it is detailed and well-developed. So, explaining one point in a PET-friendly way will always get more marks than just listing a couple of points in a superficial way without developing them.

Using a research study to challenge a concept or theory is a good way to do this. Don't worry about names and dates. But do make sure you explain how the study challenges the concept. For example, consider the study by Moncrieff *et al.* How does this study challenge the role of neurotransmitters?

Apply it

Salma's long-term relationship has been strained for many months and it has now reached breaking point. It looks like she will have to sell the house she currently owns with her partner and look for somewhere else to live, just as she is about to start a challenging new job.

1. State what is meant by 'hormone'. (1 mark)

2. Salma has been feeling stressed for quite a while. Name **one** hormone that plays a role in Salma's stress response. (1 mark)

3. Explain the role of the hormone you have identified in Salma's stress response. (2 marks)

4. Discuss whether neurochemistry can account for Salma's response. (3 marks)

Key concept 6: Evolutionary psychology

Content area A

Unit 1 Psychological approaches and applications

SPEC SPOTLIGHT

Evolutionary psychology, including the environment of evolutionary adaptation, survival of the fittest, the fight, flight, freeze response, sexual selection and genome lag.

Apply it

Huda is hoping for a big promotion at work. She has an interview with her company's CEO and has been preparing for several days. Now she is sitting outside the interview room and her name has just been called.

1. Using **one** concept from evolutionary psychology, explain how Huda might behave in the interview. **(3 marks)**

2. Discuss the extent to which evolutionary psychology can explain Huda's behaviour. **(3 marks)**

In the interview, Huda was asked for her favourite fact. She replied, 'African male lions have bushy manes of fur around their faces, whereas the females do not.'

3. Explain this difference using your knowledge of sexual selection. **(3 marks)**

The peacock's tail demonstrates the importance of sexual selection.

Evolutionary psychology	
Survival of the fittest	**Evolution** refers to how the form and behaviour of living things change over time through natural selection.
	Ancestors who had characteristics that helped them stay alive and reproduce in hard times passed their **genes** on to the next generation, so the genes were 'selected'.
	'Fittest' means the characteristics that best match ('fit') the demands of the environment (Darwin).
Environment of evolutionary adaptation (EEA)	Today we see the outcomes of natural selection – organisms are what they are because their characteristics helped them survive in particular environments.
	Human evolution mostly took place during the EEA, which ended 10,000 years ago. Our ancestors' minds and behaviour evolved from apes on four legs to hunter-gatherers surviving on the African savannah using tools and language.
	Our minds and behaviour today are still largely adapted to the evolutionary pressures of the EEA.
Genome lag	Evolutionary pressures change the human genome over thousands of years, but our world changes much more quickly.
	E.g. most of the population lives in vast cities alongside countless others, but we still have a 'small group' mentality adapted to the EEA.
Fight, flight, freeze response	The sympathetic division of the ANS is activated when we perceive a threat. This creates physiological arousal in the body to prepare us to: confront the threat (fight), run away (flight) or stay still to avoid attention (freeze).
	Ancestors who responded to threats such as predators with the **fight, flight, freeze response** were more likely to survive and reproduce, passing the beneficial genes on (i.e. natural selection).
Sexual selection	Darwin noted that some characteristics continue to exist even when they threaten an organism's survival. Such characteristics confer an advantage, making the individual attractive to potential mates.
	E.g. the peacock's tail is hard for the male bird to carry around and a big target for predators, but it is attractive to females. So, this threat to survival actually increases the male's chances of reproducing and passing on the genes that led to his success.

Key concept 6: Evolutionary psychology

One strength is support from research into partner preferences.

In many modern societies, women have a greater role in the workplace than they once did and so are less dependent on men to provide resources for them.

As a result, women's partner preferences are now less determined by resources than they might once have been.

This supports genome lag because it shows that a behaviour important to survival (choosing a mate) has been influenced by cultural changes while the genome has hardly changed at all.

Women still often confront threats by supporting each other in caring for offspring.

One weakness is that the EEA concept may not explain all evolution.

The EEA concept implies that significant human evolution stopped about 10,000 years ago, but there is evidence this is not the case.

For example, a gene allows some people to digest milk thus conferring a survival advantage, but this happened less than 10,000 years ago.

Therefore, some human characteristics may be due to outcomes of evolutionary pressures operating much more recently than the EEA, which undermines the importance of this concept.

Another weakness is evidence of gender bias in evolutionary psychology.

For instance, the fight, flight, freeze response would have been disadvantageous for an ancestor woman because it would have made it harder for her to protect her offspring.

A more adaptive response for women is 'tend and befriend', which involves them nurturing offspring and seeking support from social networks (Taylor *et al.*).

Therefore, evolutionary psychology's explanation of how we respond to threat may well be biased towards men's behaviour.

REVISION BOOSTER

The secret to making good revision notes is to keep them VERY short – in fact all you need are the key words to-be-remembered. Always be looking to reduce your revision notes. This helps make the activity more active instead of just passive. Doing this makes it much easier to construct cue/flash cards.

Then practise how you should put these key words together to write a well-expressed point. If you can't remember the full explanation, then have a look again at what we have written here and see if you can remember it better next time.

Apply it

Male robins may look gentle but they are actually incredibly aggressive. When they see another male robin, or even just a patch of red feathers, they will attack it.

1. State what is meant by 'survival of the fittest'. *(1 mark)*

2. Explain the male robin's behaviour using the concept of survival of the fittest. *(2 marks)*

Some evolutionary psychologists believe that humans are poor at coping with the modern world because we are not very well adapted to it.

3. Identify **one** way in which humans are poor at coping with the modern word. *(1 mark)*

4. Explain **one** reason why humans are poor at coping with the modern world. *(2 marks)*

5. Discuss whether evolutionary psychology can effectively explain human behaviour. *(3 marks)*

Cognitive approach to explaining aggression in society

SPEC SPOTLIGHT

- Aggression – behaviours that result in psychological or physical harm to self, others or objects in the environment; hostile, instrumental, violent and verbal/nonphysical aggression.
- Cognitive priming for aggression, hostile attribution bias; cognitive scripts and schema.

All types of aggression, apart from violent, can be expressed online.

Apply it

10-year-old Nancie wanted to get her brother Curtis told off, so she punched him on the arm. When Curtis punched her back, Nancie said, 'Mum, Curtis just hit me.'

1. Identify **two** types of aggression in this scenario. **(2 marks)**

Before she hit her brother, Nancie had been watching a football match in which there was a big fight between several of the players.

2. Explain, using **one** concept from the cognitive approach, what effect watching the football may have had on Nancie's behaviour. **(3 marks)**

Nancie frequently says to her brother, 'Stop looking so angry at me' and 'You did that on purpose.'

3. Using your knowledge of hostile attribution bias, explain Nancie's comments. **(3 marks)**

4. Assess the extent to which Nancie's behaviour can be explained by the cognitive approach. **(9 marks)**

Types of aggression

Different types of aggression	**Hostile aggression** Angry and impulsive ('hot-blooded') accompanied by physiological arousal.
	Instrumental aggression Using aggression to get what you want, planned, not accompanied by arousal ('cold-blooded').
	Violent aggression Using physical force to cause injury to others (e.g. punching, kicking).
	Verbal aggression Using words to psychologically damage another person (e.g. shouting, swearing, 'cutting' remarks), can be instrumental or hostile.

The cognitive approach

Cognitive priming for aggression	An aggressive stimulus primes aggressive thoughts, so a later related stimulus 'triggers' you to behave aggressively (e.g. you think someone is being threatening).
	Aggressive prime/stimulus E.g. watching a violent film, playing a violent game, watching others behaving aggressively. Priming usually occurs over time and is not a 'one-off' event (e.g. exposure to angry posts on social media).
	Below awareness Priming occurs without us being aware of it. This means we can be primed in one social situation and behave aggressively in another. E.g. you are primed by a TV character's aggression and later you are rude to a shop assistant.
Hostile attribution bias (HAB)	Bias towards perceiving aggression. A person with a HAB: • Interprets other people's behaviour as threatening even if it is neutral, which may lead to aggressive behaviour. • Pays special attention to other people's behaviour, expecting it to be threatening. E.g. they view an accidental push as deliberate → they become aggressive → others respond with aggression → this confirms to the person they were right to expect aggression.
Cognitive scripts and schema	Cognitive scripts are a special schema which tell us what to expect, how to behave, what the consequences might be.
	Most people have cognitive scripts for aggressive situations, developed through observing and experiencing such situations.
	Aggressive scripts are stored in memory and prime us to be 'ready' for aggression. The script is triggered when we encounter cues we perceive to be aggressive (e.g. a push).
	Aggressive people have a wider range of aggressive cognitive scripts that are easily retrieved.

Cognitive approach to explaining aggression in society

One strength is that the cognitive approach has real-world benefits.

For example, the approach can help to reduce aggressive behaviours through cognitive therapy to change HABs and thoughts that prime aggressive behaviour.

Adolescent prison inmates who underwent such therapy showed a much-reduced HAB and less aggression (rated by staff) compared with a control group (Guerra and Slaby).

This means that using the cognitive approach can help to reduce aggression and the social costs associated with it.

Someone with a hostile attribution bias is likely to interpret this neutral expression as aggressive.

Another strength is studies supporting the role of cognitive factors.

For example, a review of studies of HAB in children confirmed a significant association between HABs and aggressive behaviour (Orobio de Castro *et al.*).

A study into cognitive priming found that men behaved aggressively towards a woman confederate after listening to songs with derogatory lyrics about women (Fischer and Greitemeyer).

Therefore, there is some research evidence that cognitive factors are centrally involved in aggressive behaviour.

REVISION BOOSTER

This is the first spread of the 'contemporary issues' part of Unit 1. The exam paper includes extended open-response questions on each of the three issues: aggression, consumer behaviour and gender. These questions are worth 9 marks and are often called 'the 9-mark essay questions'. You have to provide evaluation in your answers to these (see page 4).

But here's a very important fact that affects how you revise. The command term for the question may be *Discuss*, *Analyse*, *Assess* or *Evaluate*, but don't be misled. You also have to include equal amounts of description and application in your answer as well. Don't write an answer that is all evaluation.

One weakness is that cognitive factors may not be causes of aggression.

Aggressive scripts are associated with aggressive behaviour but this comes from correlational research, which cannot show that scripts *cause* aggression.

Instead, being more aggressive may contribute to a more aggressive script. Or perhaps a non-cognitive factor causes both the aggressive script and the behaviour, e.g. learning experiences.

This means the cognitive approach is limited because correlations do not allow us to identify the true causes of aggression.

Apply it

Several people commented on Facebook below a video of the latest dance on a new entertainment show. Karina wrote, 'That was such a rubbish dance, I hated it lol.' Avril responded, 'I thought it was quite a good dance.' Karina replied, 'It's called freedom of speech, so why don't you just *$£%^?'

1. Name the type of aggression shown by Karina. *(1 mark)*

2. Give **two** concepts from the cognitive approach that could explain Karina's aggressive post. *(2 marks)*

3. Explain how the two concepts you have given could help us to understand why Karina posted her comment. *(4 marks)*

4. Evaluate the view that Karina's aggressive posting can be explained by the cognitive approach. In your answer you should consider:
   • cognitive priming
   • hostile attribution bias. *(9 marks)*

Social approach to explaining aggression in society

Content area B

Unit 1 Psychological approaches and applications

SPEC SPOTLIGHT

Influences of others, including conformity to social/group norms, stereotypes, role modelling, desensitisation, disinhibition, institutional aggression, influence of the media.

Does this expression of aggression conform to any social norms you are familiar with?

Apply it

Rocky and Apollo are discussing boxing. Rocky is a big fan. He says, 'I watch boxing a lot but I can't stand seeing women boxing. I don't mind men thumping each other but it's not right when women do it.'

1. *Using your knowledge of the social approach to aggression, explain Rocky's comment.*
   (2 marks)

Rocky watches boxing and plays boxing games on his Playstation. He has also spent time in prison for serious physical assaults.

2. *Explain how the media might influence Rocky's aggressive behaviour.* *(3 marks)*

While he was in prison, Rocky beat up other prisoners and was often beaten himself.

3. *Describe how the social approach could explain Rocky's experience of institutional aggression.* *(3 marks)*

4. *Analyse the extent to which the social approach can help us understand any of Rocky's aggression.* *(9 marks)*

Influences of others

Conformity to social/group norms	**Gender norms** In many **cultures**, **gender** norms state that men should use **aggression** to achieve social rewards, but women should be nurturing and gentle (Eagly and Wood).
	A common norm is that women should be expressive, so they may be verbally aggressive to release anger.
	Cultural norms Cultures have different norms about aggression, e.g. cases of 'intentional homicide' (murder) are more than 12 times higher in the USA than in Iceland.
Stereotypes and aggression	We fit people into categories and then think we know how they are likely to behave.
	Gender stereotypes Physical aggression is strongly associated with stereotyped masculinity, potentially leading to tolerance of harassment and violence by men against women (because it is expected).
	Ethnic stereotypes Black people are often stereotyped as aggressive, potentially leading to tolerance of racist opinions and aggressive behaviour towards black people.
Influence of the media	**Role modelling** Media provides aggressive **role models** for people to **imitate**, which is more likely when the model has characteristics the observer admires, e.g. fame, wealth.
	Desensitisation Witnessing aggressive behaviour is normally associated with physiological arousal. But people who repeatedly view aggression may get used to its effects and become desensitised. They feel less empathy for victims (Funk *et al.*).
	Disinhibition Strong social and psychological inhibitions against aggression are loosened after we **observe** aggression in the media. Media depictions make aggression seem 'normal'. Repeated exposure disinhibits viewers, creating new social norms that are more accepting of aggression.
Institutional aggression	Aggression may be caused by a prison's environment, including other people (inmates, staff). Two ways other people influence prison aggression are (McGuire):
	Gang membership This is strongly linked to inmate violence because gang leaders can exercise control over members in a prison environment. The more involved an inmate is with a gang, the more likely they are to be aggressive.
	Staff behaviour Serious violence by inmates is higher when staff are inconsistent in applying discipline, e.g. where decisions made by officers are overturned by senior managers.

Social approach to explaining aggression in society

One strength is that social influences can be applied in prisons.

For example, prison staff applying rules consistently can reduce aggression because there has to be communication between staff and with inmates (McGuire).

This is because good communication and clear rules mean inmates are less likely to develop a sense of injustice that can cause aggression.

Therefore, social influences that affect aggression can be altered to help reduce aggressive behaviour in prisons (and other institutions).

Another strength is research confirming the role of social influences.

For example, people who watched a film showing violence as socially acceptable (vengeance) later gave more (fake) shocks to a confederate (Berkowitz and Alioto).

In other research, physiological arousal associated with aggression gradually reduces in people who habitually view violent media, i.e. desensitisation (Krahé *et al.*).

This evidence suggests that media such as film and TV are key social influences on aggressive behaviour.

Prison isn't the only institution where aggression occurs but it is probably the most studied.

One weakness is that biological factors may outweigh social influences.

Some psychologists argue that biological factors such as **hormones** are at least as significant as norms, stereotypes and media in influencing aggression.

For example, castrating a male animal reduces both testosterone and aggression (Giammanco *et al.*), and human studies show testosterone and aggression are linked in both men and women.

Therefore, all of the social influences on this spread are only partial explanations of aggression and may have less effect than biological factors such as hormones.

Apply it

Gwen is part of a gang who are constantly fighting with each other and with other gangs. Gwen looks up to the gang leader, who is the best fighter of all. Gwen has seen a lot of aggression and she believes she's ready to join in.

1. *Name **one** concept from the social approach which might explain why Gwen is likely to behave aggressively.* (1 mark)

2. *Explain, using **two** concepts from the social approach, why Gwen is likely to behave aggressively.* (4 marks)

Gwen likes watching soap operas on TV. She enjoys the scenes where people are shouting at each other and sometimes pushing each other around.

3. *Describe how the social approach can explain the influence of the media on Gwen's aggression.* (3 marks)

4. *Discuss whether the social approach can explain why Gwen is likely to behave aggressively.* (9 marks)

REVISION BOOSTER

It's ironic that the time you spend *not* revising can be so beneficial to your revision. You can't revise when you're asleep, but you can still boost your revision. You'll benefit from the amount of sleep you get and the quality of it.

Make sure you get enough sleep – between 7 and 9 hours a night is recommended. One reason you need plenty of sleep is because not all sleep is the same. We sleep in stages, some of which are more beneficial than others.

In some stages of sleep, what we have learned during the day gets processed and 'consolidated' in memory, including your revision. But sleep also helps you feel better generally, it improves your mood and helps motivate you. If you sleep only for relatively short periods, you won't be getting enough of the high-quality beneficial sleep you need.

Behaviourist and social learning approaches to explaining aggression in society

SPEC SPOTLIGHT

- Operant conditioning.
- Social learning including vicarious learning.

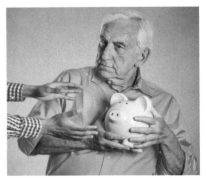

Getting someone else's possession is a tangible reward for aggressive behaviour.

Apply it

Gus has recently been promoted to senior manager of a photocopier sales company. The management team regularly shout at staff and are very unpleasant towards almost everyone. Hubert is the deputy manager and he also treats other members of staff badly, making negative comments about some people. In staff meetings, the only person Gus has good things to say about is Hubert.

1. Identify **one** example of positive reinforcement in this scenario.
   (1 mark)

2. Explain how positive reinforcement might help us understand Hubert's behaviour.
   (2 marks)

3. Using your knowledge of social learning, explain the aggressive behaviour in this scenario.
   (3 marks)

4. Evaluate operant conditioning and/or social learning as explanations of aggression in this scenario. *(9 marks)*

Operant conditioning

Positive reinforcement	Skinner proposed that behaviour is shaped by consequences: • Behaviour that is **reinforced** is *more* likely to reoccur. • Behaviour that is punished is *less* likely to reoccur. Aggressive behaviours are acquired and maintained through **positive reinforcement** because **aggression** is an effective way of gaining rewards.
Timing of rewards	Behaviours are especially strengthened when they are positively reinforced only occasionally. E.g. social media notifications – you wait for them and they are unpredictable so it feels more rewarding when they arrive. Aggressive behaviour is usually reinforced only some of the time, and is strengthened even further if there is no pattern to when it is reinforced.
Types of reward	**Tangible rewards** E.g. money, food and many other physically 'real' rewards. May reward up to 80% of children's aggressive behaviours (e.g. forcibly taking a toy, Patterson *et al.*). **Intangible rewards** E.g. pleasurable feelings, social status. Bullying is reinforced by increased status through fear. Gang members gain status through fighting. Whole societies provide status rewards (e.g. medals) for aggression in wartime.

Social learning

Observational learning and modelling	Children and sometimes adults learn aggressive behaviours through **observing** aggressive models, e.g. parents/carers, peers, media figures. They observe how the behaviour is performed and learn how to physically perform it (**modelling**). Observation of aggression alone does not guarantee **imitation**. **Vicarious reinforcement** makes it much more likely.
Vicarious reinforcement	Part of **social learning** is observing the consequences of a model's aggressive behaviour. Imitation is more likely if the observer sees the model being rewarded. The observer learns that aggression can be an effective way of gaining a desired reward. If the model's aggression is punished, the observer learns it is not effective in gaining a reward and the likelihood of imitation is reduced.

Behaviourist and social learning approaches to explaining aggression in society

One strength is that there are important applications to social policy.

Aggressive behaviours learned through direct reinforcement and exposure to family models underlie some serious crimes.

Policymakers (e.g. government) could develop programmes based on social learning and reinforcing prosocial behaviours. E.g. mentoring 'at risk' children, giving them non-aggressive **role models** to imitate.

This means the behaviourist and social learning approaches could reduce the costs to individuals and societies of human aggression in its various forms.

TV is a powerful source of aggressive role models and vicarious reinforcement for children and adults.

Another strength is strong evidence that children learn to be aggressive.

One study found that aggressive boys aged 9–12 years became friends with each other, in 'training grounds' for antisocial behaviour (Poulin and Boivin).

The boys' aggression was reinforced through rewards, e.g. praise. They experienced vicarious reinforcement by observing rewarding consequences of each other's aggression.

This study showed that aggressive behaviour readily develops in conditions predicted by the behaviourist and social learning approaches.

REVISION BOOSTER

You learned about self-efficacy earlier in this unit (see page 32). If you believe in yourself, it can boost your performance. It's about believing you are capable of doing something, in this case succeeding in an exam. Having high self-efficacy is motivating but it has other benefits too. It promotes good mental well-being generally.

So, find ways to raise your self-efficacy. Remind yourself of your past successes. Be your own coach and give yourself positive feedback, out loud if it helps. Use your imagination – visualise yourself succeeding in the exam and getting the excellent grade you deserve.

One weakness is that learning cannot explain hostile aggression.

Behaviourist theories predict that punishment of aggression makes it less likely in future, so someone who is aggressive and is attacked in return should be less aggressive in future.

But in reality the opposite is usually true and the person continues to use hostile aggression because the impulse is hard to control.

This means that alternative approaches (e.g. biological or social) may be better explanations of hostile aggression.

Apply it

Caiden hangs around the local park and shops with a group of other teenagers. The group's leader is Ade who is constantly getting into fights with others in the group. He always wins which is why he is the leader.

The other kids are always telling Ade how great he is. Caiden also thinks Ade is great and would like to be a leader like him one day. He has started shouting at and pushing some of the other kids around.

1. Identify **one** example of operant conditioning in this scenario. *(1 mark)*

2. Explain how operant conditioning might account for Ade's aggression. *(2 marks)*

3. Using the social learning approach, explain **two** reasons for Caiden's increasing aggression. *(4 marks)*

4. Assess the extent to which behaviourist and/or social learning approaches can help us to understand the aggression in this scenario. *(9 marks)*

Content area B

Unit 1 Psychological approaches and applications

Biological approach to explaining aggression in society

SPEC SPOTLIGHT

Biological, including evolution (survival of the fittest), brain structures (limbic system), biochemistry (testosterone, serotonin, dopamine and cortisol), genetics (*MAOA* gene and *SRY* gene).

To some, using aggression to compete over a parking space is a risk worth taking because 'victory is sweet'.

Apply it

Teachers are concerned about a local family. Three of the children go to the school and all have been in trouble for attacking other students. Their dad has been in and out of prison several times for assault.

1. Name **one** brain structure that may play a role in this family's aggression. (1 mark)

2. Explain **two** ways in which biochemistry may account for this family's aggression. (4 marks)

3. Explain how this family's aggression may be understood in terms of genetics. (2 marks)

4. Assess whether the biological approach can help us understand the aggression in this family. In your answer you should consider **at least two** of the following:
   • brain structures
   • biochemistry
   • genetics. (9 marks)

Biological explanations	
Evolution and aggression	Ancestors who survived to adulthood were more likely to reproduce and pass on the **genes** that contributed to their survival behaviours, e.g. **aggression**.
	Men who could 'retain' mates would pass on their genes, e.g. preventing mates reproducing with rivals by using physical violence.
Brain structures and aggression	The limbic system is a collection of brain structures that regulate emotional behaviours such as aggression, especially the amygdala.
	The amygdala has a role in assessing and responding to environmental threats. The more sensitive the amygdala, the more aggressive the person, e.g. their amygdalas react quickly and strongly to threatening stimuli (Gospic *et al.*).
Biochemistry: Testosterone	This male sex **hormone** is linked to aggression because men have higher levels than women and are generally more aggressive. Men aged 20 and over are more aggressive towards each other, when testosterone is highest (Daly and Wilson).
Biochemistry: Serotonin	This **neurotransmitter** affects aggression by influencing the orbitofrontal cortex (OFC) of the brain. Low **serotonin** in the OFC → disrupts neuron activity → causes emotional instability and reduces behavioural self-control → increases impulsive behaviours including aggression (Denson *et al.*).
Biochemistry: Dopamine	This neurotransmitter influences aggression when people compete for resources, because **dopamine** is the brain's 'reward chemical'.
	Two people in conflict with each other → high dopamine levels because they anticipate winning → **motivates** using aggression to gain victory. A dopamine boost is a reward that encourages risk-taking and impulsive behaviours like aggression.
Biochemistry: Cortisol	This stress hormone plays a role in aggression alongside testosterone. High levels of testosterone lead to aggressive behaviour, but only when **cortisol** is low. High cortisol blocks testosterone's influence on aggression (Carré and Mehta).
Genetics and aggression	**MAOA gene** Controls activity of the enzyme monoamine oxidase A, which 'mops up' neurotransmitters after a nerve impulse crosses a synapse.
	People who inherit the low-activity variant (*MAO-L*) have low enzyme activity which disrupts neurotransmitter functions. They have often been found to be highly aggressive (Brunner).
	SRY gene Indirectly influences aggression by activating testes development and triggering testosterone production in the womb (and at puberty).

Biological approach to explaining aggression in society

One strength is real-world benefits from understanding biological factors.

Each factor on this spread can be targeted for interventions. E.g. understanding the roles of hormones and neurotransmitters could lead to drugs to control and even reduce aggression.

Also, by understanding the role of genes we can develop non-biological interventions, as the influences of genes can be partly reduced by providing social and psychological support to 'at risk' families.

Therefore, the biological approach provides several potential ways of reducing the costs of aggressive behaviour to individuals and societies.

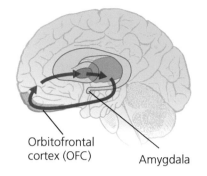

Orbitofrontal cortex (OFC)

Amygdala

A slice through the midline of the brain showing two key brain structures linked to aggression.

Another strength is research supporting the factors on this spread.

For example, brain scans show high levels of amygdala activity when individuals view images of angry faces (Coccaro *et al.*).

As another example, men using mate retention strategies in heterosexual relationships are more likely to physically assault their partners (Shackelford *et al.*).

Therefore, there is a lot of research to suggest that biological factors play a key role in aggressive behaviour.

REVISION BOOSTER

When you revise evaluation points, consider alternative approaches. The third AO3 point on this page does this, but you could take it further. You might want to argue that the biological approach is a less effective explanation of aggression than the cognitive approach. This is potentially good evaluation.

But just stating an alternative approach isn't enough. The key is to explain why you think the cognitive approach is a more effective explanation (and don't forget to link this to the specific behaviour in the scenario). There are obvious cognitive factors in aggression, such as biases in the way aggressive people think. Are these more important than genes and biochemistry?

One weakness is that there are many complex causes of aggression.

For example, the biological factors on this spread do not operate in isolation but interact with each other, e.g. brain structures and neurotransmitters.

Furthermore, biological factors contributing to aggressive behaviour also interact with non-biological factors (e.g. social and psychological) which are equally important.

This shows that the causes of aggression are extremely complex and greater than just any single biological factor.

Apply it

Ciaran is in a relationship with Livia. Ciaran is very jealous, so when he sees Livia talking to other men, he shouts at her.

He checks her mobile phone and has physically prevented her from leaving the house.

1. Explain how Ciaran's behaviour might be understood using the concept of survival of the fittest.　(2 marks)

When he was at school, Ciaran was often in trouble for hitting other students. He was easily provoked and quick to resort to aggression.

2. *Explain Ciaran's behaviour in terms of brain structures.*　(3 marks)

3. *Describe **two** ways in which biochemistry might explain Ciaran's aggression.*　(4 marks)

4. *Evaluate the extent to which the biological approach can help us understand Ciaran's aggression. In your answer you should consider the following:*
   - *brain structures*
   - *biochemistry.*　(9 marks)

Cognitive approach to consumer behaviour

SPEC SPOTLIGHT

- Schema and cognitive priming, direct and indirect attribute priming.
- Cognitive biases in information processing – authority bias, confirmation bias and brand loyalty.

This is a brand, but the product doesn't come from an actual 'Riverview Farm'.

Apply it

Bax wants to buy a new car and plans to get an expensive electric one. He watches adverts for several cars on YouTube before settling on one that he thinks is the best combination of speed and comfort.

1. *Bax's schema may have influenced his decision. Give* **one** *example from the scenario that could be part of Bax's schema for cars.* **(1 mark)**

2. *Describe how indirect attribute priming might explain why Bax chose this car.* **(3 marks)**

The car Bax has chosen is the same make as his current one. He remembers that one was quite expensive as well.

3. *Explain how* **one** *cognitive bias could help us understand why Bax chose this car.* **(2 marks)**

4. *Assess whether the cognitive approach can help us understand Bax's consumer behaviour.* **(9 marks)**

Schema and consumer behaviour

Schema and advertising	**Schema** help make the environment more predictable, but predictability is the enemy of advertising because we are less likely to recall a specific brand being advertised.
	Adverts should challenge schema not confirm them. This is 'schema incongruity', a deliberate conflict between our schema and an advert's content, e.g. a 'wacky' advert is more memorable.

Cognitive priming and consumer behaviour

Direct attribute priming	Priming features ('attributes') of a product or brand itself, e.g. advert highlights a phone's size, speed, etc.
	The consumer associates these attributes with the product and recalls the advertised brand when later thinking about phones.
Indirect attribute priming	Priming the attributes linked with a product or brand, i.e. the context of a product, not the product itself. Context is a prime that activates schema in consumers' minds, making the product more accessible in memory.
	E.g. invented brands that people associate with desirable attributes. 'Riverview Farm' does not exist but the consumer associates the brand with indirect attributes such as farming, countryside, health, etc. The consumer is primed to recall 'Riverview Farm' when thinking about healthy eating, farming, etc.

Cognitive biases and consumer behaviour

Confirmation bias	When we buy a product we look for evidence to confirm we made the right choice. E.g. we are impressed by small features and ignore the benefits of alternative brands.
	This is self-fulfilling and explains brand loyalty: 'I bought this product because it's the best; it must be the best because I bought it.'
Brand loyalty	This is important when actual differences between products are small and customers upgrade frequently. E.g. some people may buy Apple products because they are Apple products. Apple 'fans' recall good things about Apple products, but ignore competitors' products.
	Companies exploit brand loyalty, e.g. highlighting features their customers like in advertising.
Authority bias	Consumers may give more credibility to the opinion of an authority figure, e.g. an 'expert'. Toothpaste adverts often use 'dentists' to explain the benefits of the product. The authority is persuasive even when consumers suspect the 'dentist' is an actor.

Cognitive approach to consumer behaviour

One strength is evidence cognitive factors affect consumer behaviour.

For example, four groups of people tasted wine while music was played. Each group's music had different characteristics, e.g. 'powerful and heavy', 'zingy and refreshing' (North).

In fact, everyone was given the same wine to taste, but the descriptions given by the groups tended to match the characteristics of the music.

This supports priming as a key influence on memory.

Adverts on social media are 'targeted' at users. This means social media companies are finding out as much about you as they can in order to influence your buying decisions. What are the ethical implications of this?

One weakness is that the findings of research are often contradictory.

Some studies support the view that priming and biases affect consumer behaviour, but many other studies do not. The reason for this contradiction could be the problem of replication.

A study is only scientific if it can be replicated, i.e. repeat the study and get the same outcome. But in this area of research, studies have surprising results that cannot be replicated by other researchers.

This undermines the claims about the value of priming and biases in consumer behaviour.

REVISION BOOSTER

Think about how you are going to structure your 9-mark essays. It's worth it because these three questions account for one-third of the marks in the exam. What's the best way to organise AO1, AO2 and AO3? The answer is it depends mostly on your preferences.

You could write all the description first (AO1), apply it (AO2), then evaluate it (AO3). Or you could integrate these skills. So, for each point, you describe, apply and evaluate before moving on to the next point and doing the same. You can still get full marks with either approach, but try to work out during revision which suits you best.

Another weakness is that there are ethical issues involved.

For instance, the whole point of advertising is to influence people's behaviour and priming occurs without the individual's awareness.

Some adverts may be intended to influence buying choices and brand loyalties in ways consumers are unaware of, which could be interpreted as a form of deception.

This means that psychologists should think carefully about their professional involvement with techniques deliberately designed to manipulate consumers' perceptions of a product.

Apply it

Rylee always shops at the same supermarket. As far as he's concerned, nowhere else has the same combination of value and quality.

1. Explain how the concept of schema could help us understand why Rylee always shops at the same supermarket. *(2 marks)*

Rylee decides to get a new phone. He looks at several brands and models, comparing their features before choosing a brand he already uses.

2. Explain how direct attribute priming might contribute to Rylee's decision to choose this phone. *(3 marks)*

Rylee remembers seeing an advert in which a very famous celebrity praised the phone, which is partly why Rylee chose it.

3. Describe how **one** cognitive bias could explain why Rylee chose this phone. *(2 marks)*

4. Discuss the extent to which the cognitive approach can explain Rylee's consumer behaviour. *(9 marks)*

B2: Use of psychology in business to explain and influence consumer behaviour

Social approach to consumer behaviour

SPEC SPOTLIGHT

Social – the role of others, including conformity to social norms ('Bandwagon Effect', social proof).

The bandwagon was historically a vehicle used in political rallies in 19th-century America. It would carry musicians and dancers and people would jump on it to have fun.

Apply it

Tahlia is a BTEC Applied Psychology student who started her course a month ago. She wants to do well and work hard but is unsure how much effort is required. Tahlia speaks to some other students who say they are spending many hours on their homework. So, Tahlia increases the time she spends on hers.

1. *Explain how the bandwagon effect may have influenced Tahlia's behaviour.* **(2 marks)**

Tahlia wants to buy some wireless earphones but she doesn't know which ones are best. She saw an advert for Airbuds which showed lots of happy people enjoying the product. But Tahlia has noticed that the music students in the college seem to prefer Earpods.

2. *Explain how social proof might influence Tahlia's decision on the earphones she will buy.* **(2 marks)**

3. *Evaluate the social approach to explaining consumer behaviour.* **(9 marks)**

Role of others	
Conformity to social norms	People's desire to conform to social norms is often exploited by advertising.
	We signal group memberships through publicly visible behaviours, e.g. clothes, music, products. Adverts promote the message, 'If you buy this product, you are like these people.'
	Conformity to social norms is partly explained by normative social influence (NSI, see page 24).
Normative social influence and consumer behaviour	We conform to norms in order to be accepted because we have a natural desire to be liked (Deutsch and Gerard). This leads to us changing our behaviour publicly even if privately we hold a different view, i.e. compliance.
	We may buy products or brands to 'fit in' with friends and avoid ridicule or rejection. We might change our behaviour because a group's social norms dictate that as the 'price' of membership.
The bandwagon effect	Many people will do something because others are doing it ('herd mentality'). Once a product or brand is adopted by enough people, many more join in. So, companies use 'social media influencers' to promote products in the hope they will 'go viral'.
	Bandwagon advertising creates the illusion that a product is already popular and lots of people use it, e.g.Rimmel's slogan 'Live the London Look'. This influences consumer behaviour by stimulating demand for a product that was not previously there.
Social proof	Another term for informational social influence (ISI, see page 24). We may agree with others because we believe they know more than us.
	In situations where we are unsure what to do or think, we look to others for social proof of what is happening and how we should behave.
	E.g. '72% of people lost weight after following this tip' is social proof of what people are doing and it influences what we do (Cialdini).
	Social proof explains why rating systems on websites are influential and why most people are more likely to read social media posts with lots of likes than those with very few.

Social approach to consumer behaviour

One strength is conformity can be used to influence health behaviours.

For example, people who saw the sign 'More than 90% of the time, people in this building use the stairs instead of the elevator. Why not you?' were significantly more likely to use the stairs (Burger and Shelton).

The sign was effective (people conformed) because most people who read it interpreted it as social proof that the social norm is to use the stairs.

This demonstrates how social norms and social proof can help change health-related behaviours.

Another strength is research support for the bandwagon effect.

One study showed teenage students an advert for a Ralph Lauren T-shirt, associated in the experiment with a famous person.

Compared with a control group who saw the ad without the famous person, the experimental group were willing to display a significantly bigger Ralph Lauren logo on their T-shirt (Niesiobędzka).

This shows that the bandwagon effect can explain the sudden popularity of even expensive products in terms of conformity to social norms.

One weakness is effectiveness of social proof differs between cultures.

People in the USA (individualist) and Poland (collectivist) were more willing to agree with a request when told all their peers had agreed than when they were told that none of them had agreed (Cialdini *et al.*).

However, the level of agreement was much greater in Poland, suggesting that social proof is more effective in a collectivist **culture**.

This means that campaigners and advertisers who wish to use social proof should take cultural factors into account.

Before we can conform to a social norm, we have to know what the norm is. In a hotel room, the norm is to reuse towels.

REVISION BOOSTER

When you practise answering 9-mark essay questions, don't forget to work on conclusions. Some command terms require you to finish your answer with a conclusion. These are: *Assess* and *Evaluate* (whereas command terms *Analyse*, *Discuss* and *Compare* do not need conclusions). What makes a good conclusion?

A conclusion is not a summary of what you have already written. Don't be afraid to start with 'In conclusion…'. One way to write a good conclusion is to give a judgement, as long as it is supported by what you've written and by the scenario. Pick out what you think is the most important point in your answer and – this is the important bit – explain why.

Apply it

At a motorway service station, the rubbish bins all have a sign on them saying, 'Most customers use this bin for recycling plastic. Please help us care for the environment'.

The bins have a QR code on them. Cerys uses this to watch a video showing a well-known environmental campaigner putting plastic in the bins. Cerys puts her plastic recycling in the bin as well.

1. State what is meant by the 'bandwagon effect'. *(1 mark)*

2. Explain how the bandwagon effect may have influenced Cerys to use the bin. *(2 marks)*

3. Using your knowledge of social proof, explain why Cerys used the bin. *(2 marks)*

4. Discuss the extent to which the social approach can explain Cerys's behaviour. *(9 marks)*

B2: Use of psychology in business to explain and influence consumer behaviour

Behaviourist and social learning approaches to consumer behaviour

SPEC SPOTLIGHT

Use of reinforcement and association in marketing:

- Classical conditioning – emotional association with products, repetition to avoid extinction.
- Operant conditioning – positive reinforcement (buy one get one free, loyalty points).
- Social learning – the use of celebrity/influencers in advertising.

Who could resist being told to BOGOF?

Apply it

A college gives a glossy brochure to everyone who comes to an open evening. The brochure shows images of happy students enjoying their classes and smiling. Coffee is available for free as relaxing music plays in the background.

1. *Using your knowledge of classical conditioning, explain how the college hopes to attract new students.* **(3 marks)**

The college wants to increase sales in the canteen, so they introduce a loyalty scheme. Students get a point each time they buy a coffee. They get a free cake after five points.

2. *Describe, using operant conditioning, how this plan could increase sales of coffee.* **(3 marks)**

3. *After two months, sales of coffee have doubled. Assess the extent to which classical and operant conditioning can explain the increase in sales.* **(9 marks)**

Use of reinforcement and association in marketing

Classical conditioning: Emotional associations	**Classical conditioning** associates the focus of an advert (product, brand) with positive feelings (happiness, warmth). E.g., a burger advert might show attractive people or celebrities enjoying themselves in the burger restaurant. This may affect the consumer's behaviour so they buy the product or switch brands. Other desirable outcomes include a positive attitude towards the product, or greater awareness of it.
Classical conditioning: Repetition	In extinction, a conditioned response (CR) to a product weakens over time until it disappears. Extinction can be avoided through repeated pairing of the UCS and the CS. A product is repeatedly advertised in long-term campaigns, to restrengthen the association and produce the desired CR.
Operant conditioning: Positive reinforcement	Pleasurable consequences of a behaviour mean the behaviour is likely to be repeated. E.g. you have a good experience of a brand's product (easy to use, does what you want), which is rewarding and makes it more likely you will buy this brand's products again (and less likely if you have a bad experience).
Operant conditioning: Example	Companies use schemes to **reinforce** buying, e.g. BOGOF (buy one, get one free) because you feel you are getting a bargain. Loyalty schemes give points for purchases → you collect points → you exchange them for something tangible → this reinforces your loyalty → you are more likely to buy again.
Social learning: Modelling and imitation	Adverts often show people **modelling** the use of products, e.g. vacuum cleaner, car, phone. However, **imitation** of the modelled behaviour needs more than just **observation** of the behaviour.
Social learning: Vicarious reinforcement	The model in an advert enjoys using the product. We experience their **vicarious** reinforcement, imagining ourselves imitating their behaviour and enjoying the same feelings.
Social learning: Use of celebrities	Celebrities are potentially powerful models. Imitation of a celebrity model in an advert is more likely when: • The celebrity has something the consumer admires, e.g. status, attractiveness. The consumer wants to be like the celebrity, so buys products the celebrity appears to use. • The consumer believes the model is similar to themselves, e.g. **gender**, age, **personality**. This is why some adverts put celebrities in everyday situations to 'humanise' them.

Behaviourist and social learning approaches to consumer behaviour

One strength is evidence to support conditioning and social learning.

Participants in a study expressed positive views of a fictitious toothpaste brand when it was associated with positive images. The more presentations the more positive the views, highlighting the role of repetition (Stuart *et al.*).

Also, a review of 46 studies showed that attitudes towards products were more positive when they were endorsed by a celebrity (Knoll and Matthes).

This shows that conditioning and **social learning** can influence positive consumer attitudes towards a product.

One weakness is that conditioning does not explain cognitive factors.

Cognitive factors are involved because people think in different ways about products or brands. E.g. how you feel about a product advertised by Jamie Oliver depends on what you think of him.

Also, we often think carefully about products and services and make rational decisions when we buy them, which is why comparison websites exist.

This suggests that conditioning is an incomplete explanation of how marketing works.

Another weakness is that research has been mostly laboratory based.

Lab studies investigate short-term effects of advertising on a narrowly-defined behaviour. E.g. choice of snacks 20 minutes after watching an advert for a brand.

But research into the long-term effects of conditioning in the real world suggests the effects of advertising are much weaker (Schachtman *et al.*).

Therefore, the research tells us little about the effects of advertising in the real world where conditions are less controlled.

Before conditioning

The consumer experiences pleasure when they see smiling people (but not when they see the product).

 Product (NS) ➡ No response

 Smiling people (UCS) ➡ Pleasure (UCR)

During conditioning

The product is presented at the same time as the smiling people, so the consumer experiences pleasure.

 Smiling people (UCS) ➕ Product (NS) ➡ Pleasure (UCR)

After conditioning

The consumer now experiences pleasure when they see the product (without the smiling people).

 Product (CS) ➡ Pleasure (CR)

REVISION BOOSTER

Some exam questions use the command term *Describe*. You need to answer these questions in a logical order and this is something you can practise when revising.

The sentences in your answer have to follow on from each other. Using examples helps you to do this. If you start a sentence with 'For example…', chances are it will follow naturally from the previous sentence. So, make sure your revision includes examples of the main concepts.

Apply it

People in a village are planning their Christmas festival. They decide to print flyers to deliver locally.

1. *Using your knowledge of classical conditioning, explain how the flyer should be designed.* (2 marks)

2. *In the context of classical conditioning, state what is meant by extinction and explain how the villagers could prevent it.* (3 marks)

To attract visitors, they plan to sell cups of warming mulled wine.

3. *Explain **one** way in which the villagers could increase the sales of mulled wine.* (2 marks)

The festival includes turning on the Christmas lights. A TV star has agreed to switch them on.

4. *Explain, using **one** concept from social learning, how the TV star might attract more visitors.* (2 marks)

The festival is a great success and there are twice as many visitors as the previous year.

5. *Evaluate whether operant conditioning and/or social learning can explain the increase in visitors.* (9 marks)

Biological approach to consumer behaviour

SPEC SPOTLIGHT

Neuromarketing – use of technology to measure consumer decision-making, scanning techniques to detect brain changes in:

- fMRI.
- Facial coding.
- Eye tracking.

Her facial expression probably tells you all you need to know about her feelings toward cake.

Apply it

A drinks company wants to introduce a new fizzy drink to the market. It commissions a 30-second TV advert for the new drink. The drinks company hires neuromarketers to test the effectiveness of the advert. The neuromarketers use various forms of technology with a group of potential customers. The customers are also asked to decide whether they would buy the fizzy drink.

1. Identify **two** forms of technology the company could use to measure consumer decision-making. *(2 marks)*

2. Explain how the neuromarketers could use these **two** forms of technology to measure the effectiveness of the advert. *(4 marks)*

3. Assess the neuromarketers' use of technology to measure the effectiveness of the advert. *(9 marks)*

Neuromarketing	
What is neuromarketing?	**Neuroscience and marketing** Neuromarketing applies technologies that measure brain activity (neuroscience) to marketing (selling products or services). It studies people's responses to products, brands and adverts. **Brands and products** Neuromarketing studies how consumers feel about brands, what gets their attention and their decisions to buy or not buy a product.
fMRI: How it works	fMRI is a form of brain scanning which measures the activity (function) of the brain when it is 'working'. An active brain area uses more oxygen, so more blood flows to this area and this is measured by a scanning machine. The participant lies in an fMRI scanner and is shown an advert or other stimulus as their brain activity is measured in 'real time'. The scan produces 3D images showing which brain areas are most active during decision-making.
fMRI: Uses	fMRI indicates what features of an advert activate a brain area to 'push a consumer's buy button'. E.g. is the person bored or excited by the advert, do they like a product or not? The more people like a product, the higher the price that can be charged.
Facial coding: How it works	People's facial expressions may offer a window into their feelings (Darwin), but the emotional meanings of expressions are open to interpretation. The facial action coding system (FACS) measures expressions more objectively. It categorises 'micro' facial expressions from the positions of 43 facial muscles (Ekman and Friesen).
Facial coding: Uses	Electrodes attached to the face detect slight muscle movements as people watch an advert (or look at packaging, etc.). Facial movements are correlated with emotional expressions (e.g. smiling) and feelings (e.g. happiness, surprise) to show which aspects of an advert or product the consumer likes.
Eye tracking: How it works	Many brain areas are involved in vision and coordinating eye movements. So, eye movements reflect activities of these areas and are linked to cognitive functions, e.g. attention, memory.
Eye tracking: Uses	Technology follows a person's eye movements as they view a product or advert. The viewer spends most time gazing at the aspects they find most interesting, exciting or **motivating**. This is associated with brain activity. They also gaze longer at things they find confusing, identifying what might need changing in an advert or product's packaging. Eye tracking equipment is portable so it can be used in real-life situations, e.g. restaurants, supermarkets. It can also be used in a virtual reality environment, e.g. virtual supermarket.

Biological approach to consumer behaviour

One strength is that neuromarketing techniques can be the most useful.

This was shown in a study where brain activity in fMRI was closely corelated with the sales figures for songs three years later. But interestingly, the participants' conscious degree of liking was not (Berns and Moore).

This showed the fMRI was more useful than self-report (questionnaires) because sometimes people are not consciously aware of their responses (or they cannot describe them).

This suggests that the techniques of neuromarketing can sometimes reveal practically useful information about consumer behaviour.

Eye-tracking can be done in a virtual environment.

One weakness is neuromarketing fails to predict consumer behaviour.

Researchers used fMRI, eye tracking and facial coding to measure participants' responses to genuine adverts, as well as a non-neuromarketing method, focus groups (Venkatraman *et al.*).

The best technique for predicting advertising success was the focus group (participants discussed their responses to the adverts). The only effective neuromarketing technique was fMRI.

This shows that neuromarketing techniques have some usefulness but methods that don't rely on technology (e.g. focus groups) may be better.

REVISION BOOSTER

Revising with other students might seem a bit weird but could it work for you? It's obviously important you don't distract each other, so one method is to revise together silently in the learning centre/library.

Observing other students revising could be motivating for you. You can all take breaks together and talk as much as you like.

On the other hand, in a different environment, you could explain topics, concepts, theories etc to each other. Do it without notes to encourage better recall of information.

Another weakness is that neuromarketing raises ethical concerns.

For example, neuromarketing may use research findings to manipulate responses that people are unaware of and over which they have no control.

Furthermore, neuroscientific findings are sometimes used to make inflated claims in order to sell 'expertise' to companies and advertisers.

This unethical manipulation of consumers worries many researchers who believe neuromarketing should be regulated by law.

Apply it

The management team at a major supermarket wants to improve several aspects of its operations. They hire a company that specialises in neuromarketing to work with some of the supermarket's customers. The managers want to know whether they are pricing their own-brand products at the correct level.

1. Apart from eye tracking, identify **one** technique the company could use and explain how they could use it for the purpose in the scenario. *(3 marks)*

The managers also want to improve the packaging of their own-brand products. The researchers at the neuromarketing company decide to use eye tracking technology to do this.

2. Explain how the company could use eye tracking to help the management team to improve their packaging. *(3 marks)*

The managers also want to improve the supermarket's general branding, including the name and logo.

3. Describe how the neuromarketing company could use facial coding to improve the supermarket's branding. *(3 marks)*

4. Discuss the extent to which neuromarketing can help the managers to improve the supermarket's operations. *(9 marks)*

Cognitive approach to explaining gender

SPEC SPOTLIGHT

Definition of the terms 'sex' and 'gender'.

Cognitive – role of biases (alpha, beta and confirmation bias), influence on gender identity, effects on equality, discrimination and prejudice; schema in gender (gender schema theory).

Cognitive priming – sex-role stereotypes, gender roles, gender priming.

Are people who identify as androgynous similar or different from women and men? Or both? How much does it matter?

Selina was born a boy. As an adult, she identifies as a woman. However, Selina's employer insists that she be referred to as 'he' in all communications.

1. Explain **one** difference between Selina's sex and her gender.
   (2 marks)

2. Identify **one** form of bias demonstrated in this scenario.
   (1 mark)

3. Some psychologists believe such biases can have effects on equality, discrimination and prejudice. Explain the effects the bias you have identified might have on Selina.
   (3 marks)

The role of biases

Alpha bias	Two extreme **gender** biases can lead to inequality, prejudice and discrimination because they misrepresent the behaviour of women and men and fail to acknowledge their different needs (also true of non-binary and gender-fluid people).
	Alpha bias is a binary perspective that insists women and men identify closely with one gender. It usually devalues women in relation to men, and non-binary people in relation to binary.
	People who do not conform to traditional gender categories are seen as 'disordered' and needing treatment (or worse).
Beta bias	This bias insists there are no differences between women and men's behaviour (but research shows there are). This also applies to transgender women, who are not men but this difference is denied by beta bias (also true of trans men).
	This bias prevents change because it assumes everyone is the same so everyone should fit into society as it exists.
Confirmation bias	Someone with negative stereotyped views of women, men and gender-fluid people may only notice information confirming their views. Ignoring information challenging stereotypes may lead to prejudice, making it easier to accept existing inequalities.

The role of schema

Gender schema theory	The gender **schema** contains our knowledge related to gender, e.g. how men and women are expected to behave. Information consistent with gender schema is more likely to be stored and recalled (Martin and Halverson).
	E.g. a girl believes engineering is 'for men' and nursing is 'for women' → she adds information about nursing to her gender schema → she ignores information about engineering → she recalls more about nursing → her recall of engineering information may be distorted to fit her gender schema.

The role of cognitive priming

How sex-role stereotypes prime gender behaviour	Fixed views people have of men's and women's **roles** are often based on 'traditional' views of gender behaviour.
	Gender stereotypes that you accept prime you to expect certain gender-related behaviours, e.g. a job applicant with a 'man's name' will be better at maths.
How gender roles prime gender behaviour	Gender roles also prime gender-typical behaviour in both the real world and the media.
	E.g. a girl sees women/girls portrayed in TV adverts as passive → she may take on a similar role when interacting with adults.

Cognitive approach to explaining gender

One strength is that there are practical uses of the cognitive approach.

For example, there is more to explaining gender than just similarities and differences between men and women, so we should be neither alpha- nor beta-biased in our everyday interactions.

Instead, we should acknowledge both types and accept there are important similarities and differences between gender identities of all kinds.

Therefore, both forms of bias are equally misleading and we should avoid favouring one over the other.

A man in a caring role may not fit with some people's gender schema. It would challenge their sex-role stereotypes.

Another strength is evidence supporting the cognitive approach.

Participants in one study primed their gender-related schema by writing about times they behaved in stereotypically masculine or feminine ways (Fowler *et al.*).

They then undertook the cold pressor test, putting an arm into freezing water for as long as possible. Men primed by writing about feminine-typical behaviours reported less pain and **anxiety** from the test than other groups.

This finding shows that priming gender roles can have some effect on even involuntary behaviours such as the experience of pain.

REVISION BOOSTER

It's really important to spend focused revision time on understanding the difference between key terms. 'Sex' and 'gender' are often used interchangeably in day-to-day conversation, but they have different meanings in the world of psychology.

Sex refers to biological differences between males and females assigned at birth, including anatomy, hormones and chromosomes.

Gender refers to psychological, social and cultural differences between girls/women and boys/men, including attitudes, behaviours and social roles.

One weakness is the cognitive approach underplays social context.

For instance, gender-related behaviour of parents/carers and the rewards and punishments they give children may be more important than schema.

So social factors are crucial in the early years in which gender develops and are much better explained by **social learning** theory.

This failure to address how social and cognitive factors interact means the cognitive approach is an incomplete explanation.

Apply it

Baxter is 4 years old. His mum is a civil engineer and his dad is a nurse. One day as Baxter's dad dropped him off at the nursery he says, 'Daddy don't forget your yellow hat.'

1. *Describe how the cognitive approach might explain Baxter's comment.* (3 marks)

On one occasion when Baxter's dad dropped him off at nursery, one of the assistants said, 'What time will your wife pick him up?'

2. *Explain how cognitive priming of gender roles might account for the assistant's comment.* (2 marks)

A retailer is looking for checkout assistants. The senior manager says he is more interested in the male applicants because he thinks they will be better at maths.

3. *State what is meant by 'sex-role stereotype'.* (1 mark)

4. *Describe how sex-role stereotypes might explain the senior manager's comment.* (3 marks)

5. *Evaluate the extent to which the cognitive approach can help us understand gender.* (9 marks)

B3: Application of psychology to explain gender

Social approach to explaining gender

Content area B

Unit 1 Psychological approaches and applications

SPEC SPOTLIGHT

Influence of culture, cultural bias towards gender and roles, peer influences (normative and informational), conformity to gender roles.

The 'third-gender' hijras of India demonstrate just how complex gender is.

Apply it

When Farah was a young child, all of her friends were girls. They all went to the same primary school and played together in their homes. Farah didn't become friends with boys for several years.

1. Explain how Farah's gender may have been influenced by:
   (a) normative peer influences and
   (b) informational peer influences.
   (4 marks)

When Farah was 12, most of her friends were boys. She happily joined in with their games of football. Her parents were concerned that Farah was a bit of a 'tomboy' and other girls at school made spiteful comments.

2. Using the social approach, explain whether Farah will conform to a gender role.
   (3 marks)

3. Discuss the extent to which the social approach can help us understand Farah's gender.
   (9 marks)

Peer influences on gender

Gender identity in childhood	**Gender segregation** Most children can state they are a boy or a girl by age 3 years when **gender** segregation also begins. By primary school, children spend little time with other-gender peers (Egan and Perry). Same-gender peers are **models** for gender-typical behaviour.
	NSI and ISI Peers provide norms of gender-typical behaviour = NSI, e.g. 'We don't play with dolls.' Peers are also sources of information about gender-related behaviours = ISI, e.g. 'Boys don't cry.' Peers are a source of sanctions for gender-atypical behaviour (e.g. 'You're a tomboy because you like football.').
Gender identity in adolescence	Gender typicality is the extent to which the adolescent feels they are like other members of their gender category. The person reflects on their personal qualities and judges how closely they fit a gender category.
	The adolescent compares themselves with their peers, e.g. 'I am like my friends X and Y, but not like Z, so I am not a typical boy.' Some adolescents become aware they are transgender, i.e. they are not typical of their assigned (birth) sex.

Conformity to gender roles

Felt pressure for gender conformity	**NSI** The adolescent feels social pressure to conform to the norms of a gender role, from parents/carers, teachers and peers. This includes pressure not to behave in gender-atypical ways (i.e. boys should not be feminine, girls should not be masculine).
Gender non-conformity	Felt pressure causes **stress** for adolescents who do not conform to gender-role norms, because they are trying to cope with a role that many still feel is socially unacceptable. Negative outcomes are teasing, bullying, rejection (Jewell and Brown).
	Gender dysphoria and linked psychological ill health may be explained by the stress associated with a non-conforming identity (not necessarily the identity itself, Nagoshi *et al.*).

Influence of culture on gender

Culture and third genders	Several **cultures** use the term 'third gender' for people who do not fit the binary classification of woman or man.
	Five million people in India, Pakistan and Bangladesh live as transgender. Hijras in India are recognised as having legal identities in passports (indicated by the letter 'E').
	Fa'afafine of Samoa are biological males who adopt a woman's traditional gender role, e.g. work in a domestic context and dedication to the family. If a fa'afafine has sexual relations with a non-fa'afafine man, neither are considered gay.

Social approach to explaining gender

One strength is evidence supporting the social approach to gender.

For example, women in some cultures have active roles in the workplace away from the domestic environment, so old stereotypes have broken down and expectations of gender **roles** have changed (Hofstede).

But in some cultures with more traditional gender expectations, women still face pressure to adopt the role of homemaker due to social, cultural and religious demands.

This suggests that gender roles are strongly influenced by cultural context.

Our gender identity is influenced partly by the comparisons we make with our peers.

One weakness is a poor explanation of gender non-conformity.

Social influences e.g. NSI encourage gender conformity and most people in most cultures spend their lives with people who conform to gender norms and roles.

Based just on social factors, it is hard to explain how some people become non-conforming. Perhaps a cognitive element is needed, i.e. social influences depend on how we perceive them or think about them.

This suggests that other approaches may be better explanations of the nature of gender.

Another weakness is some social influences on gender are not strong.

For example, one study found that adolescent peers significantly influenced felt pressure for gender conformity, but were not a significant influence on gender typicality (Kornienko et al.).

The researchers concluded that some aspects of gender are influenced by peers (e.g. gender conformity) but others are not (e.g. gender typicality).

Therefore, the social approach does not explain all aspects of gender, such as peer influence.

REVISION BOOSTER

There are lots of techniques you can use that will help you revise effectively. But there is one that beats them all – regular self-testing. Generally speaking, if a revision technique feels easy, it doesn't help much. Highlighting, rereading notes, reorganising notes can all be useful but don't kid yourself – they are limited.

When you test yourself, you are making more of an effort to get information *out* of your memory. Each time you have a revision session (remember, no more than 20–30 minutes before a break), write down two or three quiz questions on the material. Start the next session with these questions, then add two or three more, and so on.

Apply it

Nat was born female. Their parents were quite traditional. Their dad went out to work and mum stayed at home and raised Nat and her three brothers.

Growing up, Nat did not want to adopt a traditional female role. But they felt a lot of pressure to do so, which was very stressful. By the time they were at university, Nat identified as non-binary.

1. *State what is meant by 'non-binary'.* (1 mark)
2. *Explain the influence of culture on gender.* (2 marks)
3. *Explain **two** ways in which Nat may have been influenced to conform to gender roles.* (4 marks)
4. *Evaluate the social approach to explaining gender.* (9 marks)

Behaviourist and social learning approaches to explaining gender

SPEC SPOTLIGHT

Behaviourist and social learning including the influence of the media, operant conditioning.

Children carrying out 'gender-atypical' tasks may not be as unusual as it once was.

Apply it

At primary school, Romilly's teachers praised her for her very good language skills. But when she put her hand up to answer maths questions, she was usually ignored. At home, Romilly wanted to play with her brother's toy tools but her parents told her off when she tried.

1. Explain **two** ways in which operant conditioning could have an effect on Romilly's gender. **(4 marks)**

At secondary school, Romilly decided she wanted to become an engineer. But her dad didn't want Romilly to go into a 'man's career', so eventually she became a journalist like her mum.

2. Explain how social learning might have influenced Romilly's gender. **(3 marks)**

3. Explain how Romilly's gender might have been influenced by the media. **(3 marks)**

4. Evaluate the extent to which operant conditioning and/or social learning can explain Romilly's gender. **(9 marks)**

Operant conditioning and gender

Rewards and punishments	Children behave in ways typical of their **gender** → peers and adults reward them with praise and approval → **reinforces** the behaviour. Also, gender-atypical behaviour → punished or ignored by peers and adults → weakens those behaviours.
	E.g. boys are encouraged to play with toy cars, be active and rough and avoid 'girl-type' activities. Girls are encouraged to play with dolls, to do craft activities and be passive and gentle. An active girl may be called a 'tomboy', i.e. not a 'proper' girl.
Differential reinforcement	Boys and girls are reinforced for different categories of behaviour, i.e. masculine for boys, feminine for girls.
	Fathers are most likely to apply differential rewards and punishments for gender-related behaviours (Kerig *et al.*).
	Differential reinforcement is key to learning gender identity, continuing through life and not confined to childhood (Block).

Social learning and gender

Modelling	Parents/carers **model** gender-typical behaviours for children, e.g. a mother tending to her child's needs models feminine-typical behaviour. A daughter may **observe** this and **imitate** it.
Vicarious reinforcement	Children experience the consequences of a model's behaviour indirectly. The child is likely to imitate rewarded behaviour, e.g. a girl observes her older sister being praised for looking after her doll. Imitation is less likely if the consequence is punishment, e.g. a boy observes a classmate bullied for being 'girly'.
Identification	Imitation is more likely when the observer **identifies** with the model, e.g. 'They are like me' and/or 'They are someone I want to be.' The model has qualities the observer finds rewarding (e.g. a gender-atypical model who is interesting).
Influence of the media	**Modelling** Gender-typical models are found in traditional media, e.g. TV soap operas, talent shows. Gender-atypical models are often found in online media, e.g. influencers with high status.
	Vicarious reinforcement Observers indirectly experience the consequences of media models behaving in gender-typical and gender-atypical ways, e.g. if a gender-atypical pop star is praised on TV an observer might imitate their behaviour.
	Identification An observer may imitate a gender-atypical model who they perceive as being more 'like me' than gender-typical models. High-status figures may provide gender-fluid **role models** for observers to identify with.

Behaviourist and social learning approaches to explaining gender

One strength is support from 'Baby X' studies.

The same babies were dressed half the time in 'girls' clothes' and half the time in 'boys' clothes' (Smith and Lloyd).

When dressed as boys, mothers gave them a hammer-shaped rattle and encouraged them to be active. Dressed as girls, the same babies were given a cuddly doll and reinforced for being passive.

This is evidence of a 'gender curriculum' in the home – gender-typical behaviour is reinforced differentially for boys and girls from a young age.

This is what might happen if children were just passive copiers of gender role behaviour.

Another strength is that the approach explains how gender can change.

In earlier decades, gender-atypical behaviour would have been punished or ignored, but today it is increasingly reinforced, i.e. rewarded.

For example, media portrayals (advertising, dramas, TV, online) of gender-atypical behaviour are much more common and widely accepted.

Therefore, **social learning** can explain the growth of fluid and non-binary gender identities through changes in modelling and reinforcement.

A weakness is that children are more active in acquiring gender.

If learning gender was just passively observing models, imitating them and receiving reinforcement, then children's gender identities would be the same as their parents'/carers'.

Instead, many children become much more gender-atypical than their parents, suggesting they actively construct gender rather than passively 'receive' it (e.g. adolescents seeking out gender-atypical models in the media).

This is hard for the learning approach to explain purely on the basis of reinforcement and modelling.

REVISION BOOSTER

When you eventually settle down to revise, do you find lots of other things to do instead? Does tidying your room suddenly seem like a very attractive task? Procrastination – or time-wasting – is the enemy of good revision. Here are some tips to help.

You do not have to be in the 'right mood' to start revising. If you have been procrastinating, then reset your day. Tell yourself, 'Revision starts now.' Vary your revision methods. Remind yourself why you're revising. Don't think about what you'll be doing in 30 minutes' time, or an hours' time. Just make a start. Some revision is always better than none.

Apply it

Digby and Dalia are brother and sister. Their dad plays football with Digby. Dad watches Dalia drawing and colouring with crayons. He praises Dalia for being pretty and well dressed. He praises Digby for doing well at school. When their dad once caught Digby playing with Dalia's dolls, he told the boy off and Digby never played with them again.

1. Identify **two** examples of operant conditioning in this scenario. *(2 marks)*

2. Explain **two** ways in which operant conditioning can account for Digby's gender. *(4 marks)*

Dalia follows a social media influencer who gives make-up demos on TikTok. Dalia is now pestering her parents to buy her some make-up.

3. Use your knowledge of media influence to explain Dalia's behaviour. *(2 marks)*

4. Analyse how the behaviourist and/or social learning approaches can be used to understand Dalia's gender. *(9 marks)*

Biological approach to explaining gender

Content area B

Unit 1 Psychological approaches and applications

SPEC SPOTLIGHT

Role of sex hormones (before and after birth: testosterone, oestrogen and oxytocin), evolutionary explanations for masculinity/femininity, role of chromosomes.

The hormone oxytocin is partly responsible for intense emotional bonding like this.

Apply it

Olaf has a large family and he sees himself as the main breadwinner. Other people would say he is quite masculine. He likes to 'work hard and play hard' so he is very competitive at work and when he plays rugby at the weekend.

1. *Explain the possible effects of testosterone on Olaf's gender.* **(2 marks)**

2. *Explain Olaf's gender using **one** other concept from the biological approach.* **(2 marks)**

3. *There are different approaches to explaining gender in psychology. Compare the biological approach with **one** other approach to explaining gender.* **(3 marks)**

4. *Discuss how the biological approach can be used to understand Olaf's gender.* **(9 marks)**

Role of sex hormones in gender

Testosterone	Testosterone is triggered in the womb by the *SRY* gene, which starts masculinisation of the embryo. Testosterone is linked to some differences in the brains of men and women, e.g. bigger amygdala in men (Knickmeyer and Baron-Cohen).
	Congenital adrenal hyperplasia (CAH) A genetically female foetus (XX **chromosomes**) exposed to high levels of testosterone will develop external genitalia resembling a penis.
	CAH children raised as girls often show play behaviour and toy preferences typical of boys. A small proportion of women with CAH (up to 5%) say they want to live as a man (Hines).
Oestrogen	Determines female sexual characteristics at puberty, e.g. development of reproductive tissues. Also regulates the menstrual cycle and causes increased emotionality in some women just before menstruation (PMT). Some psychologists argue PMT is a social or cultural phenomenon.
	Also involved in male puberty, e.g. growth of bones.
Oxytocin	Oxytocin is released in large amounts in women during and after childbirth. Its emotional bonding function helps new mothers feel 'in love' with their baby. It also stimulates lactation, so women can breastfeed their babies.
	It reduces the stress **hormone cortisol**, so also promotes bonding between adults ('love hormone').

Evolutionary explanations for masculinity/femininity

Dominant male theory	The most dominant ancestor males mated most often, so the **genes** that contributed to dominance survived. Male offspring developed masculine-typical traits useful in competition with other males for short-term mating (e.g. risk-taking).
Division of labour	Ancestor men and women adopted different **roles**, e.g. men were hunters and needed masculine-typical traits such as **aggression** to provide resources for female mates. Women gathered (picked fruit) and developed feminine-typical traits to ensure their reproductive success, e.g. nurturing, caring.

Role of chromosomes in gender

Turner's syndrome (TS)	About 1 in 5000 biological females inherit one X chromosome instead of two. Adults with TS do not develop a menstrual cycle, ovaries or breasts. Most identify as women and only a tiny minority experience gender dysphoria (Bondy).

Biological approach to explaining gender

One strength is explaining masculine-typical gender identity in women.

In one study of biological females, high testosterone was correlated with a masculine identity and low testosterone with a feminine identity (Baucom *et al.*).

Also, those with high testosterone saw themselves as independent, active and resourceful (masculine-typical characteristics).

These findings suggest that sex hormones may play a role in the development of **gender**.

One weakness is that gender differs across (or even within) cultures.

For example, Ashcraft and Belgrave argue African American girls **identify** with masculine-typical and androgynous gender roles.

The researchers link this finding to the structure of African American families, suggesting social context influences the learning of gender as indicated by **social learning** theory (see previous spread).

Therefore, a more useful way of looking at gender is as a combination of biological and social/cultural factors, and research should aim to identify how these interact.

Biological differences present at birth influence gender. But social, psychological and cultural influences are also 'present at birth'.

Another weakness is the tendency to view gender as binary.

The male/female binary distinction is common in the biological approach but it is contradicted by evidence of a third gender in some **cultures**.

For example, the fa'afafine of Samoa are biologically male but adopt a feminine-typical gender role. A non-fa'afafine man can have sex with a fa'afafine without either of them being considered gay.

This degree of culturally-accepted gender fluidity is difficult for the biological approach to explain.

Apply it

Leela works as a childminder because she likes being with babies and young children. She feels the job suits her because she can look after the children in her own home. Leela lives with her partner and looks after the home. She is looking forward to the day when they both have a baby together.

1. *Give* **two** *possible effects of sex hormones on Leela's gender.*   (2 marks)

2. *Most people describe Leela as feminine. Describe how evolutionary factors could be a reason for Leela's femininity.*   (3 marks)

When Leela's sister Gigi reached puberty, she did not develop a menstrual cycle or ovaries. She was diagnosed as having with Turner's syndrome. She continued to identify as a woman.

3. *Explain the role of chromosomes in Gigi's gender.*   (2 marks)

4. *Discuss the extent to which the biological approach can help us explain gender.*   (9 marks)

REVISION BOOSTER

You should aim to do three things in a typical revision session:
Review – Practise – Check.

Review – use the techniques we cover in other revision boosters in this guide, such as cue/flash cards, mind maps, memory improvement, working with others, creating quiz questions, etc.

Practise – use those cue/flash cards you have made. Answer some exam-type questions in timed conditions. There is no substitute for this. A big chunk of your revision sessions should be about answering questions.

Check – look again at your notes, this guide, etc. Did you include the right material? Identify what you did well and work further on what needs improving. You could even ask a teacher to look at the answers you have written.

A1: Psychological definition of health and ill health, addiction and stress

Defining health and ill health

SPEC SPOTLIGHT

Definitions and characteristics of health and ill health, addiction and stress.
- Health and ill health: biomedical, biopsychosocial, health as a continuum.

Apply it

Elliott is a gardener who went to his GP about a pain in his stomach. The doctor said Elliott had probably pulled a muscle while gardening. He prescribed some tablets saying, 'Take these and you'll be back to how you were before. If not, then I'll send you for a scan.' Elliott thought to himself, 'I've had pulled muscles before and it didn't feel this bad.'

1. There are two main definitions of health. Identify the definition Elliott's doctor is using and justify your answer. (2 marks)

2. The doctor recalls there is another definition of health. Name this other definition and state **one** question the doctor could ask Elliott based on this definition. (2 marks)

3. Identify **one** example from the scenario of health as a continuum. (1 mark)

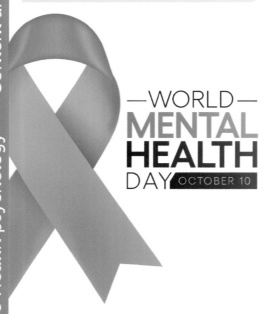

Isn't it better to prevent someone becoming unwell in the first place? The biopsychosocial approach thinks so.

Health and ill health	
World Health Organization (WHO)	**Health** is 'a state of complete physical, mental and social well-being and not merely the absence of disease or infirmity'.
	Ill health is any deviation from this healthy state.
Biomedical definition	Health is 'absence of illness', freedom from disease, pain and disability.
	Ill health ('illness') is a physical/mental disease, diagnosed by a medical professional from a person's symptoms. Treated with physical methods (drugs, surgery) to address physical/biological causes. Treatment returns person to pre-illness condition.
	Focus on biological functioning not social/ psychological causes.
	Associated with medical science/technological advances, dominant view in industrialised countries.
Biopsycho-social definition	Several interacting factors play a role in health and ill health (Engel), including:
	• **Bio**logical characteristics (e.g. **genes**, neurochemistry).
	• **Psycho**logical/behavioural characteristics (e.g. **stress**, attitudes).
	• **Social** environment (e.g. family, **culture**).
	Treatment takes all three factors into account to enhance health, rather than just make a person 'not ill'.
	Focus is on prevention and development of educational programmes to promote healthy lifestyles (e.g. exercise, lose weight, stop smoking, reduce alcohol, etc.).
	Mental ill health is not just faulty biological functioning, treatment is not just correcting this 'fault'.
Health as a continuum	The dominant biomedical view is that health and ill health are two categories (you are either healthy or ill).
	The biopsychosocial approach opposes this as too simplistic. It proposes that health exists on a continuum varying between two extremes. Over time, you can be very healthy, very ill or anywhere in between (mental as well as physical).
	Someone in extremely good health is functioning well in all or most of the social, physical and psychological areas.
	Someone with extremely poor health is not just physically ill, they may have stress and life problems as well (e.g. relationship problems, job redundancy, etc.).

Defining stress

Stress

Stressors	A stressor is any threat that creates stress.
	Physical stressors Many things in the environment create stress, e.g. temperature, noise, overcrowding.
	Psychological stressors These include major events in our lives (e.g. getting married, bereavement), everyday niggles and annoyances ('hassles'), the workplace and our personalities.
The stress response	Stress is how we respond to a stressor, physiologically and psychologically.
	Physiological stress How the body physically responds to stressors, e.g. increased heart rate, sweating, sick feeling, etc.
	Psychological stress This is the emotion you experience (usually **anxiety**) when a stressor occurs.
Perceived ability to cope	Whether you experience stress depends on how you think about the stressor and your ability to cope with it.
	Psychological stress occurs when the perceived demands of your environment exceed your perceived ability to cope.
	Example of perceived demands: students may perceive exams in different ways (as a threat or as a challenge) and this affects their response (they might feel very stressed or not at all).
	Whether you become stressed by the demands of your environment depends on your perception of the resources that are available to you.
Perception of available resources	Refers to how we *think* about our ability to deal with stressors. What coping resources do we believe we have?
	• Internal coping resources are psychological, including resilience (ability to 'bounce back') and **self-efficacy**.
	• External coping resources include social support, i.e. networks of friends, family and other people.
	Perception is key – you will not experience stress if you *believe* your coping resources can overcome the stressor (even if this is not reality).
	E.g. a student who has prepared for an exam will cope better than someone who has done little. But an unprepared student who convinces themselves they are prepared will also cope.

SPEC SPOTLIGHT

Definitions and characteristics of health and ill health, addiction and stress.
• Stress: definition of a stressor, psychological stress, stress and perceived ability to cope.

Stress isn't always stressful. Many people can cope with some stress and 'bounce back' quickly from setbacks in life.

REVISION BOOSTER

Be prepared to tackle different types of 'definition' question. You might be given a definition and have to identify it. You could be given a term and have to write a brief definition yourself. Or you might have to write a definition and explain it a bit further.

Apply it

Petra is a kitchen assistant in a busy restaurant. The kitchen gets very hot with lots of people shouting. One of Petra's jobs is to wash up and she often struggles to keep up. It's not unusual for her to be shouted at. This upsets her and she finds it hard to focus on her tasks. Petra lacks confidence and is the sort of person who prefers to be quiet. She lives on her own and doesn't have many friends.

1. *Petra is worried because she feels very stressed. Identify **two** stressors experienced by Petra.* (2 marks)

2. *Define the term 'psychological stress' and explain **one** way in which Petra is experiencing psychological stress.* (3 marks)

3. *Explain how Petra's perceived ability to cope affects her level of stress.* (3 marks)

A1: Psychological definition of health and ill health, addiction and stress

Defining addiction

SPEC SPOTLIGHT

Definitions and characteristics of health and ill health, addiction and stress.
- Behavioural and physiological addiction.

Excessive internet use is not currently recognised as an official addiction. But it might become so in a few years.

Apply it

Koji currently drinks two bottles of wine every evening. He used to drink less but his intake has gradually increased. He finds it hard to concentrate at work because he is always looking forward to drinking when he gets home. Koji feels anxious during the day but feels a lot better once he has had an alcoholic drink. He stopped drinking for a few days once but he felt terrible and was soon drinking again.

1. Identify whether Koji's addiction is physiological or behavioural and explain your answer.
   (3 marks)

2. Name **one** other behavioural addiction and **one** other physiological addiction. (2 marks)

3. Explain **one** difference between a physiological and a behavioural addiction. (2 marks)

Physiological and behavioural addiction

Addiction is a complex psychological disorder	People can become **addicted** to a substance (e.g. heroin) or a behaviour (e.g. gambling). They both produce pleasurable experiences and people persist in their addiction despite harmful consequences.
Classifying addiction	Addictions are classified into two main categories, physiological (substances) and behavioural. *International Classification of Diseases 11th edition* (ICD-11) categorises addiction as 'Disorders due to substance use or addictive behaviours': • Substance use – drugs such as cocaine, alcohol, etc. • Addictive behaviours – only gambling and video gaming are officially recognised (plus several that might be included in the future, e.g. internet use, shopping, sex).
Physiological addiction	Substance addiction has wide-ranging effects on the body. Two signs indicate someone is **physiologically addicted**: • **Withdrawal** effects – experienced when a person stops taking the substance (leads to relapse). • Tolerance – experienced when a person needs a bigger dose over time to get the same effect. Example: Is chocolate addictive? • Chocolate contains very small amounts of mood-altering chemicals. • Many chocolate-eaters show some psychological signs of withdrawal, e.g. cravings. • But tolerance does not occur so this is not a true addiction. It is probably more cultural than physiological.
Behavioural addiction	An addictive behaviour produces the same physical effects on the body as a chemical substance (e.g. tolerance and withdrawal). Example: Is excessive mobile phone use a **behavioural addiction**? • Some people show signs of dependence and withdrawal effects (when away from their mobile), e.g. cravings, anger, irritability, **anxiety**. • Tolerance does occur because they need to use the phone more often in more situations over time. • Mobile phone addiction is likely to become officially recognised in the near future.

Defining addiction

Griffiths' six components of addiction

1. Physical and psychological dependence (salience)	Addiction dominates the person's life. They are either engaging in it, thinking about it and/or craving it.
	It is impossible to lead a normal life without the substance or behaviour of addiction.
	The addiction takes up most of the person's time, so they neglect other behaviours, e.g. relationships, hobbies.
2. Tolerance	Repeatedly taking a substance means the addicted person eventually gets less of a 'buzz', so they need an increased dose.
	This is also true of behavioural addictions, where an increased 'amount' of the activity is needed to get the earlier effect.
	E.g. a person addicted to gambling places bigger bets to get the 'rush' they used to get from smaller bets.
3. Withdrawal	Effects that occur when the addictive activity is reduced or stopped. These include:
	• Physiological effects, e.g. headaches, nausea, loss of appetite, insomnia.
	• Psychological effects, e.g irritability, low mood, anxiety.
	People addicted to gambling may get stronger withdrawal effects than people who are dependent on substances (Rosenthal and Lesieur).
4. Relapse	Reverting to earlier patterns of behaviour after giving them up.
	This happens even after a very long period of abstinence, e.g. someone taking up gambling or smoking again having stopped years earlier.
5. Conflict	Two main types of conflict result from addiction:
	• *Inter*personal conflict *between* the addicted person and other people, e.g. in relationships, work, education. Occurs because the addicted person ignores the consequences of their damaging behaviour.
	• *Intra*personal conflict occurs *within* the addicted individual, e.g. loss of control from wanting to stop behaving in damaging ways but being unable to.
6. Mood alteration	A substance or behaviour can cause positive or negative mood changes on different occasions, e.g. a 'high' or 'numbness'.
	E.g. smoking is stimulating in the morning but relaxing at other times of day. This is probably due to the person's different expectations.

SPEC SPOTLIGHT

Definitions and characteristics of health and ill health, addiction and stress.

• Griffiths' six components of addiction: physical and psychological dependence (salience), tolerance, withdrawal, relapse, conflict, mood alteration.

Shopping may seem like a glamorous activity but the effects wear off quickly.

Apply it

Darian loves to buy things online. They used to have one thing delivered every day, but now there are several items at a time. Darian opens all the packages with great excitement. But once it's over they feel empty and anxious. It doesn't take long before they think about going online again. Even when they are at work, Darian is thinking about the excitement of buying things. Darian had a partner but they split up because of arguments over Darian's spending.

1. One of Griffiths' components of addiction is tolerance. Explain how Darian is experiencing tolerance. *(2 marks)*

2. Using **two** other components of Griffiths' components of addiction, explain how we know Darian is addicted to online shopping. *(4 marks)*

AO1
Description

Biological influences

SPEC SPOTLIGHT

Biological influences:
- Genetic predisposition.
- The roles of neurotransmitter imbalances.

You may inherit genes that mean you are more likely to be active. But you still need a 'trigger' to get you moving.

REVISION BOOSTER

Terminology is important because it can make your exam answers stand out. Using the right words is also more accurate. For example, 'neurotransmitter' is better than 'brain chemical' and 'antidepressants' is better than 'tablets'.

Apply it

Ursula is retired and now has lots of time to go on walks with friends. She has never smoked and has always had a positive outlook on life. She comes from a family that has experienced hard times, but they have come through and 'bounced back' from everything life has thrown at them. However, Ursula's younger brother was recently diagnosed with schizophrenia.

1. Identify **one** way in which a biological influence might affect Ursula's health. *(1 mark)*

2. Explain how the biological influence you have identified might affect Ursula's health. *(2 marks)*

3. Discuss how Ursula's health might be influenced by genetic predisposition and/or neurotransmitter imbalances. *(9 marks)*

Genetic predisposition

What is a genetic predisposition?	**Genes** contribute to **health** but do not determine it – you do not inherit a gene 'for' health or an illness.
	You inherit a predisposition which makes you more or less likely to be healthy (or ill). This is not inevitable and depends upon non-genetic factors.
	E.g. you might only become ill if you have the **genetic predisposition** and experience an environmental factor that 'triggers' the predisposition (e.g. you smoke or are stressed).
Genetic influences on health and illness	**Health** Genes affect whether we engage in physical activity, e.g. genes account for 62% of the variation in doing physical exercise (twin study by Stubbe *et al.*). People with certain genes are more likely to exercise than people without those genes.
	Physical illness Obesity is a physical disease influenced by a genetic predisposition. If one twin in an identical pair is obese, the other is highly likely to be obese as well, a much stronger correlation than in non-identical pairs (Maes *et al.*).
	Psychological disorders Many run in families, e.g. **depression** is about 37% inherited (Sullivan *et al.*). There is a genetic predisposition to develop a psychological disorder but environmental factors provide the 'trigger'.

Roles of neurotransmitter imbalances

What are neurotransmitter imbalances?	**Neurotransmitters** are chemicals that allow communication between neurons.
	Neurotransmitters are usually 'in balance', neither too high nor too low.
	But levels can become imbalanced due to genetics, **stress**, etc. This affects behaviour depending on whether the levels are too high or too low.
Physical health and serotonin	**Serotonin** is increased in the brain by short intense exercise and longer-term moderate exercise, improving sleep quality, alertness and digestion (Lin and Kuo).
Mental health and neurotransmitters	High levels of **dopamine** are associated with happiness and optimism (Mitchell and Phillips).
	Schizophrenia is a serious psychological disorder with symptoms including hallucinations. This may involve imbalances in dopamine, serotonin and other neurotransmitters in several brain areas (Kesby *et al.*).

Biological influences

One strength is correcting neurotransmitter imbalances can improve health.

For example, a structured physical activity programme can treat mild depression instead of antidepressant drugs (NICE 2009).

This kind of physical activity can improve symptoms and may alter neurotransmitter levels without the potential side effects of drugs.

Therefore, although genes cannot be altered, lifestyle and environmental changes can reduce the risk of disease and improve health in people with a genetic predisposition.

The biological approach recognises that health and ill health are not completely determined by genes. Environmental factors such as support are involved too.

Another strength is genetic predisposition includes non-genetic factors.

Some people inherit genes that predispose them to being resilient (adapt to life's problems), but they also have supportive relationships with other people (non-genetic).

So even if resilience has a genetic basis, it also depends on non-genetic environmental circumstances, which the theory recognises (Kim-Cohen and Gold).

This acceptance of non-genetic factors makes genetic predisposition a more effective (and useful) explanation of health and ill health.

REVISION BOOSTER

If you get a question with the command term *Assess*, you need to 'Make a judgement on the importance of something…'

One way of doing this is to look at the three evaluation points on the left, and decide how important they are. There are two strengths and one weakness, but this is not a football match where the highest 'score' wins. For instance, do you think the weakness is so important that it outweighs the two strengths?

Try to make this judgement on each spread and note down your thoughts.

One weakness is that the approach oversimplifies the causes of health.

It is usually inaccurate to say that a genetic predisposition influences health and ill health directly.

Instead, it makes lifestyle-related behaviours such as exercise and smoking more or less likely, which in turn affects whether someone is healthy or ill (indirect influence).

Therefore, the causes of health are complex and biological influences are not a complete explanation.

Apply it

Leah is a firefighter who has to be physically fit for her job. However, many people in Leah's family are smokers or obese. Her dad has had a heart attack and her mum has depression.

Leah does a lot of physical exercise and eats a healthy diet. Exercise makes Leah feel good, especially the five-minute bursts of intense activity. She tries to avoid stress, but this is very difficult in her job.

1. Identify **one** example of a possible genetic predisposition that might influence Leah's health. *(1 mark)*

2. Explain how genetic predisposition might influence Leah's health. *(2 marks)*

3. Describe the possible role of neurotransmitter imbalances in health and/or ill health. *(3 marks)*

4. Discuss the usefulness of understanding Leah's health in terms of biological influences. *(3 marks)*

5. Evaluate **two** possible biological influences on Leah's health. *(9 marks)*

Behaviourist approaches

SPEC SPOTLIGHT

Behaviourist approaches:
- The role of cues, positive reinforcement and negative reinforcement to explain healthy and unhealthy behaviours.
- Using operant conditioning to encourage and incentivise behaviour.

A feeling of pleasure is rewarding, but the feeling of relief we get from avoiding something unpleasant can be even more powerful.

Apply it

Yash manages a group of ambulance dispatchers. Their job is to respond to emergency calls and decide which ambulances should attend. The job can be unhealthy because it involves sitting down in a chair for long periods of time. Yash wants to find ways to encourage his staff to get out of their chairs and move around.

1. Describe **one** way in which positive reinforcement can explain why the staff stay in their chairs. **(2 marks)**

2. Describe the role of negative reinforcement in explaining the staff's unhealthy behaviour. **(2 marks)**

3. Explain **two** ways in which Yash could use operant conditioning to encourage his staff to move about. **(4 marks)**

4. Evaluate the use of operant conditioning to encourage the ambulance dispatchers to behave in more healthy ways. **(9 marks)**

Role of reinforcement

Positive reinforcement	The consequences of a behaviour are rewarded, making the behaviour more likely to happen again. This explains: • Healthy behaviours, e.g. physical exercise releases brain chemicals so you experience happiness, a pleasurable reward. You exercise again to repeat the experience. • Unhealthy behaviours, e.g. sitting on the sofa watching TV is an enjoyable experience, so you repeat the behaviour to get the same reward.
Negative reinforcement	Avoiding the unpleasant consequences of a behaviour is rewarded, making the behaviour more likely to happen again. This explains: • Healthy behaviours, e.g. thinking about missing an exercise session prompts uncomfortable feelings (guilt, hopelessness). You can avoid these by doing the exercise, reinforcing a healthy behaviour. • Unhealthy behaviours, e.g. sitting on the sofa watching TV avoids the unpleasant consequences of exercising (e.g. effort), reinforcing an unhealthy behaviour.

Role of cues

Behaviours are associated with cues	Behaviours become associated with particular stimuli, called **cues**. This explains: • Healthy behaviours, e.g wearing an item of kit which you associate with the pleasure of exercising, so just seeing the kit makes you feel happier. The kit has become a cue. • Unhealthy behaviours, e.g. smoking provides pleasurable rewards (relaxation, lower **anxiety**) which are reinforcing. Items present (lighter, ashtray) become associated with the pleasure and eventually produce a similar response on their own. They are now cues.

Using operant conditioning

Using positive reinforcement	**Positive reinforcement** encourages healthy eating by: • Receiving external feedback (e.g. praise for eating fruit). • Achieving targets (e.g. feeling good after losing weight) • Internal self-talk (e.g. encouraging yourself to reach a goal). Choose **reinforcement** carefully and tailor it to the individual, e.g. not everyone responds to praise.
Using negative reinforcement	**Negative reinforcement** encourages healthy eating because the person avoids the unpleasant feelings (e.g. guilt) associated with eating unhealthy foods. For negative or positive reinforcement, the reinforcement must come immediately after the behaviour or as close as possible.
Using punishment	Punishment encourages healthy eating by applying an unpleasant consequence to an unhealthy behaviour, e.g. a child is 'told off' for eating something unhealthy. (Note: punishment is not the same as negative reinforcement.)

Behaviourist approaches

One strength is operant conditioning can create real-world healthy behaviours.

For example, token economy is used on hospital wards to motivate patients to be physically active.

Patients are given a plastic coin (token) or something similar when they carry out a desired behaviour (e.g. exercising). The coin has no value but can be exchanged for treats so it is a reward that positively reinforces the healthy behaviour.

Therefore, operant conditioning is useful because it can lead to healthier behaviours in people who may not benefit from other interventions.

Immediate rewards are usually more powerful than long-term ones.

Another strength is research evidence supporting the effects of reinforcement.

One review looked at studies into the use of incentives to encourage exercise (e.g. going to an exercise class). Incentives included cash or vouchers (Strohacker et al.).

The review found that positive and negative reinforcement both increased exercise behaviours in children, young adults and middle-aged adults, compared with participants in a non-incentivised control group.

This suggests that reinforcement is an effective way of encouraging healthy behaviour, at least in the short term.

REVISION BOOSTER

Examiners like to see students using evidence to evaluate an approach. But the key word here is 'use', and this is a skill you should practise. Just mentioning a study is not the same as *using* it. Ask yourself these questions:

- How does the study relate to the approach?

- Does the study support the approach or challenge it?

- *In what way* does the study support or challenge the approach?

This third question is the crucial one that leads to high marks for evaluation. Mastering this skill will see a huge improvement in the quality of your evaluation.

One weakness is operant conditioning applies to a narrow range of behaviours.

Rewards for many healthy behaviours take a long time to appear. E.g. for a person trying to lose weight by dieting, the reward is weight loss at some point in the future.

A long-term reward is a very weak form of reinforcement and is often outweighed by short-term rewards for unhealthy behaviours, e.g. the pleasure we feel from eating a chocolate cheesecake.

Therefore, operant conditioning may be a less effective way of encouraging healthy behaviours than other approaches (e.g. the cognitive approach, see page 86).

Apply it

Ari is a gym member and they are there every day including weekends. They keep their kit by the front door so they see it on their way out of the house. They have several friends at the gym and enjoy exercising with them so much they never miss a session. Ari's friends are very encouraging. Ari also eats a healthy diet and just seeing fruit in the bowl makes them feel good.

1. Explain the role of cues in Ari's behaviour. (2 marks)

2. Identify **one** possible example of positive reinforcement in Ari's healthy behaviour. (1 mark)

3. Describe **one** way in which negative reinforcement may explain Ari's healthy behaviour. (2 marks)

4. Discuss the effectiveness of operant conditioning as an explanation of Ari's healthy behaviour. (3 marks)

5. Assess the extent to which operant conditioning explains Ari's healthy behaviour. (9 marks)

A2: Psychological approaches to health

Social learning approach

SPEC SPOTLIGHT

Social learning approach:
- Effects of parental and peer role models on healthy and unhealthy behaviours.
- Role models in health education.

Children imitate adults' healthy behaviours as well as unhealthy ones.

Apply it

One of Jaden's favourite activities as a child was going on bike rides with his family. He did this quite often because his parents enjoyed the rides too. When Jaden became a teenager, he stopped going on the bike rides. He became friends with a group who regularly met up to drink alcohol in the local park. This is how Jaden started drinking.

1. Identify **one** way in which parental role models may have affected Jaden's behaviour.
   (1 mark)

2. Explain **two** possible effects of peer role models on Jaden's behaviour. *(4 marks)*

3. Discuss the effects of role models on Jaden's behaviour. *(3 marks)*

4. Assess the effects of parental and peer role models on Jaden's behaviour. *(9 marks)*

Effects of parental role models	
Modelling and imitation	**Modelling** occurs when a **role model** performs a behaviour observed by someone else, e.g. a parent/carer brushes their teeth in front of their child. The parent/carer is modelling the behaviour.
	An observer **imitates** the role model's behaviour, e.g. the child brushes their teeth in the same way as the parent/carer. The child is modelling the behaviour.
	Parents/carers are 'nutritional gatekeepers' for their children: they decide what their children eat, they give opportunities for children to observe them eating, they communicate attitudes for children to adopt.
Vicarious reinforcement	An observer witnesses a model's behaviour being rewarded.
	E.g. a child watches a parent enjoy eating a chocolate bar or exercising and experiences the reward vicariously. This makes imitation much more likely than just **observation** on its own.
	Vicarious reinforcement and modelling are forms of **social learning**, i.e. we learn from observing others, especially when they are rewarded (**positive** or **negative reinforcement**).

Effects of peer role models	
Learning from someone who is your 'equal'	Our peers are a similar age and social class to us and have similar interests and experiences.
	Identification We **identify** with peers because they are similar to us, so we model our behaviour on theirs. Imitation is more likely when peers are having a positive experience.
	Social norms Peers establish what is desirable or 'normal' for the group, e.g. doing physical exercise or smoking.

Role models in health education	
Peers	Peer leaders are popular students used as role models in school-based **health** education programmes. They reinforce healthy lifestyle values and model positive health-related behaviours for others to imitate. They have more credibility with other students than parents/carers and teachers.
Healthcare professionals	Nurses are usually expected to model healthy behaviours as they have direct contact with people who benefit most and they help train future nurses.
Celebrities	Celebrities are sometimes used in health campaigns using the media to transmit the behaviour to be modelled, e.g. Kate Middleton receiving COVID-19 vaccinations. Celebrities are imitated because they have status and glamour.

Social learning approach

One strength is that health interventions based on modelling are useful.

One example is ASSIST, a peer-led school-based intervention to prevent smoking in teenagers. Peer leaders speak to other students about the risks of smoking and benefits of not smoking.

In one study, participants in an ASSIST intervention smoked less compared with a no-intervention control group (Campbell *et al.*).

This shows that peer role models can have useful positive effects on a range of health-related behaviours.

Community nurses who visit patients in their homes can be powerful role models for healthy behaviour.

Another strength is modelling explains how health behaviours develop.

For example, children in one study were more likely to sample a new food when they saw an adult eating it (Cullen *et al.*).

Other positive health behaviours (e.g. brushing teeth, doing physical exercise) are associated with parental attitudes of 'Do as I do', which is superior to 'Do as I say'.

Therefore, parents/carers who model healthy behaviours are more likely to raise children who engage in those behaviours themselves.

One weakness is that some role models in health education are ineffective.

Health educators (nurses, GPs, etc.) are officially role models of healthy behaviour but some lead unhealthy lifestyles. They may lack credibility with patients, who may not follow the educators' advice.

On the other hand, some patients can relate better to a healthcare professional who shares their struggles with unhealthy behaviours.

This suggests that modelling of behaviour in a health education context is more complex than official policies imply.

REVISION BOOSTER

We've said it before but it's worth repeating – almost all of your answers on Unit 3 will be in the context of a scenario. That's why there are two 'Apply its' on each spread in this book (usually).

Of course you need to know what 'models' are. But you should also be able to identify them when you see them in a scenario.

Try answering the Apply it questions as part of your revision. You could even try writing your own scenarios. For example, write a scenario about someone who is a 'role model in health education'.

Apply it

A sixth-form college plans to introduce a 'coping with stress' programme for students. The idea is to recruit 'student leaders' to help support other students in the college.

Zelda is a community nurse. She visits patients in their homes, mostly to provide care after surgery and help to prevent infection.

1. Give **one** possible way in which the 'student leaders' could be role models in health education. *(1 mark)*

2. Describe how Zelda could be a role model in health education. *(2 marks)*

3. Discuss the usefulness of 'student leaders' and/or Zelda as role models in health education. *(3 marks)*

4. Discuss whether the social learning approach can explain how the 'student leaders' and/or Zelda are role models in health education. *(6 marks)*

The government's Office for Health Promotion intends to design a health campaign to encourage young people to 'get fit for summer'. The campaign will be school-/college-based and supported by national advertising. A psychologist involved in designing the campaign suggests it should use role models.

5. Explain **two** ways in which the campaign could use role models. *(4 marks)*

6. Evaluate the extent to which using role models in the campaign could be effective in encouraging young people to 'get fit for summer'. *(9 marks)*

Cognitive approach

SPEC SPOTLIGHT

Cognitive approach:

- Decisions to engage in behaviours to provide relief from stress, anxiety, boredom or to mitigate impacts of other health problems.
- Resolving cognitive dissonance for behaviour change.
- Professional biases in diagnoses and treatments.

One way to resolve cognitive dissonance is to ignore any evidence that makes you feel bad.

Apply it

Ines is transgender and has a job as a dog walker which they find unchallenging. Ines is concerned about their high levels of anxiety and stays indoors a lot. They spend their time eating, even though they know it is unhealthy. Ines recently experienced chest pains so they went to the doctor. The doctor talked for most of the appointment and prescribed tablets to reduce Ines's blood pressure.

1. *Identify **two** reasons why Ines behaves in unhealthy ways according to the cognitive approach.* (2 marks)

2. *Identify **one** reason why Ines might experience cognitive dissonance and explain **one** way in which they might resolve it.* (3 marks)

3. *Explain **one** way in which professional biases may affect the doctor's diagnosis and treatment of Ines.* (2 marks)

4. *Assess the cognitive approach as an explanation of Ines's ill health.* (6 marks)

Making health-related decisions

Relief from stress, anxiety and boredom	Wanting to relieve feelings of **stress**, **anxiety** and/or boredom can lead to behaving in ways that are risky to **health**, e.g. emotional overeating ('comfort eating').
	Smoking is another example, as this can be relaxing and anxiety-reducing (due to biochemical effects of nicotine). Smoking is 'self-medication', i.e. using a drug to make yourself feel better.
	Such unhealthy behaviours are short-term coping strategies to reduce symptoms of stress, anxiety and/or boredom. But they create long-term health issues, e.g. obesity, cancer.
Mitigating other health problems	Some behaviours protect our health because they reduce (mitigate) the impact of other health issues, e.g. being physically active, eating fruit and vegetables, taking medication.
	All are associated with health and recovery from illness.

Resolving cognitive dissonance

Cognitive dissonance = discomfort from disagreement with yourself	When making decisions we sometimes have to choose between two equally (un)attractive options, so whichever we choose we think, 'Maybe I should have selected the other one.'
	Cognitive dissonance arises in e.g. smoking because you want to smoke (it is enjoyable) but you also want to give up (you know it is bad for your health).
	Two main ways to resolve cognitive dissonance:
	• Change your behaviour (e.g. find ways to stop smoking).
	• Change your belief (e.g. dismiss evidence that smoking is harmful).

Professional biases

Healthcare professionals' decisions can be biased	A bias is an inclination to believe one thing rather than another. This is usually unconscious rather than deliberate, i.e. the professional is unaware biases affect their decision-making.
	Gender bias and racial bias can affect decisions about diagnosis and treatment (of physical and psychological disorders).
	Diagnosis of women and people from ethnic minorities is often less accurate, fewer treatment options are discussed, and time spent talking to the client is shorter (Chapman *et al.*).
	Other biases are based on age, weight, social class, disability, sexuality, etc.
	Biases are cognitive because they are based on stereotypes, i.e. professionals perceive clients as members of a group and not as individuals.

Cognitive approach

One strength is the cognitive approach helps make health-related decisions.

This is because you have to think (cognitive) about your health-related decisions before you can behave in healthier ways.

E.g. you identify that you are 'comfort eating' in times of stress and make a decision to do something healthier instead, such as seeking social support from a friend.

This shows that thinking about how we usually respond to stress, anxiety and boredom can help us to behave in healthier ways.

The key to removing bias is for professionals to view their clients as individuals.

Another strength is that cognitive dissonance can help change behaviour.

In one study, dissonance was created in smokers by getting them to discuss smoking-related topics and then to write or film an anti-smoking speech (Simmons and Brandon).

These participants were more likely to make some change to their behaviour than a non-dissonance control group, e.g. they picked up anti-smoking leaflets. They also had stronger intentions to stop smoking after a month.

This shows that cognitive dissonance can be used in effective interventions that change unhealthy behaviours.

REVISION BOOSTER

Exercise your memory by practising retrieval. Students often work hard to get information *into* memory, but they spend less time getting it *out* again. But this is what you have to do in the exam. The activity of pulling information out of your memory dramatically improves your learning.

Tests and quizzes are good ways to promote retrieval. Write your own questions for each spread and swap them with other students.

You can also write down key 'trigger' words for each concept, and see how much you can recall by looking at the trigger word alone.

A further strength is that professional biases can be reduced.

One study asked white doctors and black clients to sign a contract before they met, to remind them they were 'on the same team' working together.

After 16 weeks, the clients expressed more trust in their doctors and continued with treatment longer than clients in a non-intervention control group (Penner *et al.*).

This shows that professional biases can be identified and removed by getting professionals to view their clients as individuals and not as members of a group.

Apply it

Clara is a healthcare assistant on a busy hospital ward. It's a stressful job and Clara finds it hard when patients die. She lacks confidence and finds it difficult to make friends. In her spare time, she gambles online and has lost a lot of money. Clara knows that gambling is bad for her but she can't help herself.

1. Identify **one** reason the cognitive approach would give to explain Clara's gambling. (1 mark)

2. Describe **two** ways in which the cognitive approach helps us to understand Clara's gambling. (4 marks)

3. A cognitive psychologist would say that Clara experiences cognitive dissonance when she thinks about her gambling.

   Explain **two** ways in which Clara might try to resolve her cognitive dissonance. (4 marks)

4. Discuss the effectiveness of the cognitive approach in understanding Clara's gambling. Refer to **one** other approach in your answer (9 marks)

Theory 1: Health belief model

Unit 3 Health psychology   Content area A

SPEC SPOTLIGHT

Health belief model:
• Concepts of perceived seriousness, susceptibility, cost-benefit analysis, how demographic variables such as age, gender, culture and external/internal cues affect behaviour.

Demographic variables → Perceived seriousness of an illness

Cues to action → Perceived susceptibility to an illness → Likelihood of engaging in preventive or treatment behaviour

Cost-benefit analysis
Perceived benefits | Perceived barriers

Self-efficacy

Apply it

Mila is a BTEC student who is experiencing pains in her finger joints. She knows her 82-year-old grandad has severe arthritis. Mila could go for a blood test to confirm a diagnosis of arthritis in her fingers. The health belief model (HBM) uses a variety of concepts to predict health-related behaviours.

1. Identify **one** demographic variable that might affect Mila's decision to have a blood test.
   (1 mark)

2. Explain how this demographic variable could affect Mila's decision, according to the HBM.
   (2 marks)

3. Explain how internal and/or external cues could affect Mila's decision, according to the HBM.
   (3 marks)

4. Evaluate the extent to which the HBM can successfully predict whether Mila will have a blood test.
   (9 marks)

Key concepts of the model (Rosenstock)

Basics	A decision to change (or not) health-related behaviours depends on your beliefs about health/ill health. Summed up in three questions: 1. How serious are the consequences of the illness? 2. How likely am I to get the illness? 3. What are the benefits and costs of changing?
1. Perceived seriousness	*I may change my behaviour in a healthy direction if I believe the consequences of not changing are serious.* E.g. condoms help avoid sexually transmitted diseases such as chlamydia. I do not believe this is serious enough for me to start using condoms. However, condoms also reduce the risks of HIV. I do believe this is serious enough for me to change my behaviour. The impact on factors other than health is also important. Are the consequences of not changing behaviour serious for work, family, etc.?
2. Perceived susceptibility	*I may change my behaviour in a healthy direction if I believe I am vulnerable (susceptible) to becoming ill if I don't change.* E.g. I believe HIV is a disease that affects gay men and I am not a gay man so I do not perceive myself as susceptible. I am unlikely to start using condoms.
3. Cost-benefit analysis	*I may change my behaviour in a healthy direction if I perceive the benefits of doing so outweigh the costs (barriers).* **Perceived benefits** I believe that using a condom will benefit me, e.g. it protects me against disease, it shows my partner I care. **Perceived costs/barriers** I believe that using condoms is inconvenient, e.g. they reduce pleasure, indicate lack of trust. The balance of this analysis is one factor affecting my decision to start using condoms.
Modifying factors	**Demographic variables** Age, gender, culture, etc. affect perceived seriousness, susceptibility and cost-benefit analysis. E.g. a younger man believes he is more 'at risk' from HIV than an older man does. This helps explain why the younger man uses condoms but the older one does not. **Cues to action** Predispose a person to change their behaviour (or not). Internal cues include previous experience of symptoms. External cues include advice, media campaigns. Cues increase or decrease health beliefs/perceptions that a person is susceptible to a disease and/or how serious it is. **Self-efficacy** A person's belief in their ability to change their behaviour, e.g. someone who believes they cannot use a condom has low self-efficacy so is less likely to do so.

Theory 1: Health belief model

One strength is the HBM helps develop interventions to change behaviour.

For example, one study used the HBM to encourage people to be screened for bowel/colon cancer, by reducing barriers to screening, highlighting benefits and increasing perceived susceptibility.

The researchers found this intervention was moderately successful in changing this health-related behaviour (Williamson and Wardle).

This suggests that the HBM can explain why people engage in healthy behaviours and how they can be helped to do so.

Thinking about our health triggers a lot of emotions. So decisions about health could be driven more by emotions than by rational thinking.

Another strength is that the HBM was developed by health practitioners.

Practitioners work on the 'front line' directly with people who want to change their health-related behaviours.

So the model is based on experiences of real-life health issues and behaviour change.

This makes the HBM a credible explanation that is accepted by people who want to change their behaviour and the practitioners who want to help them.

One weakness is that the HBM assumes we make rational health decisions.

For instance, the HBM assumes we weigh up the costs and benefits of an action logically, along with susceptibility, seriousness and whether we have the resources to make a change.

In reality it is unlikely we do this when we make healthy or unhealthy choices, and habits and emotions may play significant roles.

This suggests there may be other psychological factors more important in behaviour change than those included in the HBM.

REVISION BOOSTER

The health belief model is a very structured model, which is why there is a diagram on the facing page.

This is good news for your revision. It means you can arrange your notes in a structured way, for instance in a table. Use the components as headings ('Perceived seriousness', etc.). Explain each component with a different health issue from the one we have used (e.g. deciding to go for a medical scan or test).

Apply it

Lily's mother and grandmother had breast cancer. Her grandmother died and her mother recovered after having a mastectomy (an operation to remove one or both breasts).

Genetic testing shows Lily has a mutation in the gene *BRCA1*, which means she has a substantially increased risk of breast cancer. Lily has not been diagnosed with breast cancer yet, but doctors recommend she has a preventative mastectomy now in advance. This will reduce her risk of developing breast cancer by 90%.

1. *Lily has to decide whether or not to have the operation. The health belief model helps us to understand what she will decide. Identify in the scenario evidence of the concepts of:*
   a) *Perceived seriousness.* (1 mark)
   b) *Perceived susceptibility.* (1 mark)

2. *Explain the role of cost-benefit analysis in Lily's decision.* (2 marks)

3. *Describe how the health belief model can help us understand whether Lily will decide to have the operation.* (3 marks)

4. *Assess the extent to which the health belief model can help us understand what decision Lily will make.* (9 marks)

A3: Theories of stress, behavioural addiction and physiological addiction

Theory 2: Locus of control

SPEC SPOTLIGHT

Locus of control:
- Internal and external locus of control, the role of attributions in determining health behaviour.

People with an internal LoC are more likely to take control over their health behaviour, for instance by going to the dentist for a check-up.

Apply it

Ayla is a farmer. She and her partner Georgia work hard on the farm trying to make ends meet. They both feel a lot of responsibility to keep the farm running and work long hours to do so. Ayla smokes a lot and her blood pressure is high. Georgia has never smoked or had a day off work. Georgia believes that the farm will be a success because of the hard work they are putting in. But Ayla believes that there is little they can do to make the farm a success.

1. State whether Ayla has an internal or external locus of control and justify your answer using evidence from the scenario. *(3 marks)*

2. Describe the role of attributions in Ayla's and/or Georgia's health. *(3 marks)*

3. Discuss the usefulness of locus of control in understanding the health behaviour of Ayla and Georgia. *(9 marks)*

Key concepts of the theory (Rotter)	
Internal locus of control (LoC)	People with an internal **locus of control (LoC)**, ('internals') believe the things that happen to them are under their own control.
	They believe their successes and failures are due to their own actions or inactions (e.g. hard work, lack of effort).
	They take control of their mental and physical **health**, e.g. they will seek out information and support, keep appointments, etc.
External locus of control	People with an external LoC ('externals') believe the things that happen to them are out of their control.
	They believe their successes and failures occur because of luck, circumstance, other people, bad weather, etc.
	They leave their mental and physical health to chance, 'If I get ill so be it, there's nothing I can do about it.'
LoC continuum	LoC in reality is not a type, people are not usually either fully internal or fully external.
	LoC is a continuum with high internal at one end and high external at the other.
	Most people are in between these extremes, i.e. low-to-moderate internal or low-to-moderate external.
Measuring LoC	Rotter's questionnaire includes several pairs of contrasting statements, e.g.:
	• 'Sometimes I can't understand how teachers arrive at the grades they give.' (externals would agree) • 'There is a direct connection between how hard I study and the grades I get.' (internals would agree)
	The *Multidimensional Health Locus of Control Scale* measures specific health-related LoC, e.g.:
	• 'If I take the right actions, I can stay healthy.' • 'Regarding my health, I can only do what doctors tell me.'
Attributions and health behaviour	Attribution means how we explain behaviour in terms of internal and external causes (we attribute causes to behaviour).
	Internals and externals attribute the causes of their behaviour in different ways. This affects their health-related behaviours.
	E.g. **addiction**:
	• Internals attribute the causes of their behaviour as under their own control, so they avoid risk factors making them vulnerable to addiction (e.g. not too influenced by peers). • Externals attribute the causes of their behaviour as outside their control, so they do not take steps to avoid risk factors (they believe there's no point making the effort).

Theory 2: Locus of control

One strength is that the link between LoC and health is practically useful.

For example, one study measured LoC in children aged 10 years. The internals were less likely than externals to be obese or psychologically stressed 20 years later.

Having an internal LoC in childhood seems to influence health-related behaviours in adulthood, offering some protection against ill health (Gale *et al.*).

This suggests that interventions aimed at developing an internal LoC could be one way of helping people to gain health benefits.

Could this be the desk of a student with an internal locus of control?

Another strength is evidence that LoC influences health behaviour.

In one questionnaire study of university students, externals reported more study-related **stress** than internals (a significant correlation).

However, their stress was specific to studying, because externals did not experience any other forms of stress more than internals (Abouserie).

This study suggests that LoC can help explain why some students experience study-related stress and also offers a target for practical intervention.

One weakness is the role of LoC in health behaviours may be exaggerated.

Rotter pointed out that LoC is only relevant in new situations, and previous experience always influences our behaviour more than LoC in familiar situations.

For example, someone who has been influenced in the past by friends to have an alcoholic drink will likely be influenced again, even if they are highly internal.

This limits the power of LoC to predict changes in health-related behaviours.

REVISION BOOSTER

Don't forget why you are studying locus of control (or any other Unit 3 topic). It's because of what it tells us about *health behaviour*. So always make sure you are linking concepts, theories, models and topics to health behaviour.

Learn some health-related differences between internals and externals and come up with some of your own.

Apply it

Rajul knows she is addicted to smoking. Her friends have pointed out that she might get lung cancer or heart disease. Rajul knows she is at risk and would like to stop.

Her friends have bought her nicotine patches but she doesn't use them and hasn't done anything else to give up. Rajul seems to believe she is powerless to change her own behaviour. Her attitude is one of, 'Whatever will be will be, there's nothing I can do about it.'

1. Identify evidence in the scenario that shows Rajul has an external locus of control. *(1 mark)*

2. Explain how Rajul having an external locus of control affects the likelihood of her giving up smoking. *(2 marks)*

3. Explain whether locus of control is a good predictor of Rajul's health-related behaviour. *(2 marks)*

4. Explain how understanding the role of attributions in Rajul's behaviour could help her to give up smoking. *(3 marks)*

5. Discuss how locus of control theory helps us understand whether Rajul is likely to continue being addicted to smoking. *(6 marks)*

Theory 3: Theory of planned behaviour

SPEC SPOTLIGHT

Theory of planned behaviour:
- Concepts of personal attitude to behaviour, subjective norms, perceived behavioural control and their effect on behaviour.

Sometimes it can be hard to work out whether other people disapprove. Not this time though.

Apply it

Several employees at an IT company are stressed to the point where their health is affected. The company pays for them to join a stress-reduction programme. Joining is optional and several employees sign up, including Mason. Mason is very stressed and was recently diagnosed with high blood pressure.

1. The theory of planned behaviour includes several components that help us understand health behaviours. Explain how personal attitudes and subjective norms could influence Mason's decision to join the programme.
   (4 marks)

2. Explain how Mason's perceived behavioural control might affect his health behaviour. (2 marks)

3. Assess the extent to which the theory of planned behaviour can explain Mason's health behaviour. (9 marks)

Key concepts of the theory (Ajzen)

Basics	The theory of planned behaviour explains how people exercise control ('plan') to change their behaviour. Intention is the central concept. A specific **health** behaviour can be predicted from our intention to behave in that way. Intentions are formed from three key sources.
1. Personal attitudes	The balance between your favourable and unfavourable beliefs about your current behaviour. E.g. 'I drink to relax' versus 'Drinking is bad for my health'.
2. Subjective norms	Your beliefs about whether the people who matter most to you approve or disapprove of your current behaviour. E.g. you conclude: 'Most people who matter to me are very unhappy with me drinking like this', so you intend to drink less, so you are less likely to drink.
3. Perceived behavioural control (PBC)	How much you believe you can direct your own behaviour. Do you believe it is easy or hard to give up alcohol? It depends on your perception of your resources, external (support, time) and internal (skills, determination). PBC influences both intentions and actual behaviour: • Intentions – the more control you believe you have over your drinking, the stronger your intention to stop. • Behaviour – the more control you believe you have, the longer and harder you will actually try to stop.
Example: Gambling	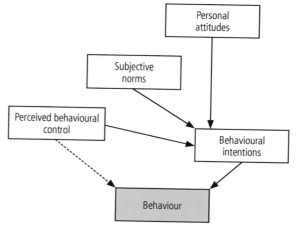

For example, the theory predicts I am likely to stop gambling if:

- My personal attitudes favour stopping (e.g. my attitude towards stopping is more positive than my attitude towards continuing).
- I believe people who matter to me approve of me stopping (and disapprove of me gambling).
- I believe I can control my behaviour (I have the resources).

These combine to strengthen my intention to stop gambling and I make a greater effort for longer in order to do so.

Theory 3: Theory of planned behaviour

One strength is that the TPB has been used to design practical interventions.

For instance, participants in one study who increased their perceived behavioural control (PBC) were more likely to give up smoking within six months (Borland *et al.*).

The lesson to draw here is that interventions that aim to increase clients' PBC are especially effective.

This shows that the TPB has been useful in helping people give up smoking (and other addictive substances such as alcohol).

'The road to hell is paved with good intentions.' Just because you intend to do something does not mean you will do it.

One weakness is that the TPB cannot explain the intention–behaviour gap.

For example, teenagers in one study who intended to give up gambling often did not actually give it up (Miller and Howell).

Researchers have tried to reduce this 'gap' by adding many factors to the TPB to improve its prediction of behaviour from intentions, but this means it is not recognisable as the TPB.

Therefore, many psychologists agree that it is 'time to retire the theory of planned behaviour' (Sniehotta *et al.*).

Another weakness is that the TPB does not predict long-term change well.

A review of studies found that the strength of correlation between intentions and behaviour depended on the length of time between the two.

For example, intention to stop drinking was a good predictor of actually stopping within five weeks but not beyond five weeks (McEachan *et al.*).

This means the TPB is not applicable to many real-world behavioural changes which often take place over longer periods of time.

REVISION BOOSTER

You can summarise the major components of the TPB very briefly (e.g. for any addiction):

- Personal attitudes: Do I like it or not?
- Subjective norms: Do others approve or disapprove?
- Perceived behavioural control: Can I give up or not?

Make these summaries your starting points and build on them.

Apply it

Mo agrees when family members say he is addicted to smoking. He smokes to relax, although his friends, family and partner do not smoke.

He smokes outside at work with a small group of people and they share gossip about people they work with.

Mo realises smoking damages his health but he also enjoys it.

1. The theory of planned behaviour includes several concepts to explain health-related behaviour. Identify from the scenario **one** example of each of the following:
   a) Personal attitudes. *(1 mark)*
   b) Subjective norms. *(1 mark)*

2. Mo is seriously considering giving up smoking. Describe how the theory of planned behaviour explains whether Mo will be able to give up smoking. *(3 marks)*

3. Discuss the extent to which the theory of planned behaviour helps us to understand whether Mo will give up smoking.
   (9 marks)

An NHS Trust appoints a team to design a health campaign to encourage young people to reduce their drinking. At the first meeting the team decide to base the campaign on the theory of planned behaviour. They identify three aspects of the theory that they will incorporate into the campaign, which are: personal attitude to behaviour, subjective norms, perceived behavioural control.

4. For each aspect of the TPB, identify a practical way in which the campaign could encourage young people to reduce their drinking. *(3 marks)*

5. Explain how subjective norms and perceived behavioural control could be effective in helping young people to reduce their drinking. *(4 marks)*

Content area A

Unit 3 Health psychology

Theory 4: Self-efficacy theory

SPEC SPOTLIGHT

Self-efficacy theory:
- Mastery experiences, vicarious reinforcement, the effect of social persuasion and emotional state on self-efficacy and likelihood of behavioural change.

Role-playing is a good way to develop self-efficacy through mastery experiences, for example in social situations.

Apply it

Harv is a laboratory-based researcher at a large university. He has a big workload with several responsibilities including supervising students. Harv knows that his colleagues are also under pressure but they seem to be much better at handling the stress.

1. Self-efficacy theory includes several concepts to explain health behaviour. Two are mastery experiences and emotional state. Explain how mastery experiences and emotional state could affect Harv's self-efficacy. **(4 marks)**

2. Harv joins a stress support group at work. The person who runs it has been leading such groups for many years. She helps people to learn techniques to help cope with stress. Describe how self-efficacy theory helps us understand whether Harv will improve his coping skills. **(3 marks)**

3. Discuss the effectiveness of self-efficacy theory in explaining Harv's health behaviour. **(6 marks)**

Key concepts of the theory (Bandura)

Basics	**Self-efficacy** is the belief we have in our ability to successfully perform an action or task. • High self-efficacy – we expect to succeed so we are **motivated** to try hard. • Low self-efficacy – we expect to fail so we avoid the challenge, or give up quickly. Awareness of our self-efficacy comes from four sources.
1. Mastery experiences	Self-efficacy is increased by having a past history of performing a task successfully, because: • We learn we are capable of performing the task or improving our skills. • We expect to succeed again in the future. Constantly failing at a task reduces our self-efficacy (we expect to fail in the future). E.g. children with Type I diabetes learn to inject insulin correctly. Successful experience increases self-efficacy, meaning the child has more belief in their ability. Self-efficacy is developed by giving a person opportunities to experience success. Task difficulty should be a bit beyond current skill level to provide a challenge (too far beyond will guarantee failure).
2. Vicarious reinforcement	Observing another person (**model**) doing a task successfully increases our own self-efficacy (or decreases it if the model fails). The model is very influential if we **identify** with them (e.g. perceive them as similar to us). Group-based **health** programmes (e.g. WeightWatchers) provide **vicarious reinforcement**. Observing others being successful is rewarding ('If they can do it, so can I').
3. Social persuasion	Verbal persuasion (using words is a form of social persuasion) increases self-efficacy. E.g. a trainer giving motivating feedback to someone exercising, after recovering from a heart attack, increases their belief that they can succeed. Effectiveness depends on the perceived credibility of the persuader. E.g. a qualified and experienced trainer who is trusted by the client will enhance self-efficacy. Social persuasion is less influential than mastery experiences and vicarious reinforcement, but is easier to provide.
4. Emotional states	**Stress**, **anxiety** and fear can reduce self-efficacy. E.g. someone exercising in a gym for the first time believes they are being observed and evaluated so they expect to 'fail', reducing self-efficacy making failure more likely (self-fulfilling). A good trainer removes emotional obstacles (e.g. by relaxation and social persuasion), so the client focuses on task success.

Theory 4: Self-efficacy theory

One strength is the theory offers a range of strategies to change behaviour.

For example, for mastery experiences a task should be broken down into achievable elements. Also, relaxation training can be used to reduce anxiety and improve performance.

Such strategies suggested by self-efficacy theory are often quite different from the ones suggested by other behaviour change theories.

Therefore, self-efficacy theory provides several uniquely useful interventions for improving people's lives.

A task that is slightly beyond a child's current skills leads to high self-efficacy because it is challenging but also achievable.

Another strength is the large body of evidence supporting the theory.

A review of studies found that people with high self-efficacy were more likely to be successful in changing their health behaviours in areas such as weight control, smoking and exercise.

Experimental studies in the review also showed that self-efficacy can be increased and lead to behaviour change (Strecher *et al.*).

This shows that self-efficacy is a consistent predictor of short-term and long-term health-related behaviour change.

One weakness is that the theory assumes high self-efficacy is always positive.

However, researchers in one study found that raising students' self-efficacy increased their performance in a puzzle-based game but decreased performance when they repeated the game.

The reason for this finding is that the students' high self-efficacy caused them to become overconfident, so they made less effort on the task next time (Vancouver *et al.*).

This suggests the theory is less effective because it does not predict some of the negative effects of high self-efficacy.

REVISION BOOSTER

Try the revision technique of 'Just a Minute', based on the classic radio game. You have to talk on a topic for one minute without hesitation, repetition or deviation. So, no pauses, no repeating yourself and no diversions into other topics.

Once you've revised a topic thoroughly, you'll be able to do this with just a list of key trigger words or phrases. Eventually you won't even need the list. It works because you are effectively explaining the topic to yourself, so you become more aware of what you do and don't understand.

Apply it

Connie has joined Gamblers Anonymous, a support group for people addicted to gambling. Connie likes the idea that people at the meetings explain their own experiences of gambling. It means they don't feel like they are on their own.

Connie finds the other people very encouraging. One person in the group has not gambled for more than two years. The weekly meeting has a very relaxed atmosphere and is like a calm spot in Connie's hectic life.

1. Self-efficacy theory claims that social persuasion influences self-efficacy. Explain how social persuasion could predict whether Connie will stop gambling. (2 marks)

2. Explain how vicarious reinforcement might affect Connie's self-efficacy. (2 marks)

3. Assess the extent to which self-efficacy theory helps us understand whether Connie will continue to be addicted to gambling. (9 marks)

Theory 5: Transtheoretical model

SPEC SPOTLIGHT

Transtheoretical model:
- Precontemplation, contemplation, preparation, action, maintenance.

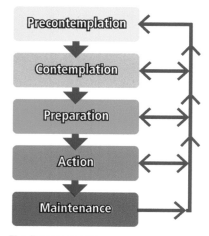

The five stages of the transtheoretical model.

Apply it

Mak is addicted to online shopping. His 30th birthday is in six months and he doesn't like the idea of still being addicted to shopping by then. On the other hand, he really enjoys the excitement of opening all those packages.

1. The transtheoretical model views behaviour change as going through a series of stages. Identify the stage of the transtheoretical model that Mak is currently at. (1 mark)

2. Describe how Mak might behave in any later stage of the transtheoretical model. (2 marks)

3. Discuss the effectiveness of the transtheoretical model in predicting whether Mak will overcome his shopping addiction. Refer in your answer to **one** other theory or model. (9 marks)

Key concepts of the model (Prochaska and DiClemente)

Assumptions	The model makes four assumptions about change: • People change their behaviour through five stages. • Change is not a single event but a cyclical process, e.g. return to earlier stages, skip stages. • People differ in their readiness to change, e.g. thinking about it, doing something, deciding to do nothing, etc. • Choice of intervention depends on the stage. Some are useful at an early stage but less so later on.
1. Precontemplation *'Ignorance is bliss'*	The person is not thinking about changing their behaviour in the next six months, because of: • Denial – they don't believe they need to change, or • Demotivation – they've tried before and failed. A useful intervention is to help the person consider the need to change their behaviour in a healthy direction.
2. Contemplation *'Sitting on the fence'*	The person is considering changing their behaviour in the next six months. They are aware of the need to change (e.g. risk of cancer) but also aware of the costs (e.g. less enjoyment), so they have not yet decided to change. This may cause psychological discomfort (**cognitive dissonance**, see page 86). A useful intervention is to encourage cognitive dissonance by emphasising the benefits of change.
3. Preparation *'OK, I'm ready for this now'*	The person decides to change their behaviour in the next month because they conclude the benefits of changing outweigh the costs. But they haven't decided how and when. A useful intervention is to help construct a plan or present options (e.g. joining a weight-loss club, calling a helpline, etc.).
4. Action *'Let's do this'*	The person has done something to change their behaviour in the last six months. This could be: • Formal and structured, e.g. therapy. • Informal but meaningful, e.g. cutting up cigarettes or pouring alcohol down the sink. The action must substantially reduce risk (e.g. giving up cigarettes rather than just switching to low-tar versions). A useful intervention is to help the person develop the coping skills they need to maintain behaviour change.
5. Maintenance *'Stay on track'*	The person has maintained a change for more than six months, so it becomes a way of life. A useful intervention is to help prevent relapse by applying learned coping skills (e.g. avoid situations with triggering **cues**, use support).

Theory 5: Transtheoretical model

One strength is the model is useful because of its positive view of relapse.

It is a positive view because the model considers relapse as a normal and inevitable part of behaviour change and not as a failure.

The model recognises that change takes multiple attempts and suggests interventions to get clients 'back on track' after relapse.

This means that the model is more acceptable to clients because they can see it is realistic about relapse.

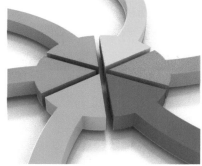

The word 'trans' means 'across'. So the transtheoretical model brings in ideas and concepts from across different theories of behaviour change.

Another strength is that the model views behaviour change as dynamic.

For example, overcoming an **addiction** is not usually an 'all-or-nothing' event. It takes time and is a continuing process of various stages.

The order and duration of these stages vary from person to person, and some people 'revisit' earlier stages more than others.

Therefore, the transtheoretical model is effective because it matches the experience of many people who try to change their behaviour.

REVISION BOOSTER

Sometimes a question asks you to 'refer to another theory or model in your answer'. This is your chance to compare, which is an evaluative skill. You need to do more than just mention another theory or model. The comparison needs to be *meaningful*.

Basically, you are using another theory/model to evaluate the theory/model that the question is about. For instance, the transtheoretical model has a positive view of relapse (see top left). But what about the other theories or models? Are they just as positive? Try in your revision to highlight these points of similarity or difference.

One weakness is that the 'cut-off points' for each stage are arbitrary.

For instance, someone planning to stop smoking in 30 days' time is in the preparation stage, but someone planning to stop in 31 days' time is in the contemplation stage.

There is no logical reason for this cut-off point, which matters because the recommended interventions are different at each stage.

This suggests that the transtheoretical model has little usefulness for understanding changes over time and for treatment recommendations.

Apply it

Kali smokes a lot of cigarettes but she tells her friends that she is perfectly healthy and could give up at any time. However, Kali's friends know she has tried to give up before but has never managed it.

1. *One of the stages of the transtheoretical model is precontemplation. Explain **one** reason we can say that Kali is at the precontemplation stage.* *(2 marks)*

Kali's friend Molly also smokes. Unlike Kali, Molly realises her smoking is potentially bad for her health, but she also enjoys it.

2. *Identify **one** piece of evidence that Molly is at the contemplation stage of the transtheoretical model.* *(1 mark)*

3. *Explain **one** way the transtheoretical model could be used to help Kali and **one** way it could be used to help Molly.* *(4 marks)*

4. *Evaluate the extent to which the transtheoretical model can predict whether Kali and/or Molly will continue to be addicted to smoking.* *(6 marks)*

Causes of stress: Life events and daily hassles

SPEC SPOTLIGHT

Causes of stress:
• Definition and role of life events and daily hassles in stress.

Even when there's fun, a new arrival can be stressful because you have to adjust.

Apply it

When Gregor left university a year ago, he moved to a different part of the country to start a new job. He was in a serious relationship with someone at university but that ended. Gregor takes the bus to work but sometimes it doesn't turn up so he is late. He has so many things to do he isn't getting much sleep and he feels more disorganised than he was as a student. Gregor feels a lot more anxious these days and has more coughs, colds and sniffles.

1. Gregor has experienced several life events in the past year. Explain what is meant by 'life events'. **(2 marks)**

2. Identify **two** life events Gregor has experienced. **(2 marks)**

3. Gregor knows he is stressed. Explain the role of life events in Gregor's stress levels. **(3 marks)**

4. Evaluate the role of life events in the stress Gregor is experiencing. **(6 marks)**

Role of life events in stress

What are life events?	Major events that happen from time to time, e.g. getting married/divorced, bereavement, new addition to the family.
	They cause **stress** because we have to make a psychological adjustment to cope with a changed situation. Bigger events need more adjustment so are more stressful, even when they are positive.
	The effects of **life events** 'add up', so if two occur together you have to make an even bigger adjustment.
Measuring life events	The *Social Readjustment Rating Scale* (SRRS, Holmes and Rahe) is a list of 43 life events, each given a number of Life Change Units (LCUs) reflecting the amount of adjustment needed to adapt. E.g. death of close friend = 37 LCUs, divorce = 73 LCUs.
	You indicate all the life events you have experienced in a set period of time and add up all the LCUs to get a 'stress score'.
Life events and ill health	Someone scoring under 150 LCUs has a 30% probability of experiencing a stress-related illness in the following year. Between 150 and 299 LCUs is 50% probability. Over 300 LCUs is 80% probability (Rahe).

Role of daily hassles in stress

What are daily hassles?	Relatively minor irritations and frustrations that happen every day (e.g. losing keys). They are stressful because they happen often and their effects 'add up'.
	We think about hassles very negatively and believe we may not be able to cope, e.g. it is easy to lose your keys and the consequences can be serious.
Measuring daily hassles	The Hassles Scale lists 117 **daily hassles** from categories such as work, **health**, family, friends, etc. (Kanner *et al.*).
	You select all the hassles you have experienced on that day and indicate severity on a scale of 1 to 3 (somewhat, moderately or extremely severe). You add up severity scores to get a total score for that day or period of time.
Daily hassles and ill health	Daily hassles threaten health because we experience so many.
	Hassles can make us ill through their link with life events, because a life event disrupts daily routines and creates a lot of hassles.

Causes of stress: Life events and daily hassles

One strength is both concepts are measured using self-report methods.

The SRRS and Hassles Scale are completed by people to report their own life events and hassles because this is the most direct way to measure these concepts.

Furthermore, using self-report also encourages honesty, unlike a face-to-face interview. The alternative of observing people's behaviour over time is not as practical or convenient.

These factors mean we are confident that life events and daily hassles are useful ways of understanding stress because our measurements of them are valid.

Losing your keys is a hassle but it can have big consequences.

Another strength is that the roles of both concepts are supported by evidence.

For example, people who developed asthma experienced more life event stress than people who did not develop asthma (Lietzén et al.).

Furthermore, a study in a work context found that hassles were stronger predictors of poor health, poor job performance and absence from work than life events (Ivancevich).

Therefore, the evidence suggests that life events and hassles are both sources of stress, but hassles may play a greater role in ill health.

REVISION BOOSTER

Alternative theories are great for evaluation. A question might ask you to evaluate a theory (or model). A good way to do this is to compare it with a related theory.

For instance, you could make an argument that daily hassles are more stressful than life events (or vice versa). You could bring in research evidence to support this argument.

But beware the danger – don't get sidetracked into writing too much about the alternative theory. You can use it, but your main focus should be on the theory in the question.

One weakness is that life events and hassles involve retrospective recall.

These causes of stress are measured by participants recalling life events and hassles they have experienced over a certain time period, e.g. one month or one year.

However, life events happen rarely so may be hard to recall from long ago. Daily hassles are common but minor, so are easily forgotten. So, some people underestimate the number of life events and hassles they experience.

This means that research might not accurately reflect the impacts of life events and hassles on stress or health.

Apply it

After Jak got divorced they didn't have much money. They ended up living in a shared house but don't really like the people they live with. Cooking meals is inconvenient because Jak can't get into the kitchen, so they eat a lot of takeaways and now they're worried about their weight.

Jak misplaced their car keys and took ages to find them again, which meant they couldn't go to the shops. Jak has taken a few days off work because they feel ill and depressed.

1. Jak has experienced several daily hassles. Explain what is meant by a 'daily hassle'. *(2 marks)*

2. Give **two** examples of daily hassles Jak has experienced. *(2 marks)*

3. Jak feels under stress. Explain the role of daily hassles in the stress Jak is feeling. *(2 marks)*

4. Explain **two** differences between life events and the daily hassles Jak has experienced. *(4 marks)*

5. Assess the role of daily hassles in Jak's stress. Refer to life events in your answer. *(9 marks)*

Causes of stress: Role of the workplace

SPEC SPOTLIGHT

Causes of stress:
- Role of the workplace in stress: role conflict, effect of the environment, level of control.

Disagreements over roles in the workplace can lead to conflict.

Apply it

Luisa works in a factory making medical equipment. The individual parts arrive to her on a conveyor belt from different sources. She has to quickly fit them together and pass them on to other workers for the next stage. Luisa's part of the factory is sometimes very noisy. It's easy for her to lose concentration and for each item she gets wrong she loses some pay.

1. Identify **two** ways in which Luisa's workplace may be causing her stress.   **(2 marks)**

2. In the context of Luisa's workplace, explain what is meant by 'level of control'.   **(2 marks)**

3. Apart from control, explain **one** other reason why Luisa is experiencing stress in her workplace.   **(2 marks)**

4. Discuss the role of Luisa's workplace as a cause of her stress.   **(3 marks)**

5. Evaluate the extent to which Luisa's workplace plays a role in her stress.   **(9 marks)**

Role of the workplace in stress	
Role conflict	Two types of role conflict are common in workplaces.
	Intra-role conflict Occurs when an employee faces competing demands within their **role** in the workplace ('intra' means 'within'). E.g. roles are poorly defined and the employee reports to two managers with differing objectives and they insist the employee performs incompatible tasks.
	Inter-role conflict Occurs when an employee has two different roles with competing demands ('inter' means 'between'). E.g. a parent/carer combining childcare with working late hours, or a student with part-time job hours that conflict with college.
Effects of the work environment	Two common environmental stressors have negative effects in the workplace.
	Temperature Hot workplaces are linked with **stress** and **aggression** (Parsons). Being too cold can also be stressful because it is a negative stimulus.
	Noise Loud sounds in workplaces can be stressful because noise is unpleasant. This is especially true when the noise is unpredictable and the employee cannot control it.
	Health and safety laws regulate workplace conditions to minimise stress but are not always fully implemented.
Level of control	**Workload** Overload (too much work) is linked to ill health, job dissatisfaction and absenteeism, especially when employees feel they have no control over workload. Having control acts as a 'buffer' protecting against the stress of work overload.
	Perception of control An employee's perception (i.e. belief) of their job control has more effect on stress than the actual reality. An employee may have little real control over their work but if they believe that they do, this protects them from stress.
Research into control	Research known as the 'Swedish sawmill study'.
	There were two groups of employees:
	• 'Finishers' prepared the wood, a skilled complex job with no control because it was machine-led.
	• 'Cleaners' maintained the sawmill and had more control and flexibility, e.g. they could decide where to work.
	The finishers had higher levels of stress **hormones**, stress-related illnesses and absenteeism, partly because of a lack of control over their job demands (Johansson *et al.*).

Causes of stress: Role of the workplace

One strength is there are practical ways to reduce stress in the workplace.

For example, giving employees some control over their jobs helps reduce workplace stress and therefore negative consequences such as ill health and absenteeism.

Also, a job with a variety of tasks provides a sense of control. Clear job roles and lines of management help avoid role conflict. Steps can be taken to reduce noise and keep the temperature comfortable.

These applications show how research can lead to changes that improve the well-being and quality of life of employees.

She's relaxed because she believes she's in control of her workload.

Another strength is that studies show the importance of job control in stress.

A study of 10,000 British civil servants found that lack of control was a significant workplace stressor but work overload was not (Bosma *et al.*).

Employees with low job control at the start of the study were more likely to have heart disease five years later (see also the sawmill study by Johansson *et al.*). This was true even after lifestyle factors were accounted for.

These findings show that lacking job control is a significant stressor that can lead to serious stress-related illnesses.

One weakness is that the impact of workplace stress varies by culture.

In individualist **cultures** (e.g. US, UK), lack of job control is seen as stressful. But in collectivist cultures (e.g. China), having control is seen as more stressful (Györkös *et al.*).

Also, conflicts between work and non-work roles are more likely in individualist cultures (Billing *et al.*). The workplace causes of stress on this spread may therefore only apply to individualist cultures, reflecting cultural ideals of personal rights and fairness.

This suggests that role conflict and lack of control are not universal features of the workplace that contribute to stress in all circumstances.

REVISION BOOSTER

Remember the difference between identifying something and explaining it.

You *identify* something by just saying what it is, e.g. one way in which a workplace is stressful. You *explain* something by giving more information, e.g. by saying how the workplace is stressful.

So, to explain something, identify or define it first, then provide additional information, which could be an example. This is why *Explain* questions are worth more marks than *Identify* questions.

Apply it

Shan is a single parent who has two young children and works full-time as a police officer. He has to organise his day very carefully to make sure the children get to the nursery on time in the morning.

He relies a lot on his parents and friends. If other people are late then Shan is late to work. Shan was asked to work evening shifts but he had to refuse. He thinks this is one reason why he has never been promoted.

1. Shan feels he is under a lot of stress. Explain how role conflict may contribute to Shan's stress. *(2 marks)*

2. Apart from role conflict, describe **one** other way in which Shan's workplace may be causing him stress. *(2 marks)*

3. Discuss the extent to which Shan's workplace plays a role in his stress. *(3 marks)*

4. Assess the role of Shan's workplace as a cause of his stress. *(9 marks)*

Causes of stress: Role of personality

SPEC SPOTLIGHT

Causes of stress:
- Definition and role of personality in stress.

Hardy people enjoy challenges and cope well with stressful situations.

Apply it

Siv is a volunteer in a food bank, organising food collections and fund-raising activities. She's known for her dedication to the cause, and has even dressed up as Wonder Woman on many occasions. Siv was the first in her town to open her house to a refugee family from Ukraine. She says she really enjoys life because she never knows what exciting things she will be doing from one day to the next. People like talking to Siv because she is 'laid back' and always seems to have time to listen.

1. With reference to Siv, explain what is meant by 'personality'.
   (2 marks)

2. Siv has never experienced much stress. Identify **two** ways in which Siv's personality may play a role in her low stress levels. (4 marks)

3. Discuss the extent to which Siv's personality plays a role in her low stress levels. (3 marks)

4. Assess the role of Siv's personality in contributing to her low stress levels. (6 marks)

Role of personality in stress

Defining personality *Personality is a collection of traits*	**What is personality?** Characteristics people describe when they explain what they are like, e.g. 'I am outgoing, friendly, daring, impulsive…', the traits of an extravert **personality**. Personality does not change much from one situation to another (it is consistent) or over time (it is enduring). **Personality and stress** Someone's personality can make the difference between them developing a stress-related illness or remaining healthy. Two kinds of personality involved in how **stress** affects us are described below.
Hardiness *A hardy personality protects against stress and ill health (Kobasa)*	Hardiness has three key components, called 'the Three Cs': • **Commitment** Hardy people are deeply involved in relationships and activities, throwing themselves into life with a sense of purpose. They believe that if something is worth doing, it's worth doing fully, even if it is stressful. • **Challenge** Hardy people are resilient, welcome change as an opportunity and recognise life is unpredictable, but this is exciting to them. They believe that stressful situations help us to learn, which is better than retreating into an easy life. • **Control** Hardy people strongly believe they are in charge of events. They make things happen rather than things happening to them. They actively try to influence their environment even in times of stress, rather than being powerless observers of life. **Hardiness and stress** Hardy people have high levels of the Three Cs. They are less likely to experience stress-related illnesses because they perceive stressors as less threatening.
Type A personality *A pattern of behaviour associated with coronary heart disease (Friedman and Rosenman)*	People with Type A personalities have high levels of: • **Competitiveness** They are ambitious, motivated by achievement, view life in terms of goals and challenges. • **Time urgency** They are fast-talking, impatient, view artistic and creative activities as a waste of time. • **Hostility** They are aggressive, intolerant, easily angered. **Type A and stress** Type A people are more vulnerable to stressors than Type Bs (see below), having higher blood pressure, cholesterol and stress **hormones**. Hostility causes Type As to have raised physiological arousal, making them prone to heart disease. **Type B personality** Type B people are more relaxed, 'laid back', tolerant and less competitive and hostile than Type As. Type Bs are better at coping with stress, less physiologically aroused and less likely to develop stress-related illnesses.

Causes of stress: Role of personality

One strength is that targeting hardiness and Type A can reduce stress.

This could involve increasing people's levels of the Three Cs, e.g. thinking optimistically and viewing setbacks as challenges to overcome.

It also helps to encourage people at risk of stress-related illnesses to shift their behaviour from Type A to Type B, e.g. slowing down, doing one task at a time, practising patience.

There are several practical ways in which understanding personality can help people cope better with stress and avoid stress-related ill health.

Type As' time urgency leads them to 'juggle' many things at once.

One weakness is that it is unclear what hardiness and Type A really are.

For example, the Three Cs overlap significantly and some researchers believe hardiness is nothing more than control and that challenge should be abandoned altogether (Hull *et al.*).

Also, Type A is much too broad and some researchers argue that only hostility is linked to stress/illness and other Type A traits are irrelevant (Carmelli *et al.*).

This means that hardiness and Type A lack validity and do not explain the link between personality and stress.

REVISION BOOSTER

When you revise, you should test yourself and practise writing exam answers. But bear in mind that almost all exam questions include scenarios. Get into the habit of applying your knowledge to scenarios. That's why all the Apply its in this guide also include a scenario.

If a scenario is about Damo's personality (see below), you need to write about Damo's personality and not about personality in general. The examiner has to read your answer and know you are writing about Damo.

Remember that the scenarios are there for a reason, so use information from the scenarios throughout your answers.

Another weakness is that both concepts are measured by self-report.

The problem with this is that self-report questionnaires measuring hardiness and Type A suffer from social desirability bias.

People complete questionnaires to exaggerate their hardiness traits (seen as desirable) and minimise their Type A traits (seen as undesirable).

Therefore, self-report measures of hardiness and Type A rely on the socially desirable views people have about themselves and so are not accurate measures of personality.

Apply it

Damo has started many new hobbies in the past few years but never seems to stick with any of them. He has some friends but isn't bothered one way or the other whether they stay in touch. Sometimes he phones his mum when he remembers.

Damo works as a hospital receptionist. He has his way of doing things and doesn't like it if colleagues try to organise things differently. He gets annoyed with his colleagues easily and can be quite impatient. Damo is always rushing around but never seems to get anything useful done.

1. *Damo feels he is very stressed. Identify **two** aspects of Damo's personality that may be contributing to his stress.* (2 marks)

2. *Explain **two** reasons why Damo's personality may be contributing to his stress.* (4 marks)

3. *Discuss the role of Damo's personality as a cause of his stress.* (3 marks)

4. *Evaluate the extent to which Damo's personality plays a role in his stress.* (9 marks)

Physiological responses to stress

Unit 3 Health psychology   Content area B

SPEC SPOTLIGHT

Physiological responses to stress, to include:

- General adaptation syndrome (GAS).
- Role of the sympathomedullary (SAM) and the hypothalamic-pituitary-adrenal (HPA) system in chronic and acute stress.
- Role of adrenaline in the stress response.

Limitation of viewing stress as a purely physiological response:

- Gender differences in physiological responses.
- More than two responses, the 'freeze' response and role of cognitions.
- Fight or flight response is maladaptive in modern society.
- Role of personality, variation in level and type of hormones released.

Apply it

Cal hates their job. Every morning they wake up dreading the drive into work and spending the day with people they do not get on with. They have felt this way for months and don't know what to do. Cal has a permanent cold and can't sleep.

1. Identify evidence that Cal is experiencing chronic stress. *(1 mark)*

2. Explain the role of the hypothalamic-pituitary-adrenal system in Cal's stress response. *(2 marks)*

3. Assess the limitations of viewing Cal's stress as a purely physiological response. *(9 marks)*

The body's response to stress: General adaptation syndrome (GAS)

Selye's research *Rats subjected to various stressors*	Selye found that the rats' bodily responses were always the same to any stressor (e.g. extreme cold, surgical injury). **Stress** is a *general* response of the body to any stressor. It is *adaptive* (helps the body cope with stressors in the short term). It is a group of responses that occur together (*syndrome*).
Stages of the GAS *The stress response is always the same*	**Stage 1 – Alarm reaction** When a stressor is recognised the hypothalamus in the brain triggers **adrenaline**/noradrenaline in readiness for **fight or flight**. If stressor ends, return to normal. **Stage 2 – Resistance** If the stressor continues, a longer-term response starts using the body's resources (e.g. glucose, **hormones**). The body appears to be adapting to the stressor, but is deteriorating, e.g. the immune system is less effective. **Stage 3 – Exhaustion** Resources to resist the stressor are now depleted and the person re-experiences the initial symptoms (e.g. sweating, raised heart rate). Adrenal glands may be damaged and the immune system compromised. Stress-related illnesses are now likely, e.g. coronary heart disease.

The body's response to stress: A more modern approach

Acute stress: Sympatho-medullary (SAM) system *Controls fight or flight, the body's immediate stress response*	• *Sympatho* refers to the sympathetic branch of the **autonomic nervous system (ANS)**, triggered by the hypothalamus when a stressor is perceived. • *Medullary* refers to the middle (medulla) of our two adrenal glands. The hypothalamus signals the adrenal medullas to release the hormone adrenaline (and noradrenaline) into the bloodstream. Hormones circulate in the blood and stimulate target organs, e.g. the heart. When the stressor stops, the parasympathetic branch of the ANS takes over with opposite effects to the sympathetic branch, returning the body to the rest and digest state.
Chronic stress: Hypothalamic-pituitary-adrenal (HPA) system *The body's longer-term stress response starting the same time as the SAM*	• *Hypothalamic* refers to the hypothalamus which activates the HPA system by releasing into the bloodstream the hormone corticotropin releasing factor (CRF). • *Pituitary* gland detects CRF and releases a hormone called adrenocorticotropic hormone (ACTH) into the bloodstream. • *Adrenal* glands (outer portion called the adrenal cortex) are stimulated by ACTH to release **cortisol**. Cortisol helps the body's **stress response**, e.g. affecting glucose metabolism to provide an energy source. But long-term it also damages the body because it suppresses the immune system. The hypothalamus and pituitary monitor when cortisol exceeds a set point, reducing CRF and ACTH. These lower levels are detected by the adrenal cortex, which then reduces cortisol (a negative feedback loop).

Physiological responses to stress

One weakness is that the stress response is different for men and women.

Fight or flight may apply only to men. It would be risky for our women ancestors because running away (or fighting) could leave their offspring defenceless (Taylor).

'Tend and befriend' was more adaptive for women. A threat was met with nurturing (tending) of offspring and befriending of other women to provide social support.

This suggests that explanations of stress in terms of the GAS, SAM and HPA are biased towards men's physiology.

Another weakness is that the acute response is not just fight or flight.

Fight or flight means confronting a stressor or running away from it, but there is another response in which the individual **freezes**.

Some animals become paralysed when faced with a predator. Some humans become 'dissociated'. Both are adaptive because a predator loses interest in a non-responsive prey.

This suggests that fight or flight is just part of a more complex response to acute stressors.

The body's physiological stress response.

A further weakness is that the body's stress response is maladaptive today.

Fight or flight was once a useful adaptive response to confronting a hungry animal, but does not help us cope with modern stressors, e.g. being stuck in a traffic jam.

Also, stressors for our ancestors were usually acute (ended quickly), but modern stressors are often chronic (with damage to the body from the HPA response).

This means that the physiological stress response is actually maladaptive in the modern world because it can do us harm.

REVISION BOOSTER

The evaluation on this spread is a bit unusual because there are four points instead of the traditional three. Each point corresponds to the four 'limitations of viewing stress as a purely physiological response' on the specification.

You can use these points to answer any question on the physiological response to stress. But you might get a question specifically on the limitations, e.g. about gender differences in physiological responses. So, make sure you revise them thoroughly.

Another weakness is the response is affected by non-physiological factors.

The physiological response varies depending on **personality**, e.g. extraverts produce less cortisol compared with introverts (Xin *et al.*).

Coping also depends on personality, e.g. extraverts seek social support more than introverts, which reduces extraverts' physiological response.

This shows that portraying the stress response as physiological diminishes our understanding and may prevent us from uncovering potentially useful treatments.

Apply it

Flo used a cash machine to get some money out of her bank account. But a message flashed up saying she was overdrawn. She felt sick, her heart was beating fast and she started sweating. Then Flo remembered her month's salary was going into her account the next day and she felt much better.

Caleb hates the thought of bedtime. He knows that tonight, just like the past six months, he won't be able to sleep because the baby will be crying. Caleb has a painful headache that just won't go away.

1. *Identify evidence that Flo experienced acute stress.*   (1 mark)

2. *Explain the role of the sympathomedullary system in Flo's stress response.*   (2 marks)

3. *Using an example from the scenario, compare acute and chronic stress.*   (3 marks)

4. *Some psychologists believe there are limitations to viewing stress as a purely physiological response. Explain* **one** *limitation of viewing Caleb's stress as a purely physiological response.*   (3 marks)

5. *Discuss the limitations of viewing Flo's and Caleb's stress as a purely physiological response.*   (6 marks)

Stress and physical ill health

SPEC SPOTLIGHT

The link between stress and physical ill health:

- Short-term (headache, stomach upset, fatigue).
- Long-term (heart attack, stroke, hypertension).

Short-term stressors, such as being stuck in traffic, can be physically and psychologically draining.

Apply it

Kasper works as a lifeguard on a popular beach. When someone gets into trouble in the water it's a very stressful situation. When it's over Kasper goes back to calmly waiting and watching. He has no idea when his skills will be called upon. Kasper feels fatigued and has stomach problems.

Adi had to move back in with their parents a year ago because they couldn't afford anything else. Adi relies on food banks and can't pay their share of the bills. They hardly ever go out with their friends because they can't pay their way.

1. Identify **two** short-term effects of stress on Kasper.   (2 marks)

2. Identify **two** long-term effects of stress Adi is at risk of experiencing.   (2 marks)

3. Using evidence from the scenarios, explain the link between stress and physical ill health.   (3 marks)

4. Evaluate the extent to which Kasper's physical ill health can be explained by stress.   (6 marks)

Stress and physical ill health: Short-term effects	
Headache	Short-term effects are the consequences of **fight or flight**, the acute **stress response** controlled by the SAM system. Muscles tense in the neck and jaw when we experience a stressor. Muscles relax once the stressor is over but we may develop a tension-type headache if the stressor is repeated.
Stomach upset	**Stress** affects the gastrointestinal tract (the gut) with several symptoms, e.g. nausea, vomiting and diarrhoea. Repeated acute stress is linked to digestive disorders, e.g. inflammatory disorders such as Crohn's disease are worsened by stress.
Fatigue	When an acute stressor stops, muscle tension is relieved but the person is left with muscular fatigue (physical tiredness). Fatigue also has a psychological element (a feeling of exhaustion, lack of energy). When short-term stressors repeat, this can 'build up' physical and psychological fatigue over time.
Indirect effects	The above outcomes are also caused by stress indirectly, e.g. acute stress disrupts sleep, which in turn can cause headaches, stomach problems and fatigue.

Stress and physical ill health: Long-term effects	
Hypertension	Long-term effects are caused by the HPA system and **cortisol**. Stress raises blood pressure temporarily, but it is unclear whether it causes blood pressure to remain permanently high (hypertension). Stress likely contributes to hypertension indirectly (see below).
Heart attack	Stress contributes to atherosclerosis (blood vessels narrowing). Cortisol causes inflammation of vessel walls, so clumps of cholesterol (plaques) stick and blood has less room to flow. If a plaque ruptures in a coronary (heart) artery this can cause a blood clot to block the artery. Blood cannot flow to the heart, depriving the heart muscle of oxygen and stopping the heart, a myocardial infarction (heart attack).
Stroke	A blood clot can form in a cerebral (brain) artery, blocking it and depriving part of the brain of oxygen. The physical damage is an ischaemic stroke. Symptoms depend on the part of the brain damaged, including speech problems, one-sided paralysis (e.g. arm, leg, facial muscles), loss of vision.
Indirect effects	Lifestyle factors increase the risk of atherosclerosis, including lack of exercise, poor diet, smoking. These are behavioural responses to chronic stress, leading to high blood pressure, heart attack and stroke.

Stress and physical ill health

One strength is that understanding stress can prevent and treat ill health.

For example, we can use stress-reduction techniques to perceive stressors (e.g. exams) as challenges rather than disasters, to reduce the physical effects.

We can minimise indirect effects, e.g. not using smoking and overeating as negative coping mechanisms. We can also treat hypertension with medication.

This means that people can learn ways to reduce stress and make changes to their lifestyles that improve their quality of life.

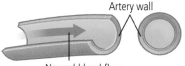

Normal artery — **Artery cross-section**
Artery wall
Normal blood flow

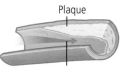

Narrowing of artery — **Artery cross-section**
Plaque / Plaque
Abnormal blood flow / Narrowed artery

An artery can become narrower and eventually blocked by a cholesterol plaque, leading to a heart attack or a stroke.

One weakness is gender differences in how people respond to stressors.

For example, atherosclerosis (narrowing of blood vessels) and heart disease are slower to develop in women than in men (up to ten years later, Rozanski *et al.*).

This protective effect may be explained by higher levels of oestrogen in women, so chronic physical effects are reduced in women relative to men.

This shows that the link between stress and physical illness is complex and not yet fully understood.

REVISION BOOSTER

Try making memory improvement a regular part of your revision. Here's one that's well-suited to topics like this. This is a list-like topic with six effects of stress. To remember short-term effects, you need to link headache, stomach upset and fatigue.

One way is to create a mental image of someone under stress having these symptoms. Draw this image in your revision notes. Another way is to put the words into a sentence of your own, the more bizarre the better. There are more memory-improving suggestions later in this guide.

Another weakness is that the short-term/long-term divide is simplistic.

There is overlap between acute and chronic effects. Intense acute stressors can trigger heart attacks, e.g. cardiac emergencies trebled during some football matches in the 1996 World Cup (Wilbert-Lampen *et al.*).

Also, long-term chronic stress can cause headaches and fatigue. We should look at how acute and chronic stress affects different bodily systems to get a more coherent picture.

Therefore, a more practically useful approach is to consider all the short-term and long-term physical effects of stress together.

Apply it

Mahsi is telling her grandchildren about when she collected her exam results many years ago. They were pinned up on the noticeboard for everyone to see. She got out of bed at 6 am because she couldn't sleep and walked to school feeling anxious all the way. She felt her heart beating faster and faster as she approached the noticeboard. After it was all over Mahsi had a splitting headache.

Anton is a carer for his mother who has dementia and cannot look after herself. Anton has been doing this for two years and rarely gets much time to himself. He is always 'on call' and has to respond any time of the night or day. Although he loves his mum it is difficult for Anton because she is beginning to forget who he is.

1. *Explain the link between stress and Mahsi's headache.* (2 marks)
2. *Give* **one** *other short-term physical effect that stress might have had on Mahsi.* (1 mark)
3. *Anton has been diagnosed with hypertension. Give* **one** *other physical effect that stress may have on him.* (1 mark)
4. *Justify your answer to question 3.* (2 marks)
5. *Discuss the link between stress and physical ill health. Refer in your answer to both Mahsi and Anton.* (9 marks)

B2: Physiological addiction

Smoking: Biological approach

SPEC SPOTLIGHT

Smoking – biological approach:
- Initiation: genetic predisposition to addiction, dopamine receptors.
- Maintenance and relapse: role of dopamine, nicotine regulation, tolerance, withdrawal symptoms.

The first cigarette of the day is satisfying because it prevents the start of withdrawal symptoms.

Apply it

Almost everyone in Rees's family smokes. Rees remembers the first cigarette he ever had made him feel really good. These days he enjoys smoking after meals and in the evening because it makes him feel relaxed. Although he tried to cut down, Rees now realises he is smoking more than ever. The last time he gave up he lasted about a week before he started up again.

1. Explain **one** way in which biological factors may play a role in the initiation of Rees's smoking. **(2 marks)**

2. Describe the role of dopamine in the maintenance of Rees's smoking addiction. **(2 marks)**

3. Identify evidence that Rees is experiencing tolerance. **(1 mark)**

4. Evaluate the biological approach to understanding Rees's smoking addiction. **(6 marks)**

Biological explanation of smoking addiction	
Initiation: Genetic predisposition	A **genetic predisposition** means your inherited **genes** make you more likely to start smoking. Genes may be a risk factor for nicotine **addiction**. If so, we would expect to find that smoking runs in families. But this is not inevitable because non-genetic factors are also important.
	A review of twin studies found that genetic influences contribute 53% to the risk of smoking initiation (Carmelli *et al.*), with other studies ranging from 11% to 75% (Lodhi *et al.*).
Initiation: Dopamine receptors	The **neurotransmitter dopamine** is the brain's 'pleasure and reward' chemical. Neurons in the ventral tegmental area (VTA) of the brain have receptors on their surfaces which are activated by molecules of dopamine. Nicotine molecules can attach to these dopamine receptors.
	On inhaling tobacco smoke, nicotine molecules reach dopamine receptors in seconds, which triggers a release of dopamine in the nucleus accumbens (NA).
	Feelings of pleasure (the 'buzz') are rewarding because of the dopamine release – the first step in being 'hooked'.
Maintenance and relapse: Role of dopamine	Nicotine molecules continue attaching to receptors in the VTA and dopamine is released in the NA, producing more pleasure and reward.
	Pleasure from the dopamine release **positively reinforces** the smoking behaviour, making it more likely to happen again.
Maintenance and relapse: Nicotine regulation and withdrawal symptoms	Going too long without smoking produces **withdrawal symptoms**, including headache, sore throat, **anxiety**, cravings.
	Dependent smokers continue all day, and nicotine molecules continually attach to dopamine receptors, activating neurons.
	This keeps nicotine in the bloodstream at a level that avoids withdrawal (nicotine regulation), the main **motivation** for continuing to smoke or relapsing (i.e. **negative reinforcement**).
Maintenance and relapse: Tolerance	Sensitivity of dopamine receptors reduces over time, so the person has to smoke more to restimulate receptors to previous levels and get the sensations they used to.
	Tolerance occurs to mood-changing effects (e.g. less 'buzz') and to the negative effects of nicotine (fewer headaches).

Smoking: Biological approach

One strength is the practical benefits in helping people stop smoking.

Methods to stop smoking take advantage of the biological mechanisms of addiction, e.g. replacing nicotine from cigarettes with substitutes such as patches, gum and inhalers.

This works because most damage to **health** from smoking does not come from nicotine. Also, replacement can be reduced over time (e.g. smaller patches), a controlled reduction of the dopamine 'hit'.

This shows that the biological explanation can provide practical interventions to reduce the damage and costs caused by smoking.

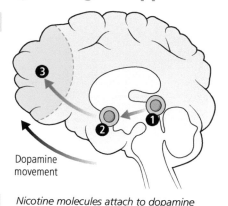

Dopamine movement

Nicotine molecules attach to dopamine receptors in the ventral tegmental area (1). This stimulates release of dopamine in the nucleus accumbens (2) and also in the frontal cortex (3).

One strength is evidence supporting the biological explanation of smoking.

Light and heavy smokers were given cigarettes containing lower-than-usual amounts of nicotine. This meant if they smoked the same number of cigarettes as they usually did, they would have lower levels of nicotine than they were used to.

Heavy smokers increased their rate of smoking more than light smokers did to make up the bigger nicotine deficit. This demonstrates the role of nicotine regulation (Schachter).

Therefore, the biological approach is an effective explanation because this finding matched a prediction of nicotine regulation in the maintenance of smoking.

REVISION BOOSTER

The word 'effectiveness' sometimes appears in exam questions. Something is effective if it works. So, if you are asked to consider the effectiveness of a theory, you're being asked if it explains the behaviour, in this case smoking addiction. A good way to answer this is to use research evidence. That's science – it's evidence that tells us whether a theory works or not. Let's say you're making an argument that the biological approach is an effective explanation of smoking. You can develop the argument by bringing in a research study. You don't have to remember the researchers' names. Instead, explain how the research supports (or in some cases does not support) the theory.

One weakness is not everyone who starts to smoke becomes dependent.

According to the biological approach, everyone who smokes should become dependent because smoking gives a dopamine-based 'hit'.

But a category of occasional smokers called 'chippers' show no withdrawal symptoms or cravings and no nicotine dependence even though they have smoked for decades (Shiffman *et al.*).

This finding is difficult for the biological approach to explain because it suggests some people smoke for non-biological reasons.

Apply it

Gisele has smoked cigarettes for 20 years. When she wakes up she feels a bit anxious and really looks forward to the first cigarette of the day. She feels much calmer afterwards. Gisele made a big effort to give up for the sake of her health. But it made her feel terrible and very anxious so she started smoking again quite soon.

1. *Explain how nicotine regulation maintains Gisele's smoking addiction.* (2 marks)

2. *Explain how the biological approach can help us understand Gisele's experience of relapse.* (2 marks)

3. *Discuss the role of biological factors in Gisele's smoking addiction.* (3 marks)

4. *Assess the effectiveness of the biological approach as an explanation of Gisele's smoking addiction.* (9 marks)

B2: Physiological addiction

Smoking: Learning approach

SPEC SPOTLIGHT

Smoking – learning approach:

- Initiation: parental and peer role models, positive reinforcement.
- Maintenance: negative reinforcement, i.e. removal of withdrawal symptoms, classical conditioning and association between sensory information and nicotine effects.
- Relapse: classical conditioning, conditioned cues, self-efficacy.

Children observe role models from an early age.

Apply it

Noah has an early memory of his parents having a party where lots of people were smoking. As a teenager his group of friends all smoked. He watched carefully how they did it. Everyone cheered when Noah smoked his first cigarette. That was when he really became part of the group and he's still friends with most of them. Now he is trying to give up and hasn't smoked for two days. He is keeping his lighter in his pocket 'for good luck'.

1. Explain **one** way in which learning may play a role in the initiation of Noah's smoking addiction. (2 marks)

2. Explain how the learning approach can help us understand whether Noah will relapse. (2 marks)

3. Discuss how the learning approach can help us to understand Noah's smoking addiction. (3 marks)

4. Evaluate the role of learning in Noah's smoking addiction. (6 marks)

Learning explanation of smoking addiction

Initiation: Parental and peer role models	Initiation is explained by **social learning**. A child or adolescent observes a parent/carer and/or peers smoking, who provide **role models** to **imitate**.
	The role model gets pleasure from smoking, and this is also experienced by the observer as **vicarious reinforcement**. This makes it more likely they will smoke, expecting to experience the same rewards.
Initiation: Positive reinforcement	From operant conditioning, if a consequence of a behaviour is desirable then it will be repeated. **Positive reinforcement** refers to a pleasurable reward.
	Nicotine is a reinforcer through its physiological effects on the **dopamine** reward system. Enjoyable sensations reward the smoking behaviour, so more smoking is likely.
Maintenance: Negative reinforcement	In **negative reinforcement**, the consequence of a behaviour is still desirable (rewarding) but the behaviour is escape from something unpleasant.
	When a smoker cannot smoke, they soon experience unpleasant **withdrawal symptoms** (e.g. **anxiety**). Smoking again removes these symptoms, negatively reinforcing smoking and maintaining the dependence.
Maintenance: Classical conditioning	The smoker learns an association between the sensations of smoking and its pleasurable effects.
	Sensations include the smell of smoke, the 'catch' at the back of the throat, the feel of a cigarette between the lips and fingers. These start as neutral stimuli but are repeatedly paired with the pleasurable effects, becoming conditioned stimuli capable of triggering a response on their own without nicotine.
Relapse: Conditioned cues	The pleasurable effect of smoking is called a primary reinforcer. It is rewarding in itself (not learned) through its effects on the brain's dopamine reward system.
	But smoking is accompanied by conditioned **cues** (or secondary reinforcers) such as objects, people, places, which become associated with the primary reinforcer (pleasure) through **classical conditioning**. These cues become rewarding in their own right, without the need to smoke.
	When an ex-smoker encounters a conditioned cue, they experience some of the pleasure they used to get from smoking, triggering a craving which can be strong enough to lead to more smoking (relapse).
Relapse: Self-efficacy	**Self-efficacy** refers to a person's confidence in their ability to stop smoking and continue to abstain.
	Someone with low self-efficacy will make less effort to quit, be more reluctant to do so, expect to relapse, fail to seek support and revert to smoking at the first obstacle.

Smoking: Learning approach

One strength is the approach has practical benefits to help stop smoking.

One study of aversion therapy found that 52% of smokers were still abstaining one year later compared to 25% who abstained without therapy (Smith and Caldwell).

Aversion therapy works through counterconditioning, i.e. associating smoking with an unpleasant stimulus (e.g. a sick feeling from rapid smoking).

Therefore, treatments based on the learning approach are cost-effective and improve quality of life.

Another strength is evidence supporting the role of conditioned cues.

For example, a review included 41 studies, in which smokers and non-smokers were presented with images of smoking-related cues (e.g. lighters, ashtrays, packets).

Smokers reacted strongly to these images, with increased physiological arousal (e.g. heart rate) and high levels of craving (Carter and Tiffany).

These findings are consistent with predictions about conditioned cues, showing that smokers do respond to such cues which predisposes them to relapse.

There are lots of cues to smoking that can trigger cravings

REVISION BOOSTER

Students sometimes find it hard to grasp what negative reinforcement is. It often gets confused with punishment. In punishment, something undesirable is applied to reduce the likelihood of a certain behaviour. For example, you pinch yourself hard every time you think of a cigarette, which means you think about cigarettes less often. But in negative reinforcement, something undesirable is *removed* or *avoided*, which increases the likelihood of a certain behaviour. For example, you avoid a headache by smoking a cigarette, which means you are more likely to smoke again next time.

One weakness is the learning approach cannot explain all nicotine addiction.

For example, many young people observe others smoking and enjoying it (vicarious reinforcement), but do not start smoking themselves.

Furthermore, only about 50% of adolescents who start smoking become **addicted**, with others smoking occasionally without withdrawal when they stop.

This shows that there must be several causes of smoking initiation and maintenance, which is hard for the learning approach to explain in terms of social learning or conditioning.

Apply it

Willow has noticed there are times she gets anxious and irritable when she can't smoke, e.g. at work. She plays with her lighter and the packet of cigarettes to help her calm down, but it also makes her crave a cigarette even more. Her family complain about the smell of the smoke but she finds it comforting and relaxing. Willow has tried to give up many times but the friends she meets at the pub all smoke and she likes being with them in their little group outside the back door.

1. Describe the role of negative reinforcement in Willow's smoking addiction. *(2 marks)*

2. Explain how classical conditioning maintains Willow's smoking addiction. *(2 marks)*

3. Explain how the learning approach can help us understand Willow's smoking addiction. *(3 marks)*

4. Discuss the learning approach to understanding Willow's smoking addiction. *(3 marks)*

5. Assess the effectiveness of the learning approach in explaining Willow's smoking addiction. *(9 marks)*

B2: Physiological addiction

Alcohol: Cognitive approach

SPEC SPOTLIGHT

Alcohol – cognitive approach – self-medication model:

- Initiation – use of alcohol as mitigation for current issue, use of substances for specific effects.
- Maintenance – assumption about management of the problem, stress relief.
- Relapse – counterproductive, increase of stress levels, 'solving' problem causes relapse.

It's not unusual for some people to use alcohol to help them be more sociable.

Apply it

Bo is addicted to alcohol. They live on their own and often feel lonely because they don't have any close friends. They get anxious in social situations and have had panic attacks in the past. They remember being quite lonely as a child as well. Someone from work invited Bo to a party and the only way they could enjoy it was to drink beforehand.

1. Give **two** reasons from the cognitive approach why Bo started drinking alcohol. *(2 marks)*

2. Explain the role of self-medication in Bo's alcohol addiction. *(2 marks)*

3. Discuss how the cognitive approach can help us to understand Bo's alcohol addiction. *(3 marks)*

4. Assess the effectiveness of the self-medication model in explaining Bo's alcohol addiction. *(9 marks)*

Self-medication model of alcohol addiction (Khantzian)

Initiation: Mitigation for current issue	Someone traumatised in childhood (e.g. neglect, loss of a parent/carer) may experience a psychological disorder as an adult, e.g. **depression, anxiety**.
	The person experiences emotional distress so they use alcohol to relieve ('mitigate') their distress.
	Self-medication is soothing as the person uses alcohol to manage psychological pain and become emotionally stable.
Initiation: Specific effects	The person's choice of drug is not random. There is a link between the specific emotional state and the drug used to relieve it ('specificity').
	E.g. alcohol self-medicates anxiety because it has relaxing effects. Cocaine self-medicates depression because it is a stimulant that can boost **self-esteem**.
	Drug choice may be the outcome of experimentation, i.e. someone **addicted** to alcohol may have tried other drugs first.
Maintenance: Assumptions about managing the problem	The person is too distressed to look after themselves. They have low self-esteem and lack skills to cope with **stress** or social situations.
	Self-medication with alcohol helps to regulate self-esteem, relationships or self-care (e.g. makes the person more sociable and friendly).
	Using alcohol reinforces the person's dependence as they learn they can't live without it. They progress from use to addiction.
Maintenance: Stress relief	The person cannot soothe themselves because of their experience of trauma, so using alcohol to self-medicate relieves stress but only temporarily.
Relapse: Counterproductive	Alcohol relieves stress temporarily but the stressor is still present when the effects of alcohol have worn off.
	An addicted person who reduces or stops their use experiences **withdrawal symptoms**, which creates more stress.
Relapse: 'Solving' problem causes relapse	The stress of withdrawal plus current distress makes coping hard, so the 'solution' is to drink again to manage symptoms.
	This is the 'paradox of self-medication', a cycle of distress, use, addiction, more distress, relapse, etc.
	Treatment should focus on the underlying psychological disorder, not the alcohol addiction.

Alcohol: Cognitive approach

One strength of the approach is that it can be used to help avoid addiction.

This is because the model recognises that although self-medication is a coping mechanism, it does not have to lead to alcohol addiction.

Someone using alcohol to self-medicate can be helped to develop other methods of coping, e.g. psychological therapy or even prescription drugs that are less dangerous to **health** than alcohol.

Therefore, the self-medication model can help people to manage their alcohol use before it becomes an addiction.

The paradox of self-medication is that using alcohol to cope with stress just makes things worse.

Another strength is evidence confirming the role of early trauma.

A study investigated adverse childhood experiences (ACEs) in almost 10,000 people, calculating ACE scores reflecting the amount and severity of trauma in childhood (Felitti *et al.*).

The researchers found that higher ACE scores (more trauma) predicted later addiction to alcohol and other substances (a strong positive correlation).

This shows that the self-medication model is an effective explanation of how childhood trauma is linked to addiction in adulthood.

REVISION BOOSTER

Here's another memory technique. Make a list of 'cue words' for a topic – words that trigger your knowledge. Cue words for this spread might include 'self-medication', 'trauma', 'soothing', 'specificity', etc. Make sure there is a logical order to the cue words, e.g. initiation → maintenance → relapse.

Then imagine a room you are very familiar with. In your mind, go round the room and put the cue words in different places, e.g. 'self-medication' on the light switch, 'trauma' on the hook on the back of the door, etc. Make the placements unusual. You can recall the cue words by mentally going back round your room and 'picking up' the words from their locations.

One weakness is a lack of evidence for the role of specificity.

The model states that people self-medicate with a drug that best relieves their emotional distress, so we would expect each addicted person to use one drug more than any other.

But most people who are dependent on one drug also use at least one other equally often and many young people with psychological disorders prefer drugs used by their peers (Lembke).

This means that the model may be wrong in claiming that people self-medicate with a drug that best addresses their specific symptoms.

Apply it

Bo drank a lot at their colleague's party. They felt terrible the morning after and became even more anxious than usual. They felt so bad about themself that they stopped bothering with their appearance.

Knowing they needed to change, Bo stopped drinking alcohol. However, their performance at work is suffering and their partner has moved out.

Bo still feels anxious but now also feels a failure and worries about what other people think of them.

1. Explain what is meant by 'self-medication' in relation to alcohol addiction. *(2 marks)*

2. Describe the role of stress relief in the maintenance of Bo's alcohol addiction. *(2 marks)*

3. Explain how the cognitive approach can help us understand whether Bo will relapse. *(2 marks)*

4. Explain how the self-medication model can help us understand Bo's alcohol addiction. *(3 marks)*

5. Evaluate **one** approach to explaining Bo's alcohol addiction. *(6 marks)*

Alcohol: Learning approach

Content area B

Unit 3 Health psychology

SPEC SPOTLIGHT

Alcohol – learning approach – operant conditioning:

- Initiation – positive reinforcement, positive consequences such as relaxation, increased dopamine; negative reinforcement, relief from stress, influence of role models.
- Maintenance – negative reinforcement, relief from withdrawal symptoms.
- Relapse – reduction of withdrawal symptoms, negative reinforcement.

It's not just the chemical effects of alcohol on the brain that make drinking rewarding.

Apply it

Franc is addicted to alcohol. He had his first alcoholic drink at a party when he was 14. Some friends challenged him to 'down it in one', which he did and everyone cheered and patted him on the back. When Franc saw how relaxed his friends were and how much fun they were having, he had another drink. He soon found himself talking to a girl he liked despite normally being very shy.

1. Identify **one** example of positive reinforcement in Franc's experience. (1 mark)

2. Explain the roles of positive reinforcement and negative reinforcement in the initiation of Franc's alcohol addiction. (4 marks)

3. Explain the possible role of increased dopamine in Franc's alcohol addiction. (2 marks)

4. Discuss the learning approach to understanding Franc's alcohol addiction. (6 marks)

Operant conditioning of alcohol addiction

Initiation: Positive reinforcement	Alcohol molecules attach to **dopamine** receptors on neurons in the ventral tegmental area (VTA) of the brain. Dopamine is released in the nucleus accumbens (NA) and in frontal areas, creating a sense of pleasure. The person may also receive other rewards for drinking, e.g. friends praising them in drinking games, increased relaxation. The pleasure created **positively reinforces** drinking, making it likely to be repeated. A young person observes others (**role models**) enjoying alcohol and becoming more sociable and confident. They experience rewarding effects 'second-hand' (**vicarious reinforcement**) and learn that alcohol produces positive consequences.
Initiation: Negative reinforcement	Some people begin drinking to escape stressful lives. This is a desirable consequence which **negatively reinforces** drinking, making it more likely to happen again.
Maintenance: Positive reinforcement	Ongoing rewards make drinking likely to be repeated (as above). Eventually rewards from drinking exceed those from previously rewarding activities (e.g. sex, hobbies). Drinking becomes central to the person's life and their only source of reward (called 'motivational toxicity').
Maintenance: Negative reinforcement	Not drinking alcohol causes unpleasant **withdrawal symptoms** in dependent people: • Physiological symptoms, e.g. sweating, heart palpitations, trembling. • Psychological symptoms, e.g. cravings, **anxiety**, low mood. Withdrawal symptoms are avoided by drinking again, so relief from these symptoms is negatively reinforcing – it strengthens drinking behaviour. Fear of withdrawal symptoms can be enough to trigger drinking before the symptoms even occur.
Relapse: Negative reinforcement	At any point in abstaining from alcohol, the relief from withdrawal symptoms gained by drinking again can be strong enough to provoke a relapse. Even after withdrawal is over, alcohol may still be an escape from a reality which may now be even more stressful. There is now even more reason for using alcohol to escape.

Alcohol: Learning approach

One strength is that the approach gives options for treating addiction.

For example, *Cue Exposure with Response Prevention* (CERP) treatment forces clients to confront the unpleasant consequences of drinking and not avoid them (Laberg).

The client experiences alcohol-related **cues** (e.g. glasses, bottles, an actual drink) and their effects (e.g. increased heart rate, cravings), but they are not allowed to drink to relieve these symptoms.

This shows how understanding the learning processes involved in alcohol **addiction** can be used to create potentially successful treatments.

In CERP, the client is not allowed to satisfy their cravings by drinking.

Another strength is that negative reinforcement explains relapse effectively.

The process of drinking alcohol to avoid withdrawal symptoms (negative reinforcement) may be controlled by the amygdala (Koob).

The amygdala becomes hyperactive during withdrawal, which activates the HPA system (**stress response**), making the client vulnerable to stressors and relapse more likely. So withdrawal is like a severe stress response and relapsing is a way of calming it.

This research suggests that the negative reinforcement responsible for maintenance and relapse has a biological reality in the brain.

REVISION BOOSTER

Understanding negative reinforcement could help you revise better. Revising can be a struggle, it can be hard work, inconvenient and it takes time. As with anything unpleasant, if you put it off you feel better because you are relieved. But this just makes it harder next time because your avoidance has been reinforced.

One way of overcoming this is to use positive reinforcement to counteract negative reinforcement. Try to make revision rewarding. Give yourself treats every now and again, build in short breaks. And above all remind yourself of the benefits of revision – write some down and look at them from time to time.

One weakness is operant conditioning may not be an effective explanation.

We would expect more people to become addicted if the effects of alcohol are positively and negatively reinforcing and based on a biological reward system in the brain.

Alcohol addiction is difficult for operant conditioning to explain when many people enjoy alcohol on a regular basis without becoming dependent.

This suggests that other non-conditioning factors are crucial in alcohol addiction, the most influential of these being **genes**.

Apply it

By the time Franc went to university, he was drinking a lot, believing it made him interesting and attractive. He found it hard to drag himself to lectures, his grades got worse and he gradually became more withdrawn from his friends. He would drink when he woke up to reduce his hangover. When Franc realised he might not pass his first year, he tried to stop drinking but had some really bad withdrawal symptoms.

1. Describe the role of negative reinforcement in the maintenance of Franc's alcohol addiction.   (2 marks)

2. Using the learning approach, explain why Franc might relapse.   (2 marks)

3. Discuss the usefulness of the learning approach in explaining Franc's alcohol addiction.   (3 marks)

4. Evaluate the effectiveness of the learning approach in explaining Franc's alcohol addiction. In your answer, refer to **one** other approach.   (9 marks)

Gambling: Cognitive approach

SPEC SPOTLIGHT

Gambling – cognitive approach – expectancy theory:

- Initiation – cost-benefit analysis.
- Maintenance – irrational thoughts, cognitive biases, illusions of control, exaggeration of ability.
- Relapse – recall bias and overestimation of success.

'This machine likes me!' Thinking can be irrational during gambling.

Apply it

Thea is addicted to gambling. She started playing on fruit machines because she thought she could make some money. She didn't tell her parents what she was doing. When she almost wins, she thinks the machine will pay out next time. There is one machine in the arcade that Thea plays on a lot and she feels she understands its moods. She taps the front of the machine three times before pushing the spin button.

1. Explain **one** way in which cost-benefit analysis may have played a role in the initiation of Thea's gambling addiction.
(2 marks)

2. Describe how irrational thoughts and/or cognitive biases explain the maintenance of Thea's gambling addiction. (3 marks)

3. Discuss the cognitive approach to understanding Thea's gambling addiction. (3 marks)

4. Assess how effective the cognitive approach is in explaining Thea's gambling addiction. (9 marks)

Expectancy theory of gambling addiction

Initiation: Cost-benefit analysis	A person is likely to start gambling if they expect the future potential benefits to outweigh the costs. Potential costs include financial losses, **anxiety** and disapproval from other people. Potential benefits include enjoyment, financial gain and a feeling of control. But **cost-benefit analysis** is not a rational process because it is influenced by emotions and distorted cognitions.
Maintenance: Irrational thoughts	Illogical thinking about luck and chance (e.g. the gambler's fallacy) is the mistaken belief that one random outcome can influence another random outcome (e.g. 'This coin has landed on heads three times so it must be tails next'). In a study by Griffiths, regular users of fruit machines thought about the machines irrationally as if they had personalities (e.g. 'This machine likes/hates me').
Maintenance: Cognitive biases	A person **addicted** to gambling is biased towards favourable outcomes. E.g. the 'near miss' bias in which they are constantly 'nearly winning' when they have actually lost. Near misses provide excitement and tension, rewarding feelings which maintain gambling behaviour.
Maintenance: Illusions of control and exaggeration of ability	Someone addicted to gambling may believe they can influence outcomes through their own skill or ability. E.g. they think they are experts in selecting racehorses, or believe a behaviour alters the odds in their favour (wearing a 'lucky' item of clothing). These are ways of trying to exercise control over something that cannot be controlled. In Griffiths' study, regular fruit machine users believed they could control the machine ('I'm going to bluff it') and attributed wins to their skills rather than to luck or chance.
Relapse: Recall bias and overestimation of success	A person addicted to gambling who quits may remember their gambling in a distorted way. They recall wins, forget losses, overestimate benefits and underestimate costs. This makes gambling seem more attractive than it was, so the recovering person is vulnerable to relapse because starting again does not seem 'too serious'.

Gambling: Cognitive approach

One strength is treatments for gambling addiction based on the approach.

Treatments directly address **cognitive biases** and irrational thoughts, replacing them with more rational ways of thinking, with some success in reducing gambling behaviour.

For example, one study found that correcting perceptions of randomness reduced gambling behaviour even 12 months later (Ladouceur *et al.*).

Therefore, tackling cognitive biases and irrational thoughts can be useful in reducing gambling addiction.

This is a very different environment from a lab and so is the behaviour in it.

Another strength is evidence that the approach is an effective explanation.

Griffiths found that regular gamblers express cognitive biases and irrational thoughts during gambling, in the real-world gambling setting of a fruit machine arcade.

Real-world findings are powerful and different from findings from lab studies. E.g. heart rates of users in a lab do not increase much but they do in a casino (Anderson and Brown).

This means the cognitive approach is particularly effective because it applies to situations in which people actually gamble.

REVISION BOOSTER

Revision can be daunting because there is so much to go through. The 'bite-sized' approach is very useful. Break down what you need to revise into realistic chunks and set yourself achievable targets.

One weakness is the approach cannot fully explain the role of cognitions.

If expectancy theory is correct, it is surprising there are not many more people who are addicted to gambling.

Many people have irrational thoughts and distorted cognitions about luck and chance, but very few start gambling and only about 1–3% have difficulty controlling their behaviour (Ladouceur).

This suggests that cognitive factors are not enough to explain why people start and continue to gamble, so there is a role for processes such as learning (see the next spread).

This guide is designed to help you do this – look carefully at how the topics are divided up. For example, gambling addiction is conveniently divided into initiation, maintenance and relapse. You could revise initiation and test yourself on that topic before moving on.

Apply it

Rowan spends a lot of money playing the National and EuroMillions Lotteries. They look forward all week to the draws and they feel the excitement building as they watch the numbers come out. Rowan's favourite lottery draw machine is Merlin because it looks more friendly than the others.

They choose the same numbers every week because they feel they have the best chance. On one occasion several of Rowan's numbers were out by just one or two. They have won small amounts and each time they think, 'I had a feeling my numbers would come up.'

1. *Explain **two** reasons why cognitive factors could be the cause of Rowan's gambling addiction.* (4 marks)

2. *Describe the role of cognitive factors in the maintenance of Rowan's gambling addiction.* (3 marks)

3. *Rowan hasn't played the Lottery for two weeks to save money. Using the cognitive approach, explain why Rowan might relapse.* (2 marks)

4. *Discuss how expectancy theory can help us to understand Rowan's gambling addiction.* (3 marks)

5. *Evaluate the role of cognitive factors in Rowan's gambling addiction.* (6 marks)

B3: Non-substance-related addiction

Gambling: Learning approach

SPEC SPOTLIGHT

Gambling – learning approach:

- Initiation – association between gambling and pleasure/excitement therefore behaviour strengthened.
- Maintenance – variable reinforcement schedules, behaviour strengthened due to variable success.
- Relapse – cue reactivity, cues associated with behaviour increase likelihood of relapse, i.e. walking past betting shops, gambling advertisements.

Fruit machine payouts are unpredictable, to keep you playing.

Apply it

When he was a child, Ezra's whole family watched horse races on TV. He loved watching all the people in their glamorous clothes and everyone shouting for their horse to win. Ezra eventually started betting until he was doing it several times a day. He had a big win early on and thought, 'This is easy!' His life is more disorganised and stressful as he gambles more and more.

1. Identify **one** learning factor that explains the initiation of Ezra's gambling addiction. **(1 mark)**

2. Explain the role of learning in the initiation of Ezra's gambling addiction. **(2 marks)**

3. Describe the learning approach to the maintenance of Ezra's gambling addiction. **(3 marks)**

4. Evaluate the effectiveness of the learning approach as an explanation of Ezra's gambling addiction. **(6 marks)**

Learning explanation of gambling addiction	
Initiation: Social learning	Observing **models** being rewarded for gambling is a powerful initiator (**vicarious reinforcement**). **Observation** can also be indirect through media reports of excited lottery winners, the glamour of horse racing, etc. This may trigger a desire for the same **reinforcement** in someone who hasn't gambled before.
Initiation: Classical conditioning	Intense external stimuli (flashing lights, bustling crowds, noise) and internal sensations (excitement, tension) quickly become associated with gambling (they become conditioned stimuli).
Maintenance: Positive reinforcement	Winning and the 'buzz' are rewarding. These **positively reinforce** gambling so it is likely to be repeated. A 'big win' shortly after starting gambling is a powerful reinforcer for some gamblers who continue gambling to repeat it. Near misses are also positively reinforcing because they give the gambler short-lived bursts of excitement and tension.
Maintenance: Negative reinforcement	Gambling for some people is an escape from reality, giving temporary relief from **anxiety**. This **negatively reinforces** (strengthens) the gambling behaviour.
Maintenance: Variable reinforcement	Variable reinforcement refers to when an unpredictable proportion of gambles is rewarded. E.g. a fruit machine pays out after an average of 10 spins but not on every 10th spin (too predictable). It pays after four spins, then seven spins, then 14 spins, etc. (i.e. the intervals vary). This is a highly unpredictable pattern of reinforcement leading to persistent gambling. The person keeps feeding the machine or placing bets even when they do not win for a long time.
Relapse: Cue reactivity	Conditioned **cues** are reinforcing because they are associated with arousal. E.g. adverts for gambling, the colourful look of scratchcards, the flashy environment of a casino, the intensity of a gambling website. These are cues that trigger the arousal that the person associates with gambling and still craves. Conditioned cues are everywhere in the social and media environment (e.g. walking past a betting shop), so they are a constant reminder of the pleasures of gambling and are significant risk factors for relapse.

Gambling: Learning approach

One strength is evidence the learning approach is an effective explanation.

For example, one study compared low-frequency gamblers (LFG) and high-frequency gamblers (HFG) in two betting offices in Birmingham (Dickerson).

HFGs placed their bets in the last two minutes before races started, deliberately delaying bets to prolong the rewarding excitement (LFGs waited to bet on the next race).

This shows that positive reinforcement can explain gambling behaviour in a real-life environment (rather than just in an artificial lab-based study).

Another strength is research support for the role of variable reinforcement.

In one study of HFGs and LFGs, some participants received reinforcement every time they successfully solved a puzzle (continuous reinforcement). Others received reinforcement only on unpredictable occasions (partial/variable reinforcement).

When eventually no rewards were given, HFGs continued to play for significantly longer than LFGs, even though reinforcement had stopped (Horsley *et al.*).

This finding shows how variable reinforcement may specifically influence those who are **addicted** to continue gambling even when they are losing.

One weakness is conditioning does not occur in the same way in everyone.

People respond differently to identical stimuli, e.g. some relax when they gamble, some experience arousal. Some quit and never gamble again but others relapse even though they all experience the same cues.

Furthermore, many people try gambling but are not drawn into it, even though they experience the same reinforcement as experienced gamblers.

These findings can be explained in terms of irrational thoughts and **cognitive biases**, i.e. an alternative approach (cognitive) may be a better explanation.

As of March 2022, there were 6,219 retail betting shops in the UK.

REVISION BOOSTER

Here's another memory-improvement technique that could help you revise more effectively.

When you looked at memory in Unit 1, you learned that there are different ways to encode information.

Try encoding your revision in two different ways. This sounds complicated but it's actually easy. It simply means you could use both words and visuals. Chances are your notes and revision are all about the words already, so no problem there. But look though a topic and see where you can draw an image to represent what you are revising, e.g. cue reactivity as a cause of relapse in gambling addiction.

Apply it

Orla told a colleague at work that she was feeling really stressed. Her colleague showed Orla an online fruit machine website which he said helped him to relax. Orla tried it and liked it and started to play more and more until she did nothing else in her spare time. She hardly noticed when her partner left her and the bills started piling up.

She presses play like she's on automatic pilot. She sometimes wins small amounts now and again. Orla finally tried to give up but whenever she goes on the internet for something else, she always wants to go on a fruit machine site.

1. *Explain how learning factors may play a role in the initiation of Orla's gambling addiction.* (3 marks)

2. *Describe the role of variable reinforcement schedules in the maintenance of Orla's gambling addiction.* (3 marks)

3. *Using the learning approach, explain why Orla might relapse.* (2 marks)

4. *Discuss the learning approach to understanding Orla's gambling addiction.* (3 marks)

5. *Assess the role of learning in Orla's gambling addiction. Refer to **one** other approach in your answer.* (9 marks)

B3: Non-substance-related addiction

Shopping: Learning approach

SPEC SPOTLIGHT

Shopping – learning approach:
- Initiation – role models guide on how to behave, vicarious reinforcement, role of celebrity and advertisements.
- Maintenance – association with excitement and pleasure, adrenaline rush and rewards, positive reinforcement.
- Relapse – cues associated with shopping are seen, advertisements, need to shop, relief from withdrawal symptoms/negative reinforcement.

Shopping is frequently portrayed as a rewarding and glamorous activity, especially in the media.

Apply it

Rio discovered the excitement of shopping after a big promotion at work. A friend helped them buy clothes, shoes and much more. Rio now spends lot of time in shopping centres buying things. They get excited opening bags at home but the fun soon wears off. Rio immediately starts thinking about their next shopping trip.

1. *Explain the role of learning in the initiation of Rio's shopping addiction.* **(2 marks)**

2. *Identify* **one** *example of negative reinforcement in the scenario and explain how it may maintain Rio's shopping addiction.* **(3 marks)**

3. *Discuss the learning approach to understanding Rio's shopping addiction.* **(3 marks)**

4. *Assess the role of learning in Rio's shopping addiction.* **(6 marks)**

Learning explanation of shopping addiction

Initiation: Role models and vicarious reinforcement	Someone who observes others (**models**) shopping may experience **vicarious reinforcement**. They indirectly experience the rewarding effects of shopping, e.g. enjoyment. This may trigger a desire for the same rewards in someone who hasn't shopped to the same extent before.
Initiation: Celebrities and advertisements	Consumer goods are presented in adverts as bringing pleasure or status to those who buy them (vicarious reinforcement). Celebrities are effective models because of their association with a glamorous lifestyle based on shopping. The viewer may **identify** with a celebrity, e.g. perceiving them as somehow similar to themselves, which makes **imitation** of the celebrity's buying behaviour more likely.
Maintenance: Positive reinforcement	Friends may shop together, discuss purchases, gain status or praise for buying, which all **positively reinforces** the shopping behaviour. Several features of the shopping environment are also positively reinforcing, e.g. the sounds, colours and smells of shops, or the enjoyable feedback from shopping websites.
Maintenance: 'Adrenaline rush' and rewards	Compulsive shopping may trigger the same **dopamine** reward system underlying reinforcement as substances do (although this is a very under-researched area). Dopamine is released from the nucleus accumbens into the frontal areas of the brain, triggering the rewarding 'rush' when shopping (NOTE: this has nothing to do with **adrenaline**).
Maintenance: Negative reinforcement	Compulsive shoppers feel 'empty' after a shopping binge and unpleasant feelings blocked by shopping may now resurface. The compulsive shopper keeps shopping to avoid unpleasant feelings or having to face a stressful reality.
Relapse: Cues associated with shopping	Recovering compulsive shoppers cannot avoid shopping-related **cues** which are everywhere in the environment (e.g. high street shops, TV and social media adverts, websites, etc.). Cues trigger the arousal the person associates with shopping and still craves (**cue reactivity**), so the person may relapse.
Relapse: Relief from withdrawal symptoms	Recovering compulsive shoppers experience unpleasant emotions (**anxiety**, **depression**, emptiness, boredom, guilt) that are temporarily relieved by shopping again (**negative reinforcement**). Cycle of **addiction**: destructive behaviour, recovery, relapse.

Shopping: Learning approach

One strength is the approach effectively explains how advertising works.

A review of 46 studies into celebrities in adverts found that shoppers' attitudes towards products were much more positive when the products were endorsed by celebrities (Knoll and Matthes).

Furthermore, some of the reviewed studies concluded that participants often perceived a celebrity as 'someone they like'.

This shows that identification (a **social learning** concept) plays an important role in how adverts featuring celebrities influence attitudes towards products.

Another strength is that the learning approach explains gender differences.

Research indicates that women and men who are compulsive shoppers buy different categories of products. E.g. clothes, shoes, cosmetics and jewellery for women, electronic goods and tools for men (Dittmar).

Women and men receive praise and interest for buying such culturally 'approved' **gender**-typical items. This provides positive reinforcement and makes it more likely similar items will be bought again.

This supports the view that operant conditioning plays a key role in shopping addiction.

People who endorse products on social media are called 'influencers' for a good reason.

One weakness is a relatively significant role for cognitive factors.

In one study of online shopping, positive reinforcement did not explain the differences between compulsive and non-compulsive shoppers. Other factors were necessary, e.g. anonymity and expectations (Trotzke et al.).

There are several features of shopping addiction that cannot be explained by reinforcement alone. There is a greater role for cognitive factors, which is not recognised by the learning approach.

This suggests that the learning approach is not an effective explanation of shopping addiction, unless it is combined with an alternative theory (cognitive).

REVISION BOOSTER

Make friends with psychological terminology. Learn what the technical words are and what they mean. Don't try and wing it with substitute words.

'Vicarious reinforcement' and 'withdrawal symptoms' are good examples from this spread. Sometimes you have to explain them anyway. But even when you don't, you should still use them. It shows the examiner that you understand the psychological concepts of the topic. It adds an extra dimension to your answers. So, make a list as part of your revision.

Apply it

Hamz follows several influencers on Tik Tok and enjoys watching videos of them opening things they've been sent. He then enjoys going straight onto store sites to shop online. He shows his friends his latest purchases when they come round to his house.

Because he was getting into debt, Hamz tried a 'detox' to keep off shopping sites. But he kept seeing adverts on TV for stores and products so he was soon shopping again.

1. Identify an example of vicarious reinforcement in the scenario. *(1 mark)*

2. Explain how vicarious reinforcement could cause Hamz's shopping addiction. *(2 marks)*

3. Describe how the learning approach explains the maintenance of Hamz's shopping addiction. *(2 marks)*

4. Explain how the learning approach can help us understand Hamz's experience of relapse. *(2 marks)*

5. Discuss how effective the learning approach is in explaining Hamz's shopping addiction. *(9 marks)*

B3: Non-substance-related addiction

Shopping: Cognitive approach

SPEC SPOTLIGHT

Shopping – cognitive approach – self-medication:

- Initiation – relief from boredom, psychological problem, distress, lack of self-esteem, excitement.
- Maintenance – reduction of anxiety associated with spending, continuation of boredom/anxiety relief.
- Relapse – withdrawal causes lack of excitement/boredom, increase of anxiety (due to financial worries), breakdown of coping strategies.

Shopping is an effective way for some people to forget their troubles for a while.

Apply it

One day when Edie had nothing to do, she went to a shopping centre. She enjoyed the attention from the shop assistants and found that having something interesting to do was quite exciting. But when Edie got her purchases home, she felt disappointed. Whenever she felt she was bored and needed something to do she went back to the shopping centre.

1. Explain **one** way in which self-medication may play a role in the initiation of Edie's shopping addiction.   (2 marks)

2. Describe the role of cognitive factors in the maintenance of Edie's shopping addiction.   (3 marks)

3. Discuss how the self-medication model can help us to understand Edie's shopping addiction.   (9 marks)

Self-medication model of shopping addiction

Initiation: Excitement and relief from boredom	The excitement of shopping can relieve boredom. Someone who perceives that their usual boredom is strongly relieved by shopping may develop a shopping **addiction**.
Initiation: Psychological problems, distress and lack of self-esteem	Shopping may be used as relief from emotional distress and low **self-esteem** associated with psychological disorders. Emotional distress and low self-esteem originate in childhood trauma (e.g. from neglect, loss), which may have been buried but is brought to the surface by the **stress** of a major life event such as divorce (Khantzian). 'Trauma' is a strong word but it includes anything that can give rise to later emotional distress, such as parental criticism.
Maintenance: Reduction of anxiety	Compulsive shoppers spend money which leads them into debts that cannot easily be repaid, so they experience **anxiety** when they consider these consequences. They may also face **cues** that trigger anxiety (e.g. comments from others). The anxiety can be temporarily relieved by continuing to shop (self-medicate), but this is counterproductive because serious debt makes stress worse and creates greater anxiety.
Maintenance: Continuation of boredom/anxiety relief	Compulsive shoppers' attention is very narrowly focused when they are shopping (they think of nothing else). Shopping allows them to forget their everyday lives and relieves anxiety ('mood repair' function of shopping). Anxiety and boredom return when the shopping is over, but now there is more to be anxious about (e.g. more debt) and also more reason to shop (to relieve anxiety). This is a long-term destructive addiction maintenance cycle.
Relapse: Effects of withdrawal	A compulsive shopper who stops shopping experiences the feelings of distress, anxiety and boredom they relieved by shopping.
Relapse: Breakdown of coping strategies	Shopping is a coping strategy to deal with other problems. The addiction cycle can only be broken by treating the underlying emotional distress or psychological disorder. The compulsive shopper must find another way to deal with the underlying problems. E.g. therapy emotionally stabilises them by increasing self-esteem in other areas of their life such as relationships and work so they do not need to self-medicate.

Shopping: Cognitive approach

One strength is that the approach explains shopping addiction effectively.

One study found that compulsive shoppers reported significantly more family dysfunction in their childhoods, e.g. parents/carers with anxiety, **depression** and alcoholism (Valence et al.).

Other research links childhood trauma and neglect with later emotional distress and compulsive shopping (e.g. DeSarbo and Edwards).

This shows that the cognitive approach is right to suggest that shopping may be used to self-medicate distress arising out of early trauma and neglect.

Shopping addiction may be partly learned and/or have a genetic element.

Another strength is evidence linking shopping with psychological disorders.

Compulsive shopping is co-morbid with several psychological disorders, i.e. they often occur together (Black).

For example, between 41% and 80% of compulsive shoppers also have an anxiety disorder (e.g. a phobia), between 21% and 100% have a mood disorder (e.g. depression).

This suggests that current emotional distress arises out of psychological disorders as predicted by the theory. This is powerful support when combined with the research (above) into early trauma.

REVISION BOOSTER

Practice at answering exam-type questions should be at the centre of your revision. It helps to know what the questions are asking you for. So, take a closer look at each question and using your pen (or pencil or device or whatever):

- Underline the command word (e.g. *Explain, Discuss*).

- Put a ring around the key content words such as 'cognitive approach' or 'self-medication model'.

- Finally, put a box around the main topic area, e.g. 'shopping addiction', 'relapse'.

One weakness is the approach ignores or minimises non-cognitive factors.

The cognitive approach interpretation of the above findings is that parents/carers with psychological disorders create a dysfunctional home environment which causes trauma in children.

However, another interpretation is that psychological disorders have a significant genetic component (see our Year 2 'Extended Certificate' Student book, Unit 6). So, the biological approach is potentially an effective alternative explanation.

This helps explain why these children grow up to develop depression and/or anxiety as well as shopping addiction – because the disorders share common genetic roots, not because the depression/anxiety is the outcome of trauma.

Apply it

Lukas lives on his own and has no close friends. One day he was feeling down so he started shopping online for something to do. The only thing he enjoys doing these days is searching through items and pressing the buy button.

This has all got out of hand because Lukas spends too much money and has no other hobbies or activities. He realises he really needs to stop but still goes online whenever he feels depressed.

1. *Explain the role of self-esteem in the initiation of Lukas's shopping addiction.* (2 marks)

2. *Use the self-medication model to explain the maintenance of Lukas's shopping addiction.* (3 marks)

3. *Using the cognitive approach, explain why Lukas might relapse.* (2 marks)

4. *Discuss the cognitive approach to understanding Lukas's shopping addiction.* (3 marks)

5. *Evaluate the extent to which psychological approaches can help us understand Lukas's shopping addiction. You must refer to **two** approaches in your answer.* (9 marks)

Hovland-Yale theory of persuasion

SPEC SPOTLIGHT
Hovland-Yale theory of
persuasion:
• The role of the communicator,
communication and the
recipient in persuasion.

*Experts can be persuasive because they
are seen as having credibility.*

Apply it

A UK charity conducts a campaign
to persuade people to stop or
reduce their gambling. Nina is a
research scientist who is addicted
to gambling. She sees the charity's
adverts on social media. Nina was
already thinking about giving up
because her life is a mess and she
feels bad about herself.

1. *Using your knowledge of the
   Hovland-Yale model, describe
   how the campaign could
   persuade Nina to stop gambling.*
   (3 marks)

2. *Explain **one** reason why the
   Hovland-Yale theory may not
   help us understand whether Nina
   will stop gambling.* *(2 marks)*

3. *Discuss how effective the
   Hovland-Yale model is in
   predicting whether Nina will
   stop gambling.* *(3 marks)*

4. *Evaluate the Hovland-Yale model
   as an explanation of whether
   Nina will be persuaded to stop
   gambling.* *(6 marks)*

Hovland-Yale theory of persuasion (Hovland *et al.*)

Factor 1: Communicator (source) *The first of three main factors explaining how information can persuade people to change their health attitudes or behaviour*	**Credibility** A communicator is more persuasive when they are seen as credible (i.e. believable), such as an expert. E.g. a qualified and experienced medical doctor leading an anti-smoking campaign. Credibility also comes from personal experience. E.g. a former drug user persuading young people of the dangers of drugs. A communicator is more credible if they are seen as honest and trustworthy. E.g. a celebrity who advertised unhealthy snacks lacks credibility as the leader of an anti-obesity campaign. **Attractiveness** Physically attractive communicators are more persuasive, probably due to the halo effect (a **cognitive bias**), i.e. we assume that physically attractive people also have other desirable qualities, e.g. they are knowledgeable.
Factor 2: Communication (message)	**Emotional appeal** Health messages containing a fear-related threat can change behaviour. But fear is not enough on its own – the recipient has to believe there is a way to avoid negative outcomes. E.g. a message about the dangers of smoking (fear) is more persuasive if it also explains how to quit. **One side or two?** An anti-smoking message could just say that smoking is dangerous, or it could also say that smoking brings pleasure and other benefits. Both messages can be persuasive, but it depends on the recipients. E.g. a well-informed audience would find a one-sided message biased and unpersuasive.
Factor 3: Recipients (audience)	**Intelligence** Intelligent people resist persuasion because they have the cognitive resources to process complex messages. People of low intelligence are persuadable because they do not fully understand the message or pay full attention to it. **Self-esteem** People lacking **self-esteem** are easier to persuade, so health campaigns should target people with low self-esteem for greater success.
Predicting behavioural change	Smokers are more likely to be persuaded to give up if: • The source (communicator) of the information is credible, e.g. they are seen as an expert, are trustworthy/honest, have personal experience and/ or are physically attractive. • The message (communication) includes frightening consequences but also how to avoid them and may present the benefits of smoking, depending on the audience. • The smoker (recipient/audience) has relatively low intelligence and self-esteem (the message should be tailored to them).

Hovland-Yale theory of persuasion

One strength is that evidence shows the theory can predict attitude change.

In one study, 15- and 20-year-olds were shown messages about the dangers of smoking. These varied in how threatening they were (high or low) and in how easy the message suggested it was to give up (easy or hard).

The most persuasive message was the one that combined high threat with the suggestion that it is possible to quit smoking (Sturges and Rogers).

This shows the theory is effective because the result was the one predicted – that fear is only persuasive when recipients believe they can cope with change.

Do you prefer to hear both sides of an argument before making your mind up?

A weakness is that the theory is not really a theory of behaviour change at all.

The theory explains how people change their minds (i.e. their attitudes) and many studies confirm that the source, message and recipients all contribute to changing attitudes.

But this is not the same as changing *behaviour*, because changing attitudes towards health is often not enough to cause people to *behave* in healthier ways.

Therefore, the theory does not effectively predict behavioural change because it only describes the factors involved in changing attitudes.

Another weakness is a lack of support for the theory's view of self-esteem.

One study found that people with high self-esteem were actually easier to persuade than those with low self-esteem. But the people with high self-esteem were less willing to admit to being persuaded (Baumeister and Covington).

So perhaps the relationship is not a straight line but a curve – people with moderate levels of self-esteem are harder to persuade than people with high and low levels (McGuire).

Therefore, the theory is less effective because one of its key predictions about recipients is incorrect.

REVISION BOOSTER

'Metacognition' is 'thinking about thinking'. Use your metacognition when you practise answering exam questions (and in the actual exams). All this means is 'monitor what you are writing'. It's very tempting to plunge right in as soon as you see the question. Instead, start by planning your answer.

Then, as you write, think about what you are doing by asking yourself questions as you go along. For example, 'Are my descriptions detailed?', 'Have I included examples?', 'Is my evaluation PET-friendly?', 'Have I applied this point to the scenario?'

Apply it

The UK government devises a campaign to encourage people to exercise more, called 'Let's Get Britain Moving'. As part of this, a TV advert is filmed which is fronted by a major sports celebrity who has also been a fashion model. The advert points out the dangers of being inactive and the benefits of exercise.

Ellis watches the advert and realises that they could improve their health by exercising more. But they worry that they don't have the time or motivation.

1. Using your knowledge of the Hovland-Yale theory of persuasion, identify the communicator and the recipient in this scenario.
   (2 marks)

2. Explain the roles of the communicator and the communication in the government's campaign. *(4 marks)*

3. Discuss **one** reason the Hovland-Yale theory of persuasion may be effective in predicting whether Ellis will change his behaviour.
   (3 marks)

4. Assess the effectiveness of the Hovland-Yale theory in predicting whether Ellis will be persuaded to exercise more. *(9 marks)*

Fear arousal theory of persuasion

SPEC SPOTLIGHT

Fear arousal theory of persuasion:
- Low, medium and high levels of arousal and their impact on behavioural change.

Causing a high level of fear is not the best way to get people to change their behaviour.

Apply it

Health campaigners are worried about the rise in smoking in teenagers. So, they create a presentation to take into colleges. It includes graphic images of lung disease and cancer, as well as statistics about the numbers of deaths and serious health problems caused by smoking. Remi is a regular smoker and has never tried to give up. She sees the presentation and wonders if it might be a good idea to stop smoking.

1. Explain the impact of arousal on persuading Remi to stop smoking.   (2 marks)

2. Explain **one** reason the fear arousal theory may not help us predict whether Remi will stop smoking.   (2 marks)

3. Discuss how effective the fear arousal theory might be in predicting whether Remi will change her behaviour.   (3 marks)

4. Evaluate the fear arousal theory as an explanation of whether Remi will be persuaded to change her behaviour.   (9 marks)

Fear arousal theory of persuasion (Janis and Feshbach)	
Fear as a drive	Fear can motivate people to change their behaviour because fear is accompanied by physiological and psychological arousal that we find uncomfortable (Dollard and Miller).
	We can reduce this unpleasant arousal by changing our behaviour to avoid a feared outcome. This gives relief that is rewarding and strengthens the behaviour that reduced the arousal (**negative reinforcement**).
Fear-behaviour relationship	Janis and Feshbach argue that the relationship between fear arousal and behaviour change is not a straight line but is curvilinear (see graph on facing page).
	Low fear A message that arouses little or no fear does not change behaviour. The recipient's arousal is not unpleasant enough to produce the **motivation** to change.
	Moderate fear This produces enough unpleasant arousal in the recipient to trigger the motivation to change behaviour.
	High fear This is counterproductive as it produces a lot of unpleasant arousal but does not change behaviour. It produces so much fear that the recipient believes changing behaviour will not be enough to cope with the unpleasant arousal.
Reducing the arousal state	Instead of changing their behaviour, the recipient of a high-fear message uses denial to reduce unpleasant arousal.
	For example, after watching a graphic fear-inducing anti-drink-driving film, the recipient thinks, 'I would never drink that much ... I'm a better driver than that' and concludes, 'This isn't aimed at me.'
	Denial reduces the fear-arousal state. This is rewarding so denial is strengthened (negative reinforcement) and the recipient feels better but does not change their behaviour.
Predicting behavioural change	Smokers are more likely to be persuaded to give up if they:
	• Experience a moderate amount of fear-induced arousal, e.g. by viewing an advert that shows some **health** consequences of smoking but not in too much graphic detail.
	• Understand that their current behaviour means the advert applies to them (i.e. they cannot use denial).
	• Identify a behavioural change that will reduce their unpleasant arousal, e.g. the advert shows that nicotine patches can help.

Fear arousal theory of persuasion

One strength is evidence fear is an effective motivator of behaviour change.

One study found that arousing fear in students made them more likely to get vaccinated against tetanus (changing behaviour) or intend to get vaccinated (changing attitude) (Dabbs and Leventhal).

A review of 127 studies confirmed that arousing fear can change health-related attitudes and behaviours, such as poor driving, poor dental hygiene and smoking (Tannenbaum et al.).

These findings show that using fear arousal is an effective way to change people's health behaviours.

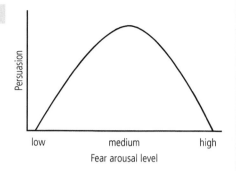

This is the relationship between persuasion and fear arousal, according to Janis and Feshbach (although their own research challenges this).

One weakness is that most research does not support the fear arousal theory.

Janis and Feshbach's own study found that low arousal produced the most behaviour change – the opposite outcome to that predicted by the theory.

This was disputed by Tannenbaum et al.'s review, which showed that high arousal generally produces the most behaviour change in a health context – also not predicted by the theory.

Therefore, some fear can be an effective motivator of behaviour change, but not in the way predicted by the theory.

REVISION BOOSTER

Use retrieval practice when you revise. Students worry about getting information *into* memory, so they spend much time 'memorising' or simply rereading notes. There's a place for this, but pay more attention to getting information *out* of memory.

Practising retrieval can improve your memory dramatically. So, test yourself, devise quizzes and consider working alongside someone else so you can test and quiz each other. And remember, the ultimate retrieval practice is writing answers to exam questions.

Another weakness is that recipients may not actually experience fear.

Fear-based health campaigns use materials (flyers, images, etc.) that are gruesome, graphic, unpleasant, etc. We assume recipients experience fear when they see these materials.

But it is hard to measure this – some recipients who change their behaviour may not experience fear. Others may experience different emotions such as anger or sadness.

Therefore, the effectiveness of health campaigns (or lack of it) could be due to other factors or emotions.

Apply it

An anti-cancer charity is creating a campaign to encourage men to check their testicles for lumps. Three members of the charity have to produce the materials but they disagree on the content.

Monty says that an undetected lump could easily lead to a testicle being removed, so the campaign should emphasise this.

Sadie thinks a lump could be a bad sign but checking regularly means it could be detected early.

Geri says the campaign should explain how rare testicular cancer is and that it's not as bad as some other cancers.

1. From the scenario, identify which suggestions will produce low and medium levels of arousal. (2 marks)
2. Using your knowledge of the fear arousal theory, explain how the campaign could persuade men to check for lumps. (3 marks)
3. Discuss the effectiveness of the fear arousal theory in predicting whether men will change their behaviour. (3 marks)
4. Assess the effectiveness of the fear arousal theory in predicting whether men will be persuaded to change their behaviour. (6 marks)

Elaboration-likelihood model of persuasion

SPEC SPOTLIGHT

Elaboration-likelihood model of persuasion:

- Use of peripheral or central route to persuasion.
- Factors of influence (role of celebrity).
- Individual differences in influence.

You probably pay more attention to health messages about diabetes if a member of your family is diabetic.

Apply it

A dangerous virus is spreading rapidly within the UK population. Health officials run a campaign to get people to wash their hands more thoroughly and frequently to help prevent the spread of the virus. The officials are divided over the most effective way to run the campaign. One official suggests basing the campaign on the elaboration-likelihood model of persuasion.

1. Using your knowledge of the elaboration-likelihood model, explain how the campaign could persuade people to wash their hands. **(3 marks)**

2. Discuss **one** reason the elaboration-likelihood model may not help us predict whether people will wash their hands. **(3 marks)**

3. Evaluate the effectiveness of the elaboration-likelihood model in predicting whether people will be persuaded to change their behaviour. **(9 marks)**

Elaboration-likelihood model of persuasion (Petty and Cacioppo)	
Process 1: Central route	I process a **health** message's content in detail, because I am interested in the issue and **motivated** by it (personal relevance). This is 'high elaboration' because I thoroughly evaluate (elaborate) the message's content.
	The central route is a direct form of persuasion, focused on the message's content (e.g. facts). It leads to long-term changes in attitudes and behaviour, and is very resistant to counterarguments.
Process 2: Peripheral route	I do not process the content of the message, because I don't have the time or the ability or I don't want to make the effort. This is 'low elaboration' because my evaluation of the content is minimal.
	I might still be persuaded by factors other than the message's content, e.g. the attractiveness of the communicator.
	The peripheral route is an indirect form of persuasion, focused on non-content factors. It leads only to short-term changes in attitudes and behaviour, easily reversed.
Factors of influence	**Personal relevance** The central route is most persuasive if an issue is personally relevant because you elaborate the message at a higher level.
	E.g. you are more influenced by a video on the importance of controlling sugar in your diet if you have family members with diabetes.
	Time and attention The peripheral route is most persuasive if you don't have much time because your level of elaboration is low if you are rushed or distracted. But other factors can still persuade you.
	E.g. you have no time to read a social media post but you notice it was posted by a celebrity you like.
	Role of celebrity Celebrities persuade through both central and peripheral routes.
	E.g. a celebrity can draw attention to the message itself and encourage you to think about it (high elaboration = central). Some people pay attention to the celebrity's attractiveness or likeability (low elaboration = peripheral).
Individual differences in influence	High or low elaboration of a message depends on your own personal characteristics because people differ in their ability and motivation to process a message centrally.
	Need for cognition (NFC) People with high NFC are motivated to think about issues deeply, enjoy analysing arguments and have the cognitive ability to pay attention to the detail of a message (others do not).

Elaboration-likelihood model of persuasion

One strength is the ELM can make health messages more persuasive.

The ELM shows that using the peripheral route in health campaigns (e.g. celebrities) can be self-defeating because changes in attitudes or behaviours are short-lived.

It is better to use both routes, e.g. someone with personal experience can get the attention of an audience (peripheral) and then use role-pay to help the audience elaborate the message (central).

This shows that the ELM is useful because it suggests practical ways of making health messages appeal to 'hard-to-reach' groups such as adolescents.

Someone with personal experience of a health issue can grab the attention of an unmotivated group.

Another strength is the ELM is an effective theory of behaviour change.

Both routes can change people's attitudes towards health but they are more likely to change their behaviour if they are persuaded by the central route.

This is because change through this route lasts longer and involves higher-level elaboration, so the central route is a better predictor of behaviour change than the peripheral route.

Therefore, the ELM is an effective explanation of why persuasion sometimes leads to behaviour change and sometimes does not.

One weakness is that ELM is based on studies with student participants.

Students have greater cognitive abilities than other groups of people in the population and they generally enjoy learning about new things.

But studies of non-students have failed to support the ELM, e.g. higher elaboration makes no difference to persuasion. This limits the extent to which findings from students can be generalised (Te'eni-Harari et al.).

Therefore, as some studies use unrepresentative samples of participants, there is some doubt over whether the ELM applies to the wider population of people.

REVISION BOOSTER

Break down your revision like we have broken down the topics in this guide. On each spread, there are a limited number of AO1 points, usually between four and six. Tackle each point one at a time and test your recall before moving on to the next one. For instance, for 'Elaboration-likelihood model' the subtopics are:

- Two processes (central route, peripheral route).

- Three factors of influence (personal relevance, time/attention, role of celebrity).

- One individual difference (need for cognition).

You could even draw a mind map of the topic, which is much easier to do once you've broken the topic down into its parts.

Apply it

Hana is addicted to online gambling. Her friends try to persuade her to stop. Amal's approach is to warn Hana about the dangers of gambling addiction and quotes some statistics. Hana says she's much too busy to listen to statistics and she's not interested anyway.

Rohan shows Hana a video of a major celebrity who was addicted to online gambling but gave it up. Hana is very interested in celebrities so listened carefully and said she would think about it.

1. *Using your knowledge of the elaboration-likelihood model of persuasion, identify the central route to persuading Hana to stop gambling.* (1 mark)

2. *Explain the role of celebrity in persuading Hana to stop gambling.* (2 marks)

3. *Identify **one** other factor of influence in the elaboration-likelihood model and explain its role in persuading Hana to stop gambling.* (3 marks)

4. *Explain **one** way in which the elaboration-likelihood model may be effective in predicting whether Hana will stop gambling.* (2 marks)

5. *Discuss the elaboration-likelihood model as an explanation of whether Hana will be persuaded to change her behaviour.* (9 marks)

C2: Treatment and management of addiction and stress

Mindfulness

SPEC SPOTLIGHT

Physiological and psychological treatment and management of addiction and stress:

- Mindfulness – attending to and regulating thoughts, feelings and emotions; being in the present; promoting healthy behaviours.

Mindfulness encourages us to become more aware of our behaviour rather than just behaving out of habit.

Apply it

Kelz is a support worker. Their workload is out of control because they are responsible for many cases, too many for them to deal with properly. Kelz feels they get no support and their colleagues are all just trying to survive each day.

Kelz works long hours and when they get home they eat takeaways and worry about the amount of alcohol they drink. They have just listened to a podcast about mindfulness.

1. Identify **two** possible ways in which mindfulness could help Kelz to be less stressed. (2 marks)

2. Explain **one** way in which Kelz could use mindfulness to promote healthy behaviours. (2 marks)

3. Discuss **one** reason why mindfulness could be an effective way for Kelz to reduce their stress. (3 marks)

4. Assess mindfulness as a way of helping Kelz to manage their stress levels. (9 marks)

Mindfulness	
What is mindfulness?	Mindfulness is a psychological approach to living involving us 'being in the present moment' rather than worrying about the future or fretting about the past.
	Mindfulness promotes mental and physical **health** because it is used to treat/manage **stress** and **addiction** positively.
Attending to and regulating thoughts and emotions	Monitor your present thoughts and feelings so you can step back from them, observe and accept them. This is so negative thoughts and feelings do not take over and control you.
Being in the present	Moment-to-moment awareness of bodily sensations, sights, smells, sounds, etc. (e.g. sensation of breathing).
Promoting healthy behaviours	Mindfulness is developed through training and practising certain techniques. Stress is reduced by applying techniques to everyday life. Experiencing the present more clearly leads to positive changes to lives and behaviour.
Mindfulness and stress *Mindfulness-Based Stress Reduction (MBSR, Kabat-Zinn)*	MBSR is a structured programme of standardised techniques based on Buddhist meditation, including: • Mindful focus – turn attention inwards and observe your own thoughts without judging them. • Body scan – become aware of different parts of your body, focus awareness on tense areas until they relax. • Mindful stretching – slowly change your body position and focus on physical sensations as you do it. MBSR reduces stress because you are less troubled by stressful thoughts as they pass through your mind. It also promotes distraction by focusing attention away from the sources of stress.
Mindfulness and addiction *Mindfulness-Oriented Recovery Enhancement (MORE, Garland)*	Addictive behaviour is often automatic (mindless). MORE helps clients with addictions become aware (mindful) of their behaviour. Chocolate exercise – the client holds a piece of chocolate under their nose and experiences automatic cravings. They switch their attention from their cravings to their breathing and the cravings subside, reducing the power of addictive **cues**. Mindfulness techniques in MORE are guided – a voice (recorded or live) gives the client direction to their meditation.

Mindfulness

One strength is that mindfulness has been successfully applied very widely.

It has been used to help lower stress levels of people receiving cancer treatment, to improve academic achievement in education settings, to increase job performance in workplaces and to increase task focus in sport (Shonin *et al.*).

Mindfulness has such wide applications because it is flexible. It has a central standard core of practice, but it can also be tailored to individuals' needs and circumstances, e.g. different causes of stress and addictions.

Therefore, mindfulness-based programmes can be used to help people in a variety of situations.

One way to become more mindful is to feel your breathing.

Another strength is evidence supporting the effectiveness of mindfulness.

A review of 34 studies of several addiction programmes found that MORE had better outcomes than other programmes, e.g. it reduced cravings and substance use (Li *et al.*).

Another review found that MBSR reduced stress more than other treatments or no treatment (Grossman *et al.*).

This shows that the central concepts of mindfulness can help to manage stress and treat addictions.

REVISION BOOSTER

When answering an extended open-response question (9- or 6-marker), it's very tempting to start with an introduction. You've no doubt heard teachers say, 'An essay should have a start, a middle and an end.' But you should resist the temptation because 'setting the scene' won't earn you any marks and will just take precious time.

On the other hand, your answer does need an 'end' (a conclusion), but only if the command word is *Assess* or *Evaluate*. In which case, make sure it's a genuine conclusion and not just a repetition or summary of what you've already written.

One weakness is that mindfulness may be 'overhyped'.

Mindfulness has caught the public imagination but evidence is often inconclusive because supporting studies have many weaknesses, e.g. they often have no control groups or just short-term outcomes (Farias and Wikholm).

The more exaggerated claims for mindfulness as a treatment for stress and addiction are not based on scientific evidence. More evidence from high-quality research is needed.

Therefore, mindfulness-based treatments may be no more effective than approaches using physical exercise or relaxation.

Apply it

Stella's life felt very stressful until a friend showed her some ways to reduce stress. Now Stella takes time each day to sit and slow down her breathing.

She breathes in through her nose and out through her mouth. She imagines her thoughts are like clouds which she observes floating past. Stella becomes aware of different parts of her body and relaxes any tense areas.

1. *One feature of mindfulness is helping to regulate thoughts. Identify **one** example of Stella using mindfulness to regulate her thoughts.* (1 mark)

2. *Explain **one** way in which Stella could use mindfulness to promote healthy behaviours.* (2 marks)

3. *Discuss **one** reason why mindfulness could be an effective way for Stella to reduce her stress.* (3 marks)

4. *Evaluate the usefulness of mindfulness in helping Stella to manage her stress levels.* (6 marks)

Talking therapies 1: Cognitive behavioural therapy

SPEC SPOTLIGHT

Physiological and psychological treatment and management of addiction and stress:

• Talking therapies including cognitive behavioural therapy (CBT).

Basic social skills, such as appropriate eye contact, can be learned in CBT.

Apply it

One reason Tate smokes is because he thinks it makes him interesting to others. He tells his friends that he's OK to smoke because he also goes to the gym regularly. Many of Tate's friends also smoke and he never refuses an offer of a cigarette.

Tate knows he's addicted and says, 'I just can't resist them.' Even when he tries to give up, he always carries his lighter around with him just in case.

1. A friend suggests Tate should try cognitive behavioural therapy (CBT). Identify **one** way that Tate might benefit from CBT. *(1 mark)*

2. Explain **one** reason why Tate could benefit from CBT. *(2 marks)*

3. Describe how CBT could help Tate to stop smoking. *(3 marks)*

4. Discuss CBT as a possible way of helping Tate to stop smoking. *(6 marks)*

Cognitive behavioural therapy (CBT)	
Basics	The cognitive approach focuses on how **addictions** are caused by irrational ways of thinking. The learning approach (behavioural) focuses on how addictions are learned.
	So, there are two elements to how CBT treats addictions:
	• The cognitive element changes the irrational thinking that underlies addictions (cognitive restructuring).
	• The behavioural element helps clients learn to avoid high-risk situations or cope better if they cannot be avoided.
Functional analysis	Client and therapist work out which distorted thoughts and irrational beliefs trigger the client's cravings and addiction-related behaviours. The client may keep a 'thought diary' to record the high-risk situations triggering such thoughts.
	This is an ongoing process which is also useful later in therapy to identify why a client still has problems coping, why they are relapsing and what skills they need to develop further.
Cognitive restructuring	The therapist challenges the client's distorted cognitions. The client may not be aware of how their faulty thinking affects their behaviour. They may believe they have been coping well.
	The therapist asks for evidence of this, so the client becomes aware of their irrational beliefs. The client has to 'own' this awareness and is not just told that their thinking is distorted.
Behaviour change	The client learns new skills to replace their main way of coping (their addiction), e.g. assertiveness training, anger management, social skills training.
	The therapist gives opportunities for the client to practise skills in a safe environment and in the real world (homework tasks).
Relapse prevention	In high-risk situations, **cues** can trigger the client's addictive behaviour. It may not be possible to avoid these so it is important to learn skills to identify the cues and cope with them.
	E.g. someone addicted to alcohol tries to avoid parties but if they cannot they identify cues such as people drinking and having fun. This triggers an irrational thought such as, 'Drinking now will make me attractive and happy.' The client learns to challenge such cues, which removes the trigger, for instance by using assertiveness to refuse a drink politely but firmly.
	The client learns the situation does not *make* them drink (or gamble, etc.). To believe it does is a distorted way of thinking.

Talking therapies 1: Cognitive behavioural therapy

One strength is CBT has clear applications to help people with addictions.

One example is to prevent relapse and break the cycle of addiction (the alternating periods of addiction, abstinence and relapse).

CBT has a realistic view of relapse built into the therapy. Relapse is viewed as a temporary setback rather than a permanent failure, providing opportunities for further cognitive restructuring and behavioural change.

This suggests that the combination of cognitive and behavioural strategies is a very useful way of treating addictions.

Another strength is evidence CBT is effective in treating drug addictions.

A review of CBT trials selected studies involving people with substance use disorders including alcohol, and compared CBT treatment with control groups including other treatments and 'treatment as usual' (Magill and Ray).

The review found a small but significant benefit for CBT in treating alcohol addiction, with 58% of the CBT clients having better outcomes than clients in control groups.

These findings are strong evidence that CBT is an effective therapy for a wide range of substance addictions.

'Being in this situation does not mean I have to drink.' A more rational way of thinking encouraged in CBT.

One weakness of CBT is a lack of any real long-term benefits.

For example, in the above study the benefits of CBT tailed off after six to nine months and reduced even further after one year.

In another review of 11 studies, there was no difference in gambling behaviour between CBT and control groups after 12 months. The researchers concluded, 'The durability of therapeutic gain is unknown' (Cowlishaw et al.).

These findings suggest that CBT is only effective as a short-term treatment of addiction.

REVISION BOOSTER

As in many areas of life, quality is more important than quantity. But many students find this hard to believe. Students often think they are doing well by writing lots and lots for questions that are only worth 1, 2 or 3 marks. Or they prefer to list several brief criticisms instead of giving, say, two in detail.

Take note of mark allocations and write in proportion to what a question is worth. Writing criticisms in detail is harder than just listing, which is why you get more marks for doing the harder skill. A detailed criticism shows real understanding.

Apply it

Kyra plays online poker on several sites. She chooses between them based on the day of the week. So, she plays one site on Saturdays because it's lucky and gives her the best chance of winning.

Kyra spends so much time playing poker that she hardly sees her friends. She would like to give up but she has to use her laptop for work and gets easily tempted.

1. *Kyra sees a psychologist who recommends she try cognitive behavioural therapy (CBT). Explain **one** reason why Kyra could benefit from CBT.* (2 marks)

2. *Describe how CBT could help Kyra to stop gambling.* (3 marks)

3. *Discuss CBT as a possible way of helping Kyra to stop gambling.* (3 marks)

4. *Evaluate the usefulness of CBT in helping Kyra to stop gambling.* (9 marks)

Talking therapies 2: Counselling and guided self-help

SPEC SPOTLIGHT

Physiological and psychological treatment and management of addiction and stress:
• Talking therapies including counselling, guided self-help.

The counsellor paying full attention to the client is a key sign of active listening.

Apply it

Sasha is a dental nurse at a large hospital. They are trying to balance a difficult job with studying for a higher qualification and looking after two young children. Sasha has found that when they are really stressed, they go online and spend a lot of money on shopping websites. A colleague points out that Sasha could get counselling at the hospital.

1. Identify **one** way that counselling could help Sasha. (1 mark)

2. Explain **two** reasons why Sasha might benefit from counselling. (4 marks)

3. Describe how counselling could help Sasha to become less stressed. (3 marks)

4. Discuss counselling as a possible way of helping Sasha to manage their stress levels. (6 marks)

Counselling

Therapeutic relationship	The relationship between client and counsellor is an alliance, with both 'on the same wavelength', working together in an open, warm and honest relationship. The client trusts the counsellor and feels safe discussing sensitive matters.
Emotional support *The client talks about their emotions related to relationships, work, childhood, etc.*	Talk must have a purpose, a recovery-focused or coping-focused goal (e.g. how can the client manage their emotions in stressful situations?). The counsellor actively listens without judging, but will not tell the client what to do. The client should find their own solutions. The client–counsellor relationship is unique, with the client able to talk honestly about their deepest feelings without fear of being criticised or ignored or worried about upsetting someone.
Relapse prevention plan	The client has space to discuss relapses and warning signs. Client and counsellor work out a plan for relapse so the client is back on a recovery path quickly (e.g. identifying lifestyle changes to help avoid relapse).

Guided self-help (GSH)

GSH basics	**Self-help** The client is their own therapist, learning CBT-related techniques and strategies and applying them in everyday life to help cope with **stress**. The source of the 'help' is materials such as printed booklets or online resources. **Guided** The client is supported by a mental health professional, who 'guides' rather than directs, so the client actively participates in their own therapy.
Practical steps: Materials	Printed or online materials form a structured programme, with information and advice about CBT techniques as well as activities for the client to practise and apply the techniques. The client works through the materials at their own pace.
Practical steps: Guided sessions *The client is supported by a Psychological Wellbeing Practitioner (PWP)*	Contact with the PWP could be on the phone, online, via email or texts, a face-to-face meeting or a group session. It can last 30 minutes up to six sessions, one per week. A guided session is structured and usually includes: • Reviewing 'homework' tasks and setting new ones. • Discussing how to apply CBT techniques in the real world. • Setting new goals for the week ahead. The PWP gives emotional support and encouragement.

Talking therapies 2: Counselling and guided self-help

One strength of counselling is it can be used to help a wide range of clients.

Counselling's wide use is mainly due to its flexibility because it usually includes a lot more than talking and puts the client's needs at the centre.

For example, it is flexible enough to include other treatments such as CBT and nicotine substitutes. It can be conducted with individuals, groups and families.

This means that clients are more likely to actively engage with counselling and stick with it.

Guided self-help is flexible enough for meetings with the PWP to be conducted online.

One weakness is a lack of evidence to support counselling's effectiveness.

The non-judgemental client–counsellor relationship is at the heart of counselling, but it is hard to measure the effectiveness of this so evidence is lacking.

In terms of **addiction** recovery, the best that can be said is that 'any therapeutic intervention tends to be more effective than none' (Joyce *et al.*).

Therefore, there is little evidence that counselling is any better than other interventions in helping clients recover from addiction.

One strength of guided self-help is that research studies show it is effective.

For example, one study randomly placed participants into a GSH intervention group or a control group (Williams *et al.*).

Stress levels reduced in both groups but by significantly more in the GSH group. This difference was maintained for six months.

Therefore, there is evidence that GSH can be effective in reducing stress in the medium term.

One weakness is that not all forms of GSH are equally effective or useful.

This is because GSH is so flexible that it 'blurs the boundaries' with other forms of therapy.

For example, the study above used GSH in a face-to-face group, very similar to 'standard' CBT (which also includes homework tasks).

This means that in some forms of GSH, it could be face-to-face contact with a therapist that is effective rather than the materials.

REVISION BOOSTER

Scenarios in exam questions are really important. You will not be applying your answer to the scenario if all you do is repeat names.

Unit 3 scenarios on the exam paper may be longer than the ones we have created for this guide. So, it's a good idea to read the scenario carefully, then the exam question. Then go back to the scenario and identify all the 'hooks' you can use in your answer. Underline or highlight them, then really engage with them throughout your answer.

Apply it

Fabian's partner was recently sentenced to a jail term, so Fabian's daily life has completely changed. He has been offered a promotion at work, which means longer hours and more responsibility. As always, Fabian feels he can't say no. Apart from a full-time job, he also volunteers at a food bank. He doesn't want to give this up as he gets satisfaction from it. He feels other people depend on him and he doesn't want to let them down.

1. *Fabian feels very stressed by his situation. Identify* **one** *way that guided self-help could help Fabian.* (1 mark)

2. *Explain* **two** *reasons why Fabian might benefit from guided self-help.* (4 marks)

3. *Describe how guided self-help could help Fabian to become less stressed.* (3 marks)

4. *Assess guided self-help as a possible way of helping Fabian to manage his stress levels.* (6 marks)

C2: Treatment and management of addiction and stress

Talking therapies 3: Stress inoculation training

SPEC SPOTLIGHT
Physiological and psychological treatment and management of addiction and stress:
- Talking therapies including stress inoculation training (cognitive preparation, skill acquisition, application and follow-through).

SIT works on the same principle as a physical inoculation that protects us against a disease.

Apply it

Arwa is a petrol tanker driver. She works long hours and is often away from home overnight. She is on a short-term contract and earns less money than she did last year. This is all very stressful for Arwa and her health is getting poorer. She contacts a psychologist who recommends stress inoculation training (SIT).

1. Identify **one** reason Arwa might benefit from SIT. *(1 mark)*

2. Describe how SIT could help Arwa manage her stress. *(3 marks)*

3. Explain **one** way in which Arwa could use SIT to promote healthy behaviours. *(2 marks)*

4. Discuss SIT as a possible way of helping Arwa reduce her stress levels. *(6 marks)*

Stress inoculation training (SIT) (Meichenbaum and Cameron)	
Stressful thinking	There are many stressful situations we cannot control, but we can control how we think about them. Thinking positively rather than negatively changes how we feel and behave, so we are happier, more optimistic and able to cope.
	The change in thinking comes first and emotions and behaviours follow.
Inoculation	SIT protects against stressors before they happen by exposing us to a little bit of **stress** in a safe environment. We learn the skills to cope with this stress and apply them when we encounter bigger stressors in the future.
Practical issues	SIT typically lasts nine to twelve sessions in a two- to three-month period, but this depends on the client. One or two sessions are for follow-up after several weeks or months.
	SIT is divided into three phases but there is overlap and clients often go back to an earlier phase before moving forwards.
Phase 1: Cognitive preparation *Client and therapist identify the stressors faced by the client*	There should be warm collaboration in this relationship rather than the therapist telling the client what to do. The therapist is supportive but the client is responsible for their own progress.
	The client learns that stressors can be overcome by seeing them as challenges rather than as threats. A stressor that might seem overwhelming can often be broken down into smaller elements that are easier to cope with.
Phase 2: Skill acquisition *The client learns skills they need to cope with stress*	The therapist has a 'toolbox' of skills, e.g. relaxation, social skills, time management and cognitive restructuring (thinking about stressful situations positively).
	Choice of skills is tailored to the client's needs, but most benefit from using self-talk including coping self-statements such as, 'You've got a plan, stick to it.' This replaces anxious internal dialogue with positive thoughts.
	The client practises these skills, e.g. they watch the therapist **model** them and then act them out in role plays.
Phase 3: Application and follow-through *The client gradually transfers their skills to everyday life*	**Personal experiments** Homework tasks are set by the therapist so the client can apply their skills in situations that are increasingly stressful. They discuss the experience in sessions and work on skill development further. As the client's control increases, the therapist's role becomes less important.
	Relapse prevention The client learns to cope with setbacks before they happen, viewing them as temporary learning opportunities and not permanent failures. The client sees that success is down to their own skills and not due to chance or other people (they develop an internal **locus of control**).

Talking therapies 3: Stress inoculation training

One strength of SIT is that it usefully meets clients' needs.

This is because it is a flexible therapy, using a wide range of stress management techniques that are suitable for many people, e.g. older people, people with learning support needs, individuals, couples, groups.

SIT can be used in different settings (work, home, online) to manage any type of stress, including the stress of racism and homophobia (Spiegler).

Therefore, SIT is very practically useful because it can be applied to new and unpredictable stressful situations.

Time management is just one of the skills that can be developed in the skill acquisition phase of SIT.

Another strength of SIT is support from several research studies.

For example, one study used a short course of SIT with students who were highly stressed and expected to perform badly in exams (Sheehy and Horan).

Compared with a control group, the students showed lower levels of stress and **anxiety** after SIT, and they performed much better in exams than expected.

These findings show that a practical and manageable SIT course can help students cope with stress and improve academic performance.

One weakness of SIT is that it is unnecessarily complicated.

SIT uses many different cognitive and behavioural techniques which are unlikely to all be equally effective, so it is hard to pinpoint exactly what it is about SIT that works.

For instance, clients develop a sense of control over stress which studies show is central to psychological well-being, so perhaps control is all that is needed.

This means that the benefits of SIT could be achieved more easily (and perhaps more cheaply) with other types of therapy.

REVISION BOOSTER

Use your knowledge of stress inoculation to help you revise. One reason for forgetting in an exam is stress. Your fight or flight response might kick in and block the thinking part of your brain (helpful when you're faced with a predator, not so much in an exam). However, you can still remember information you know well.

So, practise, practise, practise your knowledge so you learn it thoroughly. Practise answering exam questions in timed conditions because this creates a small amount of stress in a safe environment. This will inoculate you against more stress in the real exam.

Apply it

Jago finds it so hard to speak to other people that it makes him very stressed. He spoke to a therapist who suggested stress inoculation training (SIT). Together Jago and his therapist have looked at what Jago is thinking when he is in a social situation. They have broken this down into before, during and after a conversation. The therapist explains to Jago that he could view social situations as challenges and not as threats.

1. *SIT is a stress management method that has three stages: cognitive preparation, skill acquisition and application/follow-through. Identify the stage of SIT described in the scenario.* *(1 mark)*

2. *Justify your answer to question 1.* *(2 marks)*

3. *Choose **one** other stage of SIT. Explain **two** ways in which this stage could help Jago to manage his stress.* *(4 marks)*

4. *Discuss **one** way in which SIT may not be effective in helping Jago to reduce his stress levels.* *(3 marks)*

5. *SIT is often called a talking therapy. Evaluate the effectiveness of **two** talking therapies that could help Jago to manage his stress levels.* *(9 marks)*

Social support

SPEC SPOTLIGHT

Physiological and psychological treatment and management of addiction and stress:

- Social support – instrumental (practical), emotional (comfort), esteem (self-esteem).

Although there are different types of social support, there is a huge amount of overlap between them.

Apply it

Mathias is a university student who experiences anxiety. His anxiety makes his life difficult and causes him a lot of stress as a result. He finds it hard to leave his house because he is afraid he will have a panic attack in the street. Even sitting in lectures is a struggle because he finds it difficult to concentrate. Visiting the library and student union is out of the question. Mathias does have close friends but doesn't see them as much as he would like.

1. Identify **one** reason Mathias might benefit from social support. **(1 mark)**

2. Describe **two** ways in which social support could help Mathias manage stress. **(4 marks)**

3. Explain **one** way in which social support may not be effective in helping Mathias to manage his stress. **(2 marks)**

4. Discuss social support as a way of helping Mathias manage his stress levels. **(6 marks)**

Social support	
Social support basics	Our social network is a potential source of social support, i.e. people we interact with face-to-face and online to varying degrees, e.g. family members, friends, colleagues.
	Networks vary in the support they offer in times of **stress** (or to an **addicted** person). A small network may give a lot of support from just a few people. But relationships in a large network may not be close enough to give much support. The *quality* of a network may be more important than its size.
Instrumental support	This is practical help. It could be physically doing something, e.g. giving a lift to hospital, cooking a meal, providing money. Or it could be giving information, e.g. telling someone how to cope with stress, providing bus times or details of recipes.
Emotional support	This comes from expressing warmth, concern, affection, empathy or love for someone ('I'm sorry you're going through a tough time', 'I'm worried about you'). It is not meant to be practical but is offered to comfort the recipient, to help them feel better and lift their mood, especially when they are stressed.
Esteem support	This helps someone to have more faith in themselves and their abilities because we express our confidence in them ('You're so good, I know you can do this'). This increases their **self-esteem** (belief in themselves) and their self-efficacy (confidence in their abilities) and reduces stress.
Explaining the benefits	**Buffering hypothesis** Social support protects us against stress by creating psychological distance (a 'buffer zone'). Our network gives us a 'breathing space' to think about the stressor differently (cognitive). Support is a 'reserve' that reduces the impact of stressors so we cope better. But this means that support doesn't help at other times.
	Direct effects hypothesis Social support is beneficial at all times, not just during stress. It positively affects our **health** and well-being, through reducing arousal of the nervous system.
Relationships between types	The three types of support overlap considerably and we usually use more than one of them at a time. E.g. a 'shoulder to cry on' offers all three types – you are a practical helper, you make the person feel better and you increase their confidence.
	Instrumental support can appear a bit 'business-like', but also provides emotional support as it shows the supporter cares.
	All types can be given without the supporter being physically present. E.g. emotional and esteem support are common on social media networks. Different types of network can provide different types of support.

Social support

One strength is that the types of support are useful in different cultures.

One study found Asian-Americans were less likely than European-Americans to seek and use social support in times of stress, because they did not want to disrupt their communities (Taylor *et al.*).

Later research showed that practical support was more effective and useful than emotional support for Asian-Americans because it made fewer demands (Taylor *et al.*).

This shows that understanding cultural differences can make social support more useful in those different **cultures**.

Social support isn't always supportive because the supported person might not welcome it.

Another strength is evidence showing social support can help reduce stress.

For example, one study looked at the effects of giving hugs (emotional support) on the likelihood of becoming ill during stressful times (Cohen *et al.*).

Participants who had the most hugs/support were less likely to become ill and their symptoms were less severe if they did, even if they were highly stressed.

These findings show that emotional support can provide some protection against the negative effects of stress.

One weakness is that social support can backfire and have negative effects.

Sometimes support is given to make the supporter feel better, so it is not always useful or effective and depends on who provides it and when.

For example, practical information from family and friends can be inaccurate. A relative who comes with us to a hospital appointment (emotional support) can make us feel more anxious.

This suggests that social support is more useful when it is sought by the person who is stressed than when it is imposed by a well-meaning supporter.

REVISION BOOSTER

Here's your occasional reminder to make your evaluation points PET-friendly (we're reminding you because it's so important). Your evaluation points need to be 'well-developed' for your answer to get up to top marks.

- Start with P, the Point you are writing about (most likely a strength or a weakness).
- Then move on to E, which is the Explanation of the point. You could also think of it as Elaborating (another word for developing) the point, which might include Evidence or an Example.
- Finish off with T, which stands for 'Therefore…' or 'This means that…'. It's a mini-conclusion that explains why your point is a strength or weakness.

The good news is that all the evaluation points in this guide are PET-friendly.

Apply it

Celine is recovering from a gambling addiction and has not gambled for several months. She has some friends who help her. Fred drives her to meetings of Gamblers Anonymous each week. Celine feels down sometimes but when she talks to Jesse she always feels much better. There are times when Celine has been very tempted to gamble again, but Myra has pulled her through and given her the confidence to carry on.

1. One type of social support is instrumental support. Identify which friend is giving Celine instrumental support. *(1 mark)*

2. Justify your answer to question 1. *(2 marks)*

3. Explain **two** other ways in which Celine is getting social support from her friends. *(4 marks)*

4. Explain **one** way in which social support may be effective in helping Celine avoid relapse. *(2 marks)*

5. Evaluate the usefulness of social support as a way of helping Celine to continue her recovery. *(9 marks)*

C2: Treatment and management of addiction and stress

Biofeedback

SPEC SPOTLIGHT

Physiological and psychological treatment and management of addiction and stress:
- Biofeedback – physiological feedback, relaxation training.

A key element of biofeedback is relaxation training.

Apply it

When Lilia gets stressed, she experiences a lot of physical symptoms. She can feel her heart racing and thumping in her chest. She breathes more heavily and rapidly and feels sick. She gets very tense all over, especially in her neck and shoulders which means she frequently gets headaches. She often feels like this because she has a stressful job and rarely has time to relax.

1. Identify **one** reason why biofeedback might help Lilia.
   (1 mark)

2. Explain **two** ways in which Lilia could benefit from using biofeedback to reduce her stress.
   (4 marks)

3. Explain **one** way in which biofeedback may be effective in helping Lilia manage her stress.
   (2 marks)

4. Evaluate biofeedback as a method of helping Lilia to manage her stress levels.
   (6 marks)

Biofeedback	
Physiological basis	An acute stressor activates the sympathetic nervous system, which produces several physiological changes in our bodies, e.g. increased heart rate, faster breathing, muscular tension.
	These changes are involuntary, controlled 'automatically' by the sympathetic nervous system.
	Biofeedback trains a person to take control of these automatic processes, by using technology to let us see and hear our physiological functioning. This reduces the **anxiety** associated with **stress**.
Phase 1: Awareness and physiological feedback	The client is connected to a machine that converts physiological activity into signals that can be seen and/or heard.
	E.g. electrodes placed on the client's fingertips monitor heart rate and the client can see their heart rate as a graph on a screen.
	Muscular tension is measured with an electromyogram (EMG). Electrical activity of the muscles is converted into a tone heard through earphones which varies in pitch depending on how tense or relaxed the muscles are.
	A trained therapist explains what is happening at each stage, making the feedback meaningful to the client.
Phase 2: Relaxation training and control	The client learns to take control of their physiological responses.
	E.g. the client learns how to adjust their breathing to lower the line of a graph on a screen, or the pitch of a tone through earphones.
	A game-based interface may be used to **motivate** clients, e.g. getting closer to completing an on-screen puzzle every time they lower their heart rate.
	Deep relaxation training helps control some physiological responses. The client tenses a specific muscle group for a few seconds and then relaxes it. This is repeated several times before moving on to another muscle group. Deep breathing exercises help slow heart rate and visualisation helps the client imagine relaxing and calming scenes.
	Role of operant conditioning Machine feedback and praise from the therapist reward the client for achieving their goals. This **positively reinforces** the desired responses, which are more likely to be repeated in the future.
Phase 3: Transfer	The client learns to apply their skills in everyday life outside the stress-free therapy room. The client can use a portable biofeedback machine in stressful situations as they arise (and eventually can apply their relaxation skills without the machine).

Biofeedback

One strength is research evidence that biofeedback can be effective.

For example, in one study medical doctors were trained to use a biofeedback device three times a day for a 28-day period.

Mean stress scores measured by a questionnaire fell significantly over the 28 days, compared with a non-biofeedback control group (Lemaire *et al.*).

These findings suggest that biofeedback is effective in improving the psychological state of someone experiencing stress.

Modern feedback devices are much more portable and usable than they used to be.

One weakness is that biofeedback does not always give positive results.

For example, in the above study, as well as measuring psychological **stress** the researchers also measured physiological indicators such as heart rate, blood pressure and levels of stress **hormones**.

There were no significant changes in these measures over the 28 days, suggesting biofeedback had no effect on physiological indicators of stress.

Therefore, biofeedback may make the individual 'feel better' (a positive outcome), but is less beneficial for reducing physiological risk factors associated with stress.

Another weakness is biofeedback is unsuitable for some people.

Biofeedback needs effort and motivation, for example in the first phase where the client has to make an effort to understand the relationship between their physiological functioning and the signals they receive.

Also, in the transfer phase the client may not be able to apply their skills to real-world situations because their stress is so demotivating they may give up.

This suggests that biofeedback is not useful for everyone and that other treatments are better choices in some cases.

REVISION BOOSTER

Imagine this great news. In the exam, an extended open-response question comes up on a topic that you revised for ages. But hold on a minute – don't get carried away. It doesn't matter how much you know about the topic or how much you write, you can only get 9 marks at most (or 6, depending on the allocation).

Don't spend too much time on any question. There's a very good reason for keeping on track with your timing. The last three questions on the Unit 3 paper are worth 21 marks between them. So make sure you leave yourself plenty of time to answer them.

Apply it

Niall has such a lot to do at home and at work that he feels stressed most of the time.

He is always active and 'on the go' but also worried that he might not get everything done. Even when he sits down to try and relax he feels tense and anxious.

Niall's partner shows him a magazine article about biofeedback and wonders if it might help.

1. *A key part of biofeedback is relaxation training. Explain how relaxation training could help Niall be less stressed.* **(2 marks)**

2. *Apart from relaxation training, explain **two** reasons why Niall could benefit from using biofeedback to manage his stress levels.* **(4 marks)**

3. *Explain why biofeedback may not be effective in helping Niall reduce his stress.* **(2 marks)**

4. *Discuss biofeedback as a possible way of helping Niall manage stress. In your answer refer to **one** other treatment of stress.* **(9 marks)**

Skills training

SPEC SPOTLIGHT

Physiological and psychological treatment and management of addiction and stress:
• Skills training.

Clients keep a diary of their experiences of practising skills in real-world situations.

Apply it

Aiden is a compulsive shopper. They go shopping on their own and enjoy opening their bags when they get home. Aiden often does this when they have had a big argument with their partner. The arguments usually arise because Aiden would rather be shopping online than doing anything else. They also have a group of close friends who invite each other to go out shopping and 'make a big day of it'.

1. Identify **one** reason Aiden might benefit from skills training.
   (1 mark)

2. Describe how skills training could help Aiden overcome his shopping addiction.   *(3 marks)*

3. Explain **one** reason why skills training may be effective in helping Aiden with his shopping addiction.   *(2 marks)*

4. Discuss skills training as a possible treatment of Aiden's shopping addiction.   *(9 marks)*

Skills training	
Skills training basics	A skill is a learned behaviour that can help manage **stress** or control an **addiction** (examples below). We learn skills as we develop but they can also be taught through a structured programme or an unstructured self-help group. The client's **self-efficacy** increases as they practise their skills because they learn they can control their own behaviour. Coping in a high-risk situation is the result of their own actions (internal **locus of control**).
Assertiveness training	Relationship conflict is a common stressor triggering relapse in addicted people. Disagreements escalate into arguments, or the client avoids confrontation in case it develops into conflict. Assertiveness training helps the client cope with conflicts in a controlled way. This reduces the risk they will turn to addictive behaviour to relieve the stress associated with conflict.
Anger management	Some addicted people find it hard to control their emotions. Arousal is expressed as anger in stressful situations that are perceived as threatening. Clients may carry anger from childhood experiences that led to the addiction. Anger management can help a client express emotions more constructively (e.g. channelling them into creative activity).
Social skills training (SST)	Most clients benefit by developing skills to help them cope with **anxiety** in social situations. People recovering from addictions often encounter **cues** that trigger their cravings, e.g. betting shops on the high street. SST can improve verbal and nonverbal communication skills, e.g. tone of voice (firm but not angry) and eye contact.
Skills training techniques	**Group discussion** Group members can share experiences and discuss what could work and why something has not worked. They might identify high-risk situations to explore further in training, e.g. refusing a drink without becoming angry. **Modelling and role play** The therapist (or a group member) **models** a skill and clients try to **imitate** the skill in role play. This might be recorded so the whole group can watch and discuss it later. Feedback from the therapist or group highlights areas for improvement but also identifies successes. The therapist **positively reinforces** the client's behaviour with praise and encouragement. **Homework** Carefully planned tasks help the client practise their skills in the real world. Early tasks are achievable but become more challenging over time. The client keeps a diary of their experiences for discussion and feedback in sessions. **Visualisation** The client imagines situations in which they have to be assertive and mentally work through ('visualise') the steps involved in the interaction before they role-play it.

Skills training

One strength of skills training is evidence showing it can be effective.

One study randomly placed 'problem gamblers' into four treatments including CBT (with cognitive restructuring) and skills training (behavioural with no cognitive element).

Participants in all groups gambled less and spent less money up to one year later. Skills training was just as effective as CBT, which is useful because CBT does not suit everybody (Toneatto).

The findings show that gambling addiction can be treated effectively with a six-session skills training programme without including cognitive restructuring.

Someone deeply focused on their addiction is not using their social interaction skills.

Another strength of skills training is that it has long-term benefits for clients.

In the above study (Toneatto), although there was some tail-off, the reductions in gambling behaviour after skills training were still mostly present after 12 months.

These benefits are longer-term because skills training is 'future-focused', with clients learning skills they can use in any high-risk situation.

This means they are less likely to relapse or be overwhelmed by stress, a desirable outcome because the real challenge is finding solutions that work permanently.

One weakness is that skills training lacks a cognitive element.

Skills training helps stressed and addicted people without addressing underlying cognitive distortions and irrational beliefs (with some support, see above study).

But there is evidence that CBT is more effective than skills training for a wider range of people, e.g. CBT benefits the whole range of alcohol-dependent clients up to severely-dependent (Heather *et al.*).

This suggests that skills training may be more effective when used as the behavioural component of cognitive behavioural therapy rather than as a separate treatment for stress or addiction.

REVISION BOOSTER

Another way to evaluate is to consider ethical issues. These relate to the experiences clients have in treatments for stress and addiction. They include such matters as consent, physical and psychological harm and confidentiality (which you will have encountered in Unit 2).

Does skills training raise any ethical issues? For example, can assertiveness training be stressful or even harmful for someone who usually avoids confrontation? How can it be carried out ethically and sensitively? What are the issues related to confidentiality of clients?

Create your own PET-friendly evaluation points based on such ethical issues.

Apply it

Kane is looking for a job and has been to 20 interviews without success. He gets interviews because his applications are very good on paper. But in the actual interviews he gets very anxious and comes across badly.

Being unemployed and going through so many failures is making Kane feel very stressed. This is just making his interview performance worse.

1. Identify **one** reason why Kane might benefit from skills training. (1 mark)
2. Describe how skills training could help Kane reduce his stress. (3 marks)
3. Explain **one** way in which skills training may not be useful in helping Kane manage his stress levels. (2 marks)
4. Discuss the usefulness of skills training in helping Kane to manage his stress. (3 marks)
5. Evaluate the effectiveness of skills training and **one** other treatment that could help Kane to manage his stress levels. (9 marks)

Physiological treatments and exercise

SPEC SPOTLIGHT

Physiological and psychological treatment and management of addiction and stress:

- Physiological treatments – nicotine substitutes (patches, gums, tablets, inhalers, sprays); drug treatments for detoxification and withdrawal from alcohol; over the counter remedies for stress (valerian, chamomile and lavender).
- Exercise – release of endorphins.

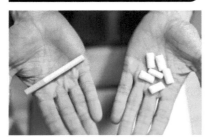

Nicotine is a chemical that can be delivered to the brain in various ways, some safer than others.

Apply it

Demi is a heavy smoker who recognises she is addicted and has tried several times to give up. She believes she smokes to help her cope with all the stressful things going on in her life and this is why she finds it hard to stop.

Demi's friend tells her there are over-the-counter remedies she can get to help her feel better. Her friend also tells her how nicotine substitutes helped her to give up smoking.

1. Describe **two** ways in which nicotine substitutes might help treat Demi's smoking addiction.
   (4 marks)

2. Explain **one** reason why over-the-counter remedies may not be useful in treating Demi's stress.
   (2 marks)

3. Discuss the effectiveness of over-the-counter remedies and/or nicotine substitutes in helping Demi. *(9 marks)*

Physiological treatments including exercise

Nicotine substitutes *(Nicotine replacement therapy, NRT)*	NRT provides a controlled dose of nicotine delivered using skin patches, chewing gum, etc. instead of tobacco. NRT is safer because harmful chemicals in tobacco smoke are absent.
	Gum, inhalers and sprays reduce cravings immediately. Patches have longer-term benefits. Combining two methods can be most effective.
	Mechanism Nicotine molecules delivered via NRT attach to **dopamine** receptors on neurons in the ventral tegmental area. This stimulates release of dopamine in the nucleus accumbens (see page 108).
	Withdrawal The nicotine dose can be reduced gradually over time (e.g. by using smaller patches). This manages **withdrawal symptoms** and improves the chances of avoiding relapse.
Drug treatments for alcohol addiction	**Disulfiram (Antabuse)** This disrupts the body's normal processing of alcohol, making the client very sensitive to it. Whenever the client has an alcoholic drink they quickly experience a severe hangover. The client learns to associate drinking alcohol with these unpleasant sensations (**classical conditioning**), so they abstain from alcohol to avoid them.
	Acamprosate (Campral) This helps the client avoid relapse after they have withdrawn and are abstaining. It stabilises the level of the **neurotransmitter** GABA in the brain, which was disrupted during withdrawal. This reduces the client's urge to drink alcohol (cravings).
Over-the-counter (OTC) stress remedies	These include valerian tablets, chamomile tea and lavender oil. All are derived from herbs and contain chemicals with similar mildly sedative (calming) effects, reducing **anxiety**, promoting relaxation and sleep.
	Herbal remedies are presented as 'natural' because they are derived from plants. But they alter the person's physiological and psychological functioning like prescription drugs do.
Exercise	Exercise helps combat negative effects of **stress** by replicating the **fight or flight** response (e.g. increased heart rate, muscular tension). This 'stresses' the body, increases the person's resilience and has a protective effect. Exercise is also a distraction, focusing away from everyday worries and anxieties.
	Release of endorphins These have specific painkilling effects but also increase production of dopamine. Exercise triggers this process and provides a short-term feeling of euphoria (the 'runner's high'). It improves mood, induces relaxation, promotes an optimistic outlook on life and improves self-image.

Physiological treatments and exercise

One strength is physiological treatments have flexible, wide-ranging uses.

Nicotine substitutes come in several forms (e.g. gum, spray) so one or two types will suit most people. Disulfiram is used outside a hospital environment in a capsule placed under the skin for slow release.

Also, OTC remedies can be used with more effective treatments to relieve stress. 'Exercise' can be interpreted flexibly to include many levels of physical activity.

Therefore, physiological treatments are useful because they can be used by many people and alongside other treatments.

Exercise can both cause injury and help recovery from injury.

Another strength is evidence showing physiological treatments are effective.

For example, a review of NRT studies concluded that all forms of NRT increase the rate of people quitting smoking by 50–60%, compared with control groups (Hartmann-Boyce *et al.*).

A review of disulfiram studies showed it was a more effective treatment for alcohol **addiction** than alternatives (Skinner *et al.*). Also, another review found that a wide range of physical activity can increase people's ability to cope with stress (Sharon-David and Tenenbaum).

Therefore, some physiological treatments are more effective than alternatives in reducing stress and addiction.

REVISION BOOSTER

An interesting thing about revision techniques is that what doesn't work for one person may well work for another. It's good to use a variety of methods to help you revise. Make them active – don't just read notes. Here are some suggestions:

- Cue cards/flashcards: one or two words on a theory, study, etc. to trigger your knowledge.
- Mind maps: organise material into a creative visual form.
- Revision groups/pairs: test each other, discuss topics with each other.
- Presentations: make some slides on a topic, so you have to organise the material.

Experiment with different techniques and you will find those that work for you.

One weakness is that physiological treatments can have harmful side effects.

They include headaches, stomach disorders and sleep difficulties for NRT and OTC remedies. Also, numbness in hands/feet and decreased mood for disulfiram, and injury and dependence on the 'runner's high' for exercise.

Side effects are usually mild, but can sometimes be serious enough to outweigh the benefits of the treatment, so the client stops using the treatment.

Therefore, the benefits of a physiological treatment need to be weighed up against the risk of side effects, which might make a psychological treatment a better option.

Apply it

Jaime is addicted to alcohol and has had no success in trying to give up. They are often drunk but when they are not they realise that their drinking is causing problems in their life that make them very stressed.

Before they started drinking, Jaime used to do a lot of running for exercise and would like to do that again. Jaime's partner thinks it is time that they went to the doctors to see if there are any drug treatments that could help.

1. Describe how drug treatments could be used to help treat Jaime's alcohol addiction. *(3 marks)*
2. Explain **one** way Jaime could benefit from exercise. *(2 marks)*
3. One feature of exercise is release of endorphins. Explain how release of endorphins might help Jaime manage their stress. *(2 marks)*
4. Evaluate drug treatments and/or exercise as ways of helping Jaime. *(6 marks)*

C3: Maintenance of behavioural change

Reasons for non-adherence 1 and 2

SPEC SPOTLIGHT

Reasons for non-adherence:
- Stress – the perceived inability to cope as a threat to behaviour change.
- Rational non-adherence, including cost-benefit analysis, financial barriers, patient-practitioner relationship.

Even if the client is listening, chances are they won't remember much afterwards.

Apply it

Esmee had an accident at work that injured her back. She has a treatment plan that involves taking four different medications and doing several exercises every day. She also has an appointment with a physiotherapist every fortnight. But the clinic is miles away so Esmee has to get there by bus which is an unexpected expense for her.

1. Explain **two** ways in which stress could be a reason for Esmee not following the treatment plan.
   (4 marks)

2. Esmee may not follow the treatment plan because she perceives she is unable to cope. Explain **one** way in which Esmee might perceive she is unable to cope. *(2 marks)*

3. Discuss stress as a reason why Esmee might not adhere to the treatment plan. *(3 marks)*

4. Evaluate stress as a reason why Esmee might not adhere to the treatment plan. *(6 marks)*

Reason 1: Stress

Four stress-related reasons for non-adherence	
	Poverty Stress can arise from poverty, e.g. not having enough money. Non-adherence is worse in lower socioeconomic groups, e.g. for diabetes medication (Mayberry *et al.*).
	Chaotic lifestyle Being disorganised (chaotic) can be stressful and stress can make people disorganised (a vicious circle). People may forget to take medication or find it hard to follow medical advice, e.g. they cannot schedule exercise or relaxation.
	Narrow attention Anxiety makes attention narrower. Clients listening to health professionals may latch onto key words and ignore the rest. E.g. the client hears 'cancer' and they pay little attention to what is said after. They miss out on information about follow-up appointments and medication, making adherence less likely.
	Memory Stress can disrupt memory and a client cannot adhere to medical advice if they cannot remember it. 40–80% of medical advice is immediately forgotten and only about half of what is remembered is correct (Kessels).

Reason 2: Rational non-adherence

| Cost-benefit analysis | A client may decide not to follow medical advice for reasons they believe are logical and make sense (i.e. 'rational'). The client weighs up the costs and benefits of following and not following medical advice.

The main benefit is that adherence reduces, eliminates or prevents the symptoms of an illness, disease or injury. |
|---|---|
| Three main costs of adherence | **Side effects** Following medical advice may have unwanted outcomes, e.g. some drugs cause dizziness and memory problems, exercise can lead to physical injury, etc.

Financial barriers Some people cannot afford to adhere to medical advice, even in countries with a 'free' healthcare system like the NHS (e.g. cost of public transport). People with private medical insurance are more likely to adhere because cost doesn't matter to them (Laba *et al.*).

Patient–practitioner relationship In a 'practitioner-centred approach' the practitioner has all the power and views treatment as non-negotiable. The client trusts the practitioner less and is less likely to adhere than in a friendly and personal 'client-centred approach'. |

Unit 3 Health psychology   Content area C

Reasons for non-adherence 1 and 2

One strength is evidence supporting the role of stress in non-adherence.

One study investigated almost 10,000 clients with diabetes and/or high blood pressure (Roohafza et al.).

The clients experiencing the highest levels of stress were less likely to adhere to medication and/or exercise advice.

This supports the view that stress can substantially increase the risk of non-adherence even in life-threatening disorders.

One weakness is that the long-term effects of stress are unclear.

For example, studies tend to look at short-term effects and not at how non-adherence changes over longer periods along with stress levels.

Presumably, adherence should increase as stress reduces (i.e. a practical application), but we do not know this for sure.

This means the role of stress is unclear and it is hard to develop practical interventions to increase adherence.

The cost and inconvenience of transport are major barriers to adherence for some people.

One strength is that rational factors are effective explanations.

One study looked at what happened in Spain when older clients had to start paying a share of their medication costs in 2012.

Adherence declined significantly for expensive drugs, but not for cheaper ones (González López-Valcárcel et al.).

This shows that non-adherence is increased by financial barriers, suggesting it has a rational basis.

One weakness is that clients usually do not make rational health decisions.

This approach assumes clients weigh up the costs and benefits of adhering to medical advice in a calm way before making a decision in their best interests.

But instead, **health** decisions are often made without a plan and the client's current emotional state influences decisions more than a **cost-benefit analysis**.

This suggests that non-adherence as a rational process cannot explain all health-related decision-making.

REVISION BOOSTER

Some revision methods make you feel busy but they are not very effective because they are passive (rereading your notes, 'typing up' your notes, using your highlighter pen on your notes). You need to use *active* methods instead.

For instance, once you've highlighted parts of your notes, what next? You could turn the highlighted notes into flashcards/cue cards and then use these to test yourself. Instead of simply rereading notes or 'typing them up', try turning them into mind maps – transform the material in some way.

Whatever active methods you use, remember the key thing is to get the material *out* of your memory – so test, test, test yourself.

Apply it

Ned has an anxiety disorder and is attending cognitive behavioural therapy sessions once a week. He has to pay for them and drive for an hour to get there. Ned has noticed that he feels a bit less anxious. He wishes the therapist was a bit more friendly, although the other clients have been supportive. Ned is wondering whether or not to continue going to the sessions.

1. *Explain how a cost-benefit analysis might affect whether Ned chooses to continue with the therapy.* (2 marks)

2. *Explain the role of financial barriers in Ned's decision whether to continue.* (2 marks)

3. *Explain why rational non-adherence could be the reason why Ned decides not to continue.* (2 marks)

4. *Discuss **one** reason why Ned may not continue with the therapy.* (3 marks)

5. *Assess rational non-adherence as a reason why Ned may not continue with the therapy.* (9 marks)

Reasons for non-adherence 3 and 4

SPEC SPOTLIGHT

Reasons for non-adherence:
- Learned helplessness – control over behaviour and outcomes.
- Lack of support – significant others, health professionals.

Learned helplessness can trap you in a downward spiral where you can't do anything to improve your situation.

Apply it

Zander is addicted to gambling, which causes him a lot of stress. He tried to stop but has failed so often he feels there's no point anymore. Zander tells himself, 'Nothing I do makes a difference.' His parents arranged for him to attend a group called Gamblers Anonymous but he immediately decided he wouldn't go.

1. Identify **one** example of learned helplessness in the scenario.
(1 mark)

2. Explain how learned helplessness may prevent Zander from going to Gamblers Anonymous.
(2 marks)

3. Discuss learned helplessness as an explanation of why Zander decides not to go to Gamblers Anonymous.
(3 marks)

4. Evaluate the role of learned helplessness in Zander's decision. In your answer, refer to **one** other explanation for his decision.
(9 marks)

Reason 3: Learned helplessness	
Basics of learned helplessness	Being ill means you repeatedly face stressful situations you feel you cannot control. Therefore, people who are ill may learn to be helpless – nothing they do makes any difference because they remain ill. Eventually they do not take opportunities to be in control even when they appear.
Link with health	A client may learn that taking control makes no difference to their **health**. So, they no longer try to behave in ways that could change their situation, e.g. they fail to take medication, do any exercise, keep appointments, etc. A person loses **motivation** and becomes passive if they think about their behaviour in these negative ways: • 'It's all my fault because I just can't do these exercises.' • 'There is nothing I can do to get better.' • 'I'll never be organised enough to take my tablets.' These are all signs of **learned helplessness** which perpetuate this way of thinking.
Downward spiral	Experience of learned helplessness can lead to **depression**, which itself makes non-adherence more likely. Non-adherence makes depression worse and reinforces learned helplessness, which again makes non-adherence more likely… and so on.

Reason 4: Lack of support	
Significant others	**Lack of practical support** Without a social network, a person may have no one to remind them to take medication, take them to hospital, show them how to access exercise videos, etc. **Lack of emotional support** Adherence is less likely when the person lacks people who can help improve their mood, or who can provide encouragement, rewards, a 'shoulder to cry on'. When relationships with significant others are stressful, a lack of such support may actually produce better outcomes for someone who needs to follow medical advice. This is because they have to rely more on support from professionals.
Health professionals	**Lack of practical support** As health professionals are experts on the benefits of adherence, a lack of information from them can lead to non-adherence by clients. **Lack of emotional support** Clients may expect professionals to provide emotional support and many professionals consider this part of their role. But there may be a 'gap' between the amount of support clients expect and professionals provide. What matters is how the client *perceives* support. If trust is low or communication poor, the client will perceive a lack of emotional support, e.g. they feel the professional does not understand them 'as a person' but only as a set of symptoms.

Reasons for non-adherence 3 and 4

One strength is that interventions can target learned helplessness.

For example, cognitive therapy helps clients to change how they perceive the link between behaviours (adherence) and outcomes (getting better).

Clients can break out of the downward spiral when they see that what they do makes a positive difference to their health.

This means that overcoming learned helplessness is a useful practical way of improving adherence.

One weakness is surprisingly little research supports learned helplessness.

A study of diabetic children found that learned helplessness was associated with worse metabolic control but not with medication adherence (Kuttner et al.).

Also, learned helplessness is linked to depression, **stress** and low **self-esteem**, so perhaps these factors cause non-adherence and learned helplessness is an indirect influence.

Therefore, learned helplessness may have negative impacts on health, but not necessarily by affecting non-adherence to medical advice.

One strength is evidence showing lack of support links to non-adherence.

For instance, adherence is lower in people who live alone, especially if they are older and have cognitive impairments (Wheeler et al.).

Also, homeless people, people who live in unstable circumstances and people with mental health issues are at risk of non-adherence.

Therefore, lack of support, in some cases from healthcare professionals, is an effective explanation of non-adherence.

One weakness is that support from professionals is just one factor.

Psychologists have noted that non-adherence is still widespread and costly in terms of ill health and finances, despite many attempts to improve it.

This is partly because most interventions only address one factor at a time, e.g. support from professionals.

This suggests that support is not enough on its own to improve adherence significantly.

Remote communication with health professionals could improve support, trust and adherence in some people.

REVISION BOOSTER

Some extended open-response ('essay') questions are worth 6 marks instead of 9. You should tackle these in the same way as you would a 9-marker because the 'levels' mark scheme is the same (just for fewer marks, of course).

The main thing to remember is that you still need to provide a balance of AO1, AO2 and AO3, even though the command word will be *Discuss* or *Assess* or *Evaluate*. Your answer will also be shorter, which might seem obvious but it's easy to get carried away in an exam. Check mark allocations carefully and don't write a 9-mark answer to a 6-mark question. It's worth practising 6-mark and 9-mark responses to the same question in your revision.

Apply it

Marin lives on their own and has no children or partner. They made lots of friends at university but everybody moved to different parts of the country after graduation. Marin gave up social media when life became too stressful and they became addicted to alcohol. They had an appointment with their GP but it wasn't very helpful. Marin hoped the GP would refer them for some treatment, but he just handed over some leaflets.

1. *Explain how lack of support from significant others may prevent Marin from giving up alcohol.* (2 marks)

2. *Identify* **one** *example of lack of support from health professionals in Marin's experience.* (1 mark)

3. *Discuss how a lack of support may cause Marin to continue being addicted to alcohol.* (3 marks)

4. *Assess reasons why Marin may not adhere to medical advice.* (9 marks)

C3: Maintenance of behavioural change

Methods used to improve adherence 1 and 2

SPEC SPOTLIGHT

Methods used to improve adherence:

- Health education/promotion – relevant to target group, improved access to information.
- Reduction of perceived threats – resistance, fears, understanding of needs, safety and security.

Adherence can be improved by modelling a health procedure behaviour such as measuring glucose in diabetes.

Apply it

A group of GPs creates a health education campaign to encourage asylum seekers to visit them for check-ups.

1. Describe how the GPs could use health education/promotion to encourage the asylum seekers to go for check-ups. **(3 marks)**

2. Health education campaigns must be relevant to the target group. Explain **two** ways in which the GPs can make their campaign relevant to the target group. **(4 marks)**

3. Explain **one** way in which the GPs could improve the asylum seekers' access to information. **(2 marks)**

4. Evaluate health education campaigns as a way of getting the asylum seekers to go for check-ups. **(6 marks)**

Method 1: Health education and promotion

Relevance to target group	People who need to follow medical advice differ from each other in several ways. E.g. some clients may have issues with memory, so health education should include opportunities to confirm the client has remembered the advice.
	Literacy skills Health education should use everyday language and limit the number of key points to two or three.
	Modelling In making lifestyle changes, some clients (e.g. people with learning disabilities) may benefit from a health professional **modelling** the behaviour. Health education aims to change behaviour, not just pass on knowledge.
Improving access to information	**Client needs** Information should be given in a form that suits the client, e.g. a printed booklet. Websites and apps are accessible to many clients, but not to all of them so alternatives are necessary.
	Health professionals Appointments with health professionals can be made via apps and websites. Pharmacists are accessible as they are on many high streets and appointments are not usually necessary. Telephone follow-ups are common and give clients the chance to ask questions they may not have considered during a face-to-face discussion.

Method 2: Reduction of perceived threats

Resistance	A client may believe they risk harm if they adhere to medical advice, so they actively resist doing so. Reducing the client's resistance can change their perception of the harmful threat.
	E.g. an intervention could encourage the client to build physical activity into their daily routine so it becomes a habit. This may lead them to reassess their perception of threat, which is more productive than trying to change their beliefs.
Understanding of needs	Clients perceive something as threatening if it prevents their needs being met. E.g. someone is part of an anti-vaccination social media group because they have a need to be accepted by a group that shares their values. A useful intervention could be to provide another source of acceptance that allows them to follow medical advice without experiencing rejection.
	Safety and security A client's need for safety and security is threatened if they must follow medical advice that they feel could be harmful. Including the client in decisions about their treatment helps them feel safer because they have some control, e.g. over their medication or diet. If the client's need for safety/security is not met they may experience fear.
	Fears The client's fears about following medical advice can be reduced by health professionals addressing them directly. E.g. fears of side effects can be discussed openly to help the client understand what the risks are. What does '1 in 1000 people experience this side effect' mean in practical terms?

Methods used to improve adherence 1 and 2

One strength is health education offers practical ways to improve adherence.

One study found that only 36% of clients understood the meaning of the phrase 'every 6 hours' (Eraker et al.).

Vague language should be avoided and instructions should be specific (e.g. who needs to do what, where, when and why).

Therefore, research can be useful in identifying barriers to adherence so that health professionals are aware of the issues that prevent compliance.

One weakness of improving access to information is that it is not enough.

Quality of information is more important than access. Improving access to incorrect information may reduce adherence.

For example, the 'information' spread by anti-vaccination groups is highly accessible but has no basis in evidence and is mostly opinion.

Therefore, improving access without considering quality can backfire and lead to non-adherence.

Understanding the information that comes with medication can reduce the client's fears about side effects.

One strength is that perceived threats is a specific method of improvement.

Many clients perceive a threat from treatments of an illness (e.g. side effects), but do not perceive enough of a threat from the illness itself.

On this basis, the health belief model (see page 88) suggests increasing the perceived threat from illness, e.g. by showing the client they are part of a vulnerable group.

This means the client will realise there are benefits to adherence that outweigh the perceived threats of harm.

One weakness is that reducing threat perception may not change behaviour.

Clients may judge risk of harm more accurately after an intervention, but this does not mean they go on to be more adherent.

E.g. a client may understand (cognitive) the risk of harm but may still be afraid (emotional) that adherence could be dangerous.

Therefore, interventions should target multiple causes of non-adherence (e.g. emotional), not just reduce the perception of threat.

REVISION BOOSTER

A poor way to revise is to start a session and just keep going until you finish. You might feel busy, but you will have lost focus, concentration and motivation long before the end. So, build lots of breaks into each revision session. Revise for no longer than 25 minutes, then take a five-minute break. After four such mini-sessions, take a longer break of 15–20 minutes.

The key is to really enjoy your breaks – don't feel guilty about them, they are helping you revise more effectively. This is called the Pomodoro technique. There are apps available that allow you to set alarms to follow such a routine.

Apply it

Neela has high cholesterol levels which put her at greater risk of heart attack and stroke. Her GP wants Neela to start taking drugs called statins which will lower her cholesterol and reduce her risk. But Neela has heard some negative things about statins and is reluctant to take them.

1. Describe how reduction of perceived threats could be an effective way to help Neela to adhere to medical advice. (2 marks)

2. Explain **one** way in which the GP could reduce Neela's resistance to taking statins. (2 marks)

3. Explain **two** ways in which a better understanding of Neela's needs would help her to adhere to medical advice. (4 marks)

4. Discuss **one** reason why reduction of perceived threats may not be effective in persuading Neela to take statins. (3 marks)

5. Assess reduction of perceived threats as a way of helping Neela to adhere to medical advice. (9 marks)

C3: Maintenance of behavioural change

Methods used to improve adherence 3 and 4

SPEC SPOTLIGHT

Methods used to improve adherence:

- Lifestyle changes – replacing unhealthy behaviours with healthy behaviours; reduction in stress, improved self-esteem and self-confidence, emotional resilience, insight into own behaviour, improved outlook on life.
- Support for behavioural change including provision of incentives, persuasive health reminders (texts, self-tracking, progress monitoring) and social prescribing.

Making one lifestyle change may lead to others, such as a healthy diet and better sleep.

Apply it

Owen smokes to relax and to appear more interesting to other people. They started smoking 20 years ago. Now, just like then, without fail they have a cigarette with a coffee to start their day.

1. Name **one** lifestyle change Owen could make to improve their health. **(1 mark)**

2. Explain how improved self-esteem and emotional resilience could help Owen to improve their health. **(4 marks)**

3. Explain **one** reason why lifestyle changes may be effective in helping Owen improve their health. **(3 marks)**

4. Evaluate lifestyle changes as a method of Owen improving their health. **(6 marks)**

Method 3: Using lifestyle changes

Reduction in stress	**Stress** lowers **motivation**, so the client feels there is no point changing their behaviour. Interventions should help clients manage stress first. E.g. some therapies help clients develop organisation skills, which makes adherence easier.
Improved self-esteem and self-confidence	Some people lack confidence in changing their behaviour and failure makes them feel bad about themselves (low **self-esteem**) and lose confidence. Interventions should boost self-esteem and self-confidence, e.g. joining an exercise group.
Emotional resilience	Emotionally resilient people 'bounce back' from setbacks and are more likely to adhere to medical advice. Resilience can be increased by developing positive relationships, taking a positive outlook on life and practising mindfulness (APA 2012).
Insight into own behaviour	Habits can prevent a person changing, e.g. sitting too much. Someone who becomes aware of unhealthy habits recognises them as 'mindless'. They gain insight into their own behaviour and the reasons why they fail to make lifestyle changes.
Improved outlook on life	Optimistic people have a positive outlook, they are hopeful and think about the good things that could happen without dwelling on past failures. They adhere to medical advice because they focus on positive changes adherence can bring (better **health**).

Method 4: Using behavioural change

Provision of incentives	Money is an incentive to change behaviour. Smokers given money to quit were three times more likely to stop smoking compared to smokers given only information (Volpp *et al.*). Money is a **positive reinforcer** of desired behaviour.
Persuasive health reminders	These increase a client's motivation by giving them support. **Persuasive texts** Remind clients of their treatment goals (e.g. don't smoke, inject insulin) at high-risk and stressful times. Texts also offer encouraging messages to improve motivation. **Self-tracking** Uses technology (e.g. mobile app) to count steps or track physiological indicators, health-related behaviours (e.g. food choices) and self-reported emotions. **Progress monitoring** Also provided by apps so a client can see improvement. This is persuasive because it increases a client's motivation when they see they are being successful.
Social prescribing	Health professionals may encourage clients to consider non-medical options, e.g. volunteering or joining support groups. A depressed client may also be lonely, so joining a volunteer group could benefit their mental health because they are mixing with other people. Social prescribing is useful when a client has complex or long-term needs.

Methods used to improve adherence 3 and 4

One strength is several lifestyle factors exist for interventions to target.

Because these factors are often linked, addressing one positively affects others, so the benefits 'add together' for a client (cumulative).

For example, if the client is more optimistic, they may also experience less stress and become more resilient and confident.

This shows that even making one lifestyle change can have positive knock-on effects, making adherence even more likely.

Joining a walking group might be a better prescription for mild depression than medication.

One weakness is that addressing lifestyle factors may not be enough.

Stressed clients often drop out of support, e.g. obese people with high stress levels giving up a support programme early (Michelini *et al.*).

So, the stressed person with obesity enters a vicious cycle. They cannot stick to support interventions to help them cope, so they do not adhere to treatment to tackle obesity either.

Therefore, adherence must be addressed directly and not just by trying to reduce stress (or any other single lifestyle method).

One strength is that behavioural change is used in persuasive eCoaching.

eCoaching uses technology to support behavioural change. It can improve adherence in several groups of clients, especially when it is personalised (Lentferink *et al.*).

Personalisation involves tailoring persuasive reminders to the client's own goals rather than taking a one-size-fits-all approach.

This shows that combining methods of supporting behavioural change is a very useful way of improving adherence.

One weakness of social prescribing is that the research base is low quality.

Most studies of social prescribing have methodological problems, e.g. no control groups, no analysis and small sample sizes (Mason *et al.*).

Also, the best quality study found that social prescribing had no positive impact on health, even though healthcare professionals recommend it.

These issues mean that social prescribing may have some small benefits but it is not as effective as some claims suggest.

REVISION BOOSTER

Plan your revision by constructing a timetable. Start with a blank timetable of all the hours you are awake. You need to add:

- All your commitments that cannot be moved – school/college, work, family, etc.

- Your available revision periods, bearing in mind that it's better to have many short periods than fewer lengthy ones.

- Your other commitments that can be moved – things you have to do but not at a fixed time.

Be flexible and make sure you include plenty of 'empty' sessions that you can use if you have to. Sir Winston Churchill once said, 'Plans are of little importance, but planning is essential.' In other words, if your plan isn't working, don't hesitate – change it.

Apply it

Alisa has an anxiety disorder which means she sometimes has panic attacks. Alisa is drinking more alcohol because she feels it calms and relaxes her.

Her clinical psychologist has discussed with Alisa the support she can give her. They agree that Alisa will start a six-week guided self-help course to reduce her anxiety. Alisa is worried she might not complete the course.

1. Describe **two** ways in which support for behavioural change could help Alisa to complete the course. (4 marks)

2. Explain how the psychologist could use incentives and persuasive health reminders to help Alisa reduce her drinking. (4 marks)

3. Explain **one** reason why using support for behavioural change may not be effective in helping Alisa. (2 marks)

4. Discuss support for behavioural change as a method of helping Alisa. (9 marks)

Glossary

Addiction A mental health issue in which a person takes a substance or engages in a behaviour that is pleasurable but eventually becomes compulsive with harmful consequences. 78–79, 90, 97, 108, 112–115, 120–123, 130–135, 143–145

Adrenaline A hormone produced by the adrenal glands as part of the body's acute (immediate) stress response (fight or flight). Adrenaline strongly stimulates heart rate and contracts blood vessels. 47, 48, 104, 120

Aggression Behaviour that is intended to cause psychological or physical injury. 23, 52–59

Anxiety A state of emotional and physical arousal. The emotions include having worried thoughts and feelings of tension. Physical changes include an increased heart rate and sweatiness. 86, 112, 122–123

Autonomic nervous system (ANS) Transmits information to and from internal bodily organs. It is 'autonomic' as the system operates involuntarily (it is automatic). It has two main divisions: the sympathetic and parasympathetic nervous systems. 46, 104

Behavioural addiction Occurs when someone compulsively continues a behaviour and experiences withdrawal when they stop it. 78

Central nervous system (CNS) Consists of the brain and spinal cord, where complex decisions are made. 11, 46

Chromosomes Found in the nucleus of living cells and carrying information in the form of genes. The 23rd pair of chromosomes determines biological sex. 42

Classical conditioning Learning by association. Occurs when two stimuli are repeatedly paired together – an unconditioned (unlearned) stimulus (UCS) and a new 'neutral' stimulus (NS). The neutral stimulus eventually produces the same response that was first produced by the unconditioned stimulus alone. 34–35, 37, 64

Cognitive biases A distortion of attention, memory and thinking. It arises because of how we process information about the world, especially when we do it quickly. This can sometimes lead to irrational judgementsandpoordecision-making. 22–23, 116–117

Cognitive dissonance An explanation for attitude change based on the concept that dissonance is an unpleasant state which occurs whenever an individual holds two cognitions (ideas, beliefs, attitudes) which are in conflict. 86–87, 96

Cortisol An important hormone produced by the adrenal cortex. It helps the body to cope with stressors by controlling how the body uses energy. Cortisol suppresses immune system activity. 48–49, 58, 104

Cost-benefit analysis An individual weighs up the balance between the perceived benefits of changing behaviour and the perceived barriers (obstacles to change). 88, 116, 146

Cues In the context of learning, cues are stimuli in the environment that become rewarding in themselves because they are associated with the pleasure experienced from engaging in a behaviour. 14–15, 82, 88, 110, 118

Cue reactivity Cravings and arousal can be triggered in, for example, people addicted to gambling when they encounter cues related to the pleasurable effects of gambling (e.g. sounds of a fruit machine). 118, 120

Culture Refers to the norms and values that exist within any group of people. 10, 23, 70–71, 101

Daily hassles The relatively minor but frequent aggravations and annoyances of everyday life that combine to cause stress, such as forgetting where you have put things and niggling squabbles with other people. 98–99

Depression Low mood beyond everyday sadness, severe enough to be diagnosed as a disorder. 48–49, 148–149

Dopamine A neurotransmitter that generally has an excitatory effect and is associated with the sensation of pleasure. 58, 108–109, 144

Evolution The changes in inherited characteristics in a biological population over successive generations. 50–51

Fight/flight/freeze response The way an animal responds when stressed. The body becomes physiologically aroused in readiness to fight an aggressor, flee or freeze. 48–50, 104–105

Gender The label of being a girl/woman or boy/man, as distinct from biological sex. 54, 68–75

Genes Inherited DNA with instructions for building physical and psychological characteristics that influence behaviour. 42–43, 80, 108

Genetic predisposition An individual may inherit an increased likelihood of developing a physical or psychological disorder. Development of the disorder is not inevitable but depends on other factors (e.g. environmental). 80–81, 108

Health Health is a positive state, in which we can face the challenges of life, overcome stress, achieve our goals and fulfil our potential. This applies to our whole lives and not just our physical state. 76, 80–91, 148–153

Hormones Chemical substances that circulate in the bloodstream and affect target organs. They are produced in large quantities, disappear quickly but have powerful effects.   47–48

Identification An individual temporarily goes along with the norms and roles of the group because they see membership as part of their identity.   26–27, 72

Imitation An individual reproduces the behaviour they observed being demonstrated by a model. It is more likely to occur when the observer identifies with the model.   11, 38, 56

Information processing Behaviour can be understood in terms of information flowing through the cognitive (mental) system in a series of stages.   10, 23

Learned helplessness If a person finds that they cannot escape an aversive situation, they eventually stop trying to escape, i.e. they learn to be helpless.   148–149

Life events Significant and relatively infrequent experiences/occasions in people's lives that cause stress. They are stressful because we have to expend psychological energy coping with changed circumstances.   98–99

Locus of control Refers to the sense we each have about what directs events in our lives.   90–91

Modelling Either an observer imitates the behaviour of a model or a model demonstrates a behaviour that may be imitated by an observer.   32, 38–39, 56, 64, 72–73, 84–85, 142, 150

Motivation Refers to the forces that 'drive' your behaviour. It encourages an animal to act. For example, hunger is a basic drive state which pushes an animal to seek food. Winning a match may drive you on to greater success, i.e. it motivates you.   36, 152

Negative reinforcement In operant conditioning, the process of learning in which a behaviour is more likely to be repeated because the consequence of the behaviour is removal of an unpleasant stimulus or situation, which is experienced as rewarding.   36, 82–83, 114–115, 120

Neurotransmitters Chemicals (e.g. serotonin) in the nervous system that transmit signals from one neuron to another across synapses.   48–49, 80

Observation Actively attending to and watching (or listening to) the behaviour of others (models).   11, 38–39

Personality Patterns of thinking, feeling and behaving that differ between individuals. These are relatively consistent from one situation to another and over time.   40, 102–103

Physiological addiction Dependence on a substance, indicated by withdrawal symptoms when the person stops taking the substance.   78–79, 108–115

Positive reinforcement In operant conditioning, the process of learning in which a behaviour is more likely to be repeated because it is pleasurable – the pleasure is rewarding.   36, 56, 82, 114

Reinforcement A behaviour is followed by a consequence that increases the probability of the behaviour being repeated.   36–37, 72–73, 82–83, 114–115, 118–119

Role models People who have qualities we would like to have and we identify with, thus we model or imitate their behaviour and attitudes.   11, 32, 39, 54, 57, 72, 84–85, 110, 114, 120

Roles The functions that individuals perform within a group – task, social, procedural or individualist roles.   30–31, 68, 71, 100

Schema A mental package of beliefs and expectations that influence memory.   16–17, 60, 68–69

Self-efficacy A person's confidence in their ability to achieve success.   32, 88, 94–95

Self-esteem How a person values themselves and the extent to which they accept and like themselves.   32–33, 112, 122, 124–125

Serotonin A neurotransmitter with widespread inhibitory effects throughout the brain. It has a key role in aggressive behaviour.   11, 48–49, 58, 80

Social learning A way of explaining behaviour that includes both direct and indirect reinforcement, combining learning theory with the role of cognitive factors.   38, 56–57, 64–65, 84–85

Stress/stress response A physiological and psychological state of arousal that arises when we believe we do not have the ability to cope with a perceived threat (stressor).   48–49, 77, 98–107, 112, 122, 130–131, 136–147

Talking therapies Interventions that aim to help a person recover from addiction or cope with stress by talking to a mental health professional about their emotions, thoughts and behaviours.   132–137

Vicarious learning/ reinforcement Occurs when a learner observes a model's behaviour being reinforced (rewarded).   11, 38–39, 56, 72, 84, 94, 120

Withdrawal symptoms A set of symptoms that develop when the addicted person abstains from or reduces their drug use.   78–79, 108, 110, 112, 114–115, 144

Notes